Lowell Thomas and Lowell Thomas Jr.

Famous First Flights

SIXTEEN DRAMATIC ADVENTURES

With a Foreword to the 2004 Edition by Buzz Aldrin,
Foreword to the 2016 Edition by Richard and Owen Garriott,
and an Introduction to the 2016 Edition by Ted Janulis

Table of Contents

Illustrations

Foreword

Just as the famous first flights described by Lowell Thomas and Lowell Thomas Jr., gripped the imagination of people around the world, mankind's first forays into space were nothing less than spellbinding to men, women, and children everywhere. How could they not be riveted by these real-life adventures, which had previously been the stuff of science fiction?

It all began on October 4, 1957, when a 184-pound satellite named Sputnik 1 became the first man-made object ever to orbit the earth. The Soviet Union's aluminum sphere spent three months circling our planet, transmitting radio signals that were analyzed to gather data about the upper atmosphere. But *Sputnik 1's* importance was less scientific than symbolic. The Cold War was fully raging in 1957, and the launch of this satellite was nothing less than the space shot heard round the world. The "Space Race" between the United States and the USSR was on.

The Soviet Union got off to a fast start, leaving the United States to eat the dust of the Communist nation's R-7 rockets. In 1959, the USSR's *Luna 1* and *Luna 2* satellites made history as the first man-made objects to orbit the sun and impact the moon, respectively. The significance of these successes was obvious and powerful: Suddenly, other heavenly bodies were within our reach.

On April 12, 1961, the Soviets achieved another enormous milestone with the launch of *Vostok 1*. Inside the capsule was cosmonaut Yuri Gagarin, the first man in space and the first to orbit the earth, a feat he completed a grand total of one time during the mission's 118-minute duration. Brief as it was, *Vostok 1*'s importance could not be underestimated: Mankind was capable of traveling in space. (Gagarin's success would not have been possible without the sacrifice of a stray dog from the streets of Moscow named Laika, who three-and-a-half years earlier had been carried into orbit on *Sputnik 2*, showing the world that a living organism could survive in a capsule in space.)

Alan Shepherd's suborbital flight on May 5, 1961, made him the first American in space; and nine months later, on February 20, 1962, John Glenn wrote his name in the history books as the first American to orbit the earth, aboard *Friendship 7*. Despite these successes, the United States was still playing catch-up.

Less than four months after Glenn's mission, Soviet cosmonaut Valentina Tereshkova became the first woman in space on June 16, 1963. A textile worker and amateur parachutist, Tereshkova orbited the earth a then-record forty-eight times during the three-day flight aboard *Vostok 6*. It would be another twenty years before the United States put its first woman, astronaut Sally Ride, in orbit.

In March 1965, the USSR achieved yet another first, when cosmonaut Alexei Leonov made the first walk in space from *Voskhod 2*. But Soviet supremacy proved short-lived. By the end of the year, *Gemini 7*, with Frank Borman and James A. Lovell Jr., aboard, stayed in space for nearly fourteen days, doubling the previous duration record. The success of *Gemini 7* meant that a manned mission to the moon was possible.

As the Soviets increasingly focused on unmanned probes to the moon and Venus in 1966 and 1967, the United States labored to fulfill the challenge made by John F. Kennedy in 1961 and send a man to the moon by the end of the decade. In December 1968, *Apollo 8*, with Frank Borman, James A. Lovell Jr., and William Anders at the controls, became the first manned spacecraft to orbit the moon. The stage was set for a mission that *The New York Times* described as "more than a step in history; it is a step in evolution."

That mission, of course, was *Apollo 11,* which famously marked the first soft landing on the moon and the first moonwalks by Neil Armstrong and myself. The date was July 20, 1969, and the largest audience in television history witnessed the first time human beings had ever set foot on another world. American supremacy in space was now unquestioned. More significantly, science fiction had become science fact. A new era had been born.

Following *Apollo 11* into the early 1970s, subsequent *Apollo* missions brought two-wheeled carts, moon rovers, and ten more astronauts to the surface of our nearest heavenly neighbor. Unmanned missions in the same decade also broke new interplanetary ground and yielded important scientific results: In 1971, *Mariner 9* became the first spacecraft to orbit another planet and went on to map, for the first time, the entire surface of Mars; the United States successfully landed two probes, *Viking 1* and *Viking 2,* on the red planet in 1976, and each broadcast a steady stream of pictures of the Martian surface; and in 1979, Pioneer 11 reached Saturn and took the first close-up photographs of the ringed planet.

In 1981, the launch of the first American space shuttle, *Columbia,* ushered in an era when a series of reusable reentry vehicles, both American and Soviet, captured the headlines. In 1990, one such shuttle, *Discovery,* deployed the Edwin P. Hubble Space Telescope, which, after some minor adjustments, revolutionized deep space astronomy for more than a decade.

The new millennium has brought with it new milestones in unmanned exploration. In 2004, the Mars lander *Opportunity* found, for the first time, evidence of water on the surface of the red planet. The discovery of life (or signs of earlier biological activity) is now a distinct possibility there.

And what "famous first flights" can we expect in the future? How about an extended lunar mission that creates the first colony of humans on the moon, made possible by a new, heavy-lift space launch system capable of sending a crew of eight astronauts into interplanetary space. If this expedition is a success, a manned mission to Mars is likely within thirty to forty years.

The fiction of Jules Verne has been turned into scientific reality in less than one hundred fifty years.

The future of space exploration is limited only by our ability to imagine.

Dr. Buzz Aldrin
Apollo 11 Astronaut
April 3, 2004

Foreword:
The New Golden Age of Spaceflight

The first fifty years of human spaceflight were the exclusive purvey of only the wealthiest of nations, those that were willing to spend enormous capital and accept substantial human risk. The first decade after Sputnik saw great advancements, from Yuri Gagarin's first human flight to Neil Armstrong and Buzz Aldrin's first landing on the moon. Yet in the fifty years since that time, less than 600 people have left the earth, and no one has left low earth orbit. It should therefore be no surprise that anything as expensive and dangerous as human spaceflight would be uncommon.

However, due to recent advances in electronics, composite materials, miniature accelerometers, and GPS units, we are now seeing a new Golden Age of space exploration. Smaller, lighter vehicles that are flying more often and with lower budgets mark this era of innovation in flight. There are also a large number of new space ventures, bringing down access cost by ten-fold, which is greatly expanding access to space. Corporations and individuals can now plan their own trips to space.

Since the beginning of the new millennium, humanity has lived continuously in space, when on November 2, 2000 the International Space Station took on its first inhabitants, Bill Shepherd of the United States and Sergei Krikalev of Russia. The Chinese also now have a space station in orbit. Multiple robotic landers, Curiosity, Spirit, and Opportunity continue to comb the surface of Mars. The spacecraft New Horizons recently visited Pluto, and NASA reports evidence of water on both Mars and Pluto. The Kepler satellite has discovered thousands of exoplanets around distant suns. And NASA is now finally poised to take humans beyond low earth orbit, even beyond the moon, which remains the farthest we have ever ventured forty years ago.

The first indication of this new Golden Age came on October 4, 2004. On that day, a private pilot named Brian Binnie flew Space Ship One, an independently designed and financed, fully reusable, sub-orbital rocket ship. It launched into space and returned safely to the earth. This was the second such flight to occur, as two weeks earlier in the same vehicle Mike Melvill became the first commercial astronaut, reaching over 100 kilometers. Burt Rutan of Scaled Composites built this ship funded by Paul Allen to win the ten million dollar Ansari X Prize with these two flights. Space Ship One now hangs in the entry gallery of the Smithsonian Air and Space Museum in Washington D.C., alongside the Wright Brothers' first airplane.

This event showed people around the world, that technology had advanced sufficiently far, to fundamentally change the mindset about what could be done in space. Now people believed that private companies could reach space and, just as importantly, that fully reusable rockets were possible. Fully reusable rockets promise huge ten- to 100-fold decreases in cost, plus similar increases in safety. These facts have now given rise to a New Golden Age of Spaceflight.

Since the last awarding of the Ansari X Prize in 2004, a vast array of new space exploration companies have sprung up, in an effort to reinvent major aspects of space flight. In 2005, Richard Branson has purchased the rights to Scaled Composite's work and is commercially developing Space Ship Two, which should soon be able to ferry sub-orbital clients to over 100 kilometers and back. Sub-orbital competition has since heated up, with companies such as Jeff Bezos's Blue Origin having re-flown their vertical takeoff/vertical landing New Shepherd vehicle in early 2016. XCOR continues to work on their Lynx sub-orbital space plane.

Orbital access is expanding and cheapening quickly too. To compete with the long serving United Launch Alliance Atlas and Delta rockets, Space X now has the Falcon 9 regularly transporting cargo to and from the ISS with their Dragon capsule. Space X has just been cleared to start crewed activities, which they will begin in 2017. More importantly, Space X has successfully landed their first stage booster after it lifted eleven satellites to orbit. Landing a huge first stage like this cuts millions of dollars off the cost of launch and so massive savings reductions and safety increases are expected.

To quantify this, a recent Soyuz or Falcon 9 launch might cost the user between seventy-five and 150 million dollars. But most of that cost is in the disposable, used-only-once rocket itself, which is destroyed on its maiden voyage. The fuel onboard is far less than 1 percent of the total cost. So as soon as we can reliably reuse the hardware stages of the rocket, ten- to 100-fold cost decreases are well within reach. Dramatic safety improvements will come at the same time, as once we are re-using the same hardware, we will have far better data to correct problems, since we will not be discarding each piece of hardware on its maiden voyage.

As the price comes down and safety goes up, there will also be an increase in flight rates. Commercial exploitation of microgravity previously thought to be too expensive or too dangerous will have a far better chance of being practical, even profitable. The development of drugs and vaccines has already begun in earnest, as affordable access to the microgravity environment grows. Asteroid mining and space-based solar power, once thought farfetched, now appear likely.

Reducing access costs ten-to 100-fold also creates huge new opportunities for the International Space Station and deep space exploration. Today ISS experiments have an incredibly high cost load to cover, from launch costs to fair burden of actual ISS operational costs. The result of this is that even the most ardent supporters of space-based research and development, much less commercial operations, are hard pressed to justify the cost benefit of such activities.

In 2016, a Space X Falcon 9 is expected to deliver a Bigelow Aerospace private inflatable habitation module to the ISS. This will be the first fully private habitat in space. Just as with the incredible drop in launch costs, this will deliver huge savings in on-orbit operational costs over time. Utilization of the current ISS, as well as future space stations, will provide greater service and greatly reduced costs.

All this commercial activity in low earth orbit allows NASA to focus on what NASA does best, which is to push the limits of human exploration and technology. NASA can afford to have a far longer timeline and pursue far more exotic technologies in search of further breakthroughs for humanity and industry. NASA's SLS systems are planned for human exploration of deep space, including the Moon, asteroids, and Mars.

Plans are now being considered which promise to move space access beyond chemical rockets. Earlier this last year Escape Dynamics wrapped up a research and development program, that demonstrated the capability to build an electromagnetic thruster capable of lifting a rocket into space with energy wholly delivered from the common electric grid, and requiring no fuel to be carried by the rocket at all. If this technology becomes available in the next decades, it could provide yet another ten-fold decrease in access costs.

Both NASA and private companies like Space X are targeting Mars. In addition to seeking evidence of life beyond earth, Mars is also considered an important place to build a human outpost, one that will help to insure the continuation of our species. Stephen Hawking has regularly stated that humankind should colonize other planets to insure the future of the species. Elon Musk says one of the primary missions of Space X is to build a Mars colony with more than one million people living on Mars as soon as possible, to ensure the survival of the species should an asteroid or super nova of a nearby star risk wiping out our home planet.

On March 2, 2016, NASA astronaut Scott Kelly and Russian astronaut Mikhail Kornienko returned to Earth after spending 340 days at the International Space Station. Kelly's time in space provides researchers with critical information for understanding how to keep astronauts healthy during an extended stay in space. Scott's identical twin Mark remained on Earth, which provided the opportunity for a twin study. This is one more step in fulfilling President Barack Obama's vision of putting American astronauts on Mars in the 2030s.

Many of the Baby Boomer generation have felt that we missed out on the twentieth-century vision of colonizing space. But, seeing human boot prints on Mars has gone from a lost dream of the Apollo age, to once again seeming an achievable dream for youngsters of today.

We are pleased to see the coming and the flourishing of this new Golden Age of Space Exploration.

Richard Garriott, private astronaut
Soyuz TMA 13

Owen Garriott, NASA astronaut (retired)
Skylab II & STS 9

Introduction to the 2016 Edition

"We have to continually be jumping off cliffs
and developing our wings on the way down."
–Kurt Vonnegut, *If This Isn't Nice, What Is?: Advice for the Young*

The history of human flight is populated with luminaries whose names have endured for generations: the Wright Brothers, Lindbergh, Earhart, Yaeger, Glenn, and Aldrin to name a few. These names have a magical effect on our imaginations, as they conjure up feats of great derring-do stretching back to ancient times, Icarus, and beyond.

As a propeller-driven world yielded to the jet age and rockets soon thereafter catapulted daring individuals into the heavens, a new breed of explorer emerged, enabled by new ideas and technologies, but anchored by the primal thirst to defy gravity and travel faster and further. While many of the major advancements in powered flight described in the coming pages were made in the first seventy years after the Wright brothers' seminal 1903 flight, there are still today vast spaces to explore and transitions underway in terms of how those horizons are reached.

Space exploration headlines, once dominated by NASA and other national agencies, now regularly feature the efforts of private companies created by Jeff Bezos, Elon Musk, and Richard Branson. If you visit the magnificent Kennedy Space Center in Cape Canaveral, Florida, you'll see that Launch Complex 39A (Pad A), which launched the Apollo 11 spacecraft on its historic flight to the moon, is now being co-developed and utilized by Space X in a public-private partnership. Within the membership of the Explorers Club, we have a symbolic representation of this evolution in Owen and Richard Garriott, the first American father/son astronaut team. Owen spent sixty days aboard Skylab in 1973 and later ten days on Spacelab-1 on a Space Shuttle mission in 1983. In 2008

Richard journeyed to the Institutional Space Station aboard the Soyuz TMA -13 as a private astronaut.

Today the challenge is to find ways to fly more efficiently and sustainably, and the race is on to develop these new and clean technologies. Both Boeing and Airbus are developing lithium batteries as a power source, and NASA is developing a series of X-Plane experimental aircraft to increase fuel efficiency and reduce noise and pollution in commercial flights. NASA has also unveiled a model of a green commercial airliner, an X-Plane, which could replace the Airbus 320 or the Boeing 737 in the near future.

To promote clean technologies, Explorers Club members Bertrand Piccard and Andre Borschberg are flying around the world in a solar powered plane. Solar Impulse has completed eight legs of its proposed around-the-world tour, covering nearly half the journey already; the plane is in Hawaii as we go to press, preparing for the completion of its historic voyage.

Other technologies are driving great change in the twenty-first century experience. Drones, unmanned planes that are remotely operated, have transformed warfare and high-tech surveillance. They also have civilian, recreational, and business uses and it's not hard to imagine our lives in the not too distant future being fulfilled by the visions of Buck Rogers, Star Trek, and one of my personal favorites, the Jetsons of cartoon fame.

We live in exiting times, and I'm mindful that my words will age quickly under a continuing splash of new and exciting inventions and milestones. Whatever form they take however, it seems likely these future achievements will be powered by the same urge expressed by John Gillespie Magee many years ago, the desire to slip the "surly bonds of earth." At the Explorers Club, we celebrate that spirit and look forward to seeing that vibrant and dynamic future realized.

—Ted Janulis
President
The Explorers Club
April 2016

Acknowledgments

Famous First Flights That Changed History, by Lowell Thomas and Lowell Thomas Jr., is Volume III in The Explorers Club Classic Series and a worthy choice. The year 2003 marked the centennial of the Wright brothers' first flight, and the year 2004 marked the centennial year for The Explorers Club. We continue these celebrations with this edition. A new foreword by Lowell Thomas Jr. updates powered flight, and *Apollo 11* astronaut Buzz Aldrin gives us an update of space flight. Both men are esteemed members of The Explorers Club.

For more than fifty years, Lowell Thomas was an integral part of The Explorers Club, and he was instrumental in the club acquiring its magnificent headquarters, the Lowell Thomas Building, in New York. Today, The Explorers Club Lowell Thomas Award is given to groups of outstanding explorers—and there is the Lowell Thomas Capital Campaign Building Fund, to which Lowell Thomas Jr. has graciously donated the proceeds from the sale of this book.

Each book in the Classics Series is the result of a collaborative effort involving Explorers Club members and staff who give appropriately of their time and ideas. Our informal committee for this edition consisted of members Gary Hermalyn, who suggested this book; Catherine Nixon Cooke; Jonathan Conrad; Richard Wiese, who is Club President (and the son of Richard Wiese Jr., who in 1959 first flew solo across the Pacific Ocean); and Milbry Polk. Clare Flemming, Curator of Research Collections, provided a first edition of this book from The Explorers Club Library, and Jeff Stolzer contributed editorial expertise. A special thanks goes to Lowell Thomas Jr., for granting us permission to republish his fine book.

Lindley Kirksey
Imprint Committee
The Explorers Club
April 23, 2004

Acknowledgments to the 2016 Edition

Famous First Flights That Changed History, by Lowell Thomas and Lowell Thomas Jr., is Volume III of the Explorers Club Classic Series. In collaboration with Jay Cassell, Editorial Director at Skyhorse Publishing, the Explorers Club is pleased to be reprinting our 2004 edition of this book with new updates by club members Dr. Owen K. Garriott, Richard Garriott, and Ted Janulis.

We again want to thank Lowell Thomas Jr. for granting us permission to reprint his fine book. He is again graciously donating the proceeds from the sale of this book to the Lowell Thomas Capital Building Fund, established in honor of his father and for whom our headquarters building in New York is named.

Even a reprint of our own book had behind the scenes efforts by many. A special thanks goes to Anne Donaghy, daughter of Lowell Thomas Jr.; Explorers Club President, Ted Janulis; Executive Director, Will Roseman; Curator of Collections, Lacey Flint; George Gowen; and Veronica Alvarado.

Jay Cassell stepped forward to keep our Classic Series books in print. These books represent our continuing commitment to excellence in exploration.

—Lindley Kirksey Young
The Explorers Club
March 2016

Prologue:
A Word Before the Takeoff

I am delighted that The Explorers Club has resurrected this book that my late father and I put together in 1965. He would be immensely pleased, too, for he was one of the most active and supportive Club members over a span of some fifty years. For his many contributions to the field of exploration and scientific research he was awarded The Explorers Club Medal—its highest honor. Later on, an award in his name was created to honor outstanding explorers. As for me, I have been a Club member since 1948, although a rather inactive one.

Writing about these famous first flights was my father's idea. It seemed to make sense to do so jointly because both of us had been involved in aviation during most of our lives; he as a radio news commentator and author of several books about aviation, most notably *The First World Flight* of which he was the official historian; and I as a bush pilot since earning my wings with the Air Force in 1944, then later, as a member and historian of the first flight around the world over both the North and South Poles.

From the days of Kitty Hawk and that historic first flight by the Wright Brothers, man has been soaring with the birds. That is, during the era of which we were writing, the speed and ceiling of planes kept them so near Earth that the term "bird man" had real meaning.

A few years after Wilbur and Orville Wright made their first short flights in 1903, the airplane really began to show what it could do. It truly came of age when the first long-distance flights were made.

Of these, the one acknowledged to be the first major long-distance aviation milestone was achieved when a Frenchman, in his fragile little airplane, made the first flight across the English Channel.

Following that event—and for a period of about half a century—flights in propeller-driven aircraft were made over longer and longer distances, soon crisscrossing all the continents, and spanning the seven seas.

The finale, the climax to this era, came with the first flight ever made around the globe by way of both Poles. And it was that bit of circumnavigation that inspired the writing of this book. Our purpose was to tell the stories of what we believed were the most important long-distance "firsts," including that Double Pole flight that was made so suddenly and without benefit of publicity.

Actually, the two of us have played a part in four of the sixteen flights in this book. Also, between us we have known most of the daring young men who blazed these historic trails through the skies. As a result of our personal knowledge and our acquaintance with nearly all of these airmen, we hoped to tell these stories with rather special enthusiasm—and not entirely with information passed on to us by others.

When a flight, even an all-important "first," is a success, it often is accomplished almost without incident. So, we also told something of the stories of those who failed and of whom you may not have heard at all. As you will discover, nearly every chapter is an account of a great air race. And, as we all know, failure often—in fact, usually—is more dramatic than success.

With the coming of jet and rocket propulsion, man now has gone far beyond the realm of the eagle and the high-soaring condor. He has indeed become a "space man." The advances made since my father and I wrote this book are enormous, with many more firsts; but most of them of a different nature. That is, technology, computers and the like are increasingly replacing the human pilot. At this writing we have jet airliners which from shortly after takeoff can climb, level off, proceed to a distant destination and land, all on their own, relegating the crew to mere supervisors. And our military has for some time been using pilotless airplanes to hover over battle grounds, transmitting data to their bases via satellite. Known as the UAVs, such as the Predator and Global Hawk, these robot planes can even drop precision weapons on the enemy, guided by GPS (global positioning by satellite). And just think of the "firsts" in space! First landing on the moon in 1969; the Mars spacecraft in 1976. Not to mention supersonic flight. And engineers are now developing hypersonic craft that will be able to soar into near-space, to orbit the earth then descend for a landing wherever there's an adequate airport. It has been said that to fly a commercial version of such an air/space craft half way around the world would take only two hours.

Well, someone else will have to write about that. However, there are a few new "firsts" of the romantic sort that are akin to what we have written about in this book, and which I want to mention. The first man-powered aircraft flew across the English Channel in 1979, with Bryan Allen at the controls. He powered the propeller of this frail lightweight machine by pumping pedals as though on a bike. Paul MacCready, an aeronautical engineer, created the plane.

Then there was the first solar-powered flight across the English Channel in 1980. Steven Ptacek's craft weighed all of 210 pounds, averaging thirty miles an hour, and made the crossing in five hours and thirty minutes.

Incredible as those two flights were, my favorite of recent times was the first non-stop 'round the world flight—*without any refueling*. That occurred in 1986 when Dick Rutan and Jeana Yeagar flew a unique lightweight aircraft made of composite material, designed and built by Burt Rutan, westward from the Edwards Air Force Base in California, 25,000 miles around the world in *nine* days. Their twin-engine plane (one small piston engine up front, the second pushing from the rear) carried a forward "canard" wing instead of the usual horizontal stabilizer and elevator at the tail. Its wings spanned one hundred and ten feet and contained most of the 1,209 gallons of gasoline needed for the flight. Named "Voyager," the crew had to endure a cabin space measuring two feet wide and seven and a half feet long—about the size of a coffin! While Dick worked the controls and the radio, Jeana would try to catch some sleep in that tiny space; and vice-versa.

Voyager averaged 122 miles an hour, its route taking it over the Philippines, the southern tip of India, central Africa, Central America and up the California coast to the point of origin. It has been said that of those one thousand plus gallons of gas, only eighteen remained on landing.

Surely that flight of Voyager was one of the most remarkable ever. For it, aviation's most prestigious award, the Collier Trophy, was presented to pilots Rutan and Yeagar, and to designer Burt Rutan and crew chief Bruce Evans.

Now for our first aerial adventure, let's make that first long-distance flight, from France to England, with Louis Bleriot.

Lowell Thomas Jr.
December 2003
Anchorage, Alaska

Famous First Flights

CHAPTER I

A 22-Mile Flight
That Startled the World

Early one morning in July 1909, the passengers on a boat plowing through the choppy English Channel from Calais to Dover were astonished to see an airplane bobbing up and down on the water, its pilot calmly smoking a cigarette while he awaited rescue by an approaching naval vessel.

The unperturbed flier was twenty-six-year-old Hubert Latham of Paris who, only minutes before, had taken off from the French coast in the hope of being the first man to fly an airplane across the Channel, and win a prize of £1000 offered by the London *Daily Mail*. But his sleek-looking Antoinette flying machine had developed engine trouble only seven miles out, forcing him to glide down to the water for a graceful, though somewhat splashy landing.

As eager hands were extended to lift him on board a French torpedo boat, Latham at least had the consolation of knowing he had achieved one "first." Even though he had failed to span the Channel, history would record that he was the first pilot ever to successfully land an airplane on water and keep it afloat. And through the years to come, he would be known as the founding father of a long line of aviators, and astronauts, who would be "picked up after falling in the drink," including hundreds who went down in the Channel during two World Wars.

Latham didn't even get his feet wet. When he returned to Calais with his slightly damaged plane, a waiting crowd gave him an enthusiastic reception and insisted that he kiss the Queen of the Port, a buxom, red-cheeked fishergirl who obviously wanted to lure a dashing young aviator into her net. With the crowd shouting its approval, he performed this cheerful chore, and then promptly set in motion plans to repair his plane and tow it back to the coast for another try. There was precious little time to waste in bussing pretty girls because the Channel flight was anything but a one-man contest.

For several weeks that summer the stage had been set for aviators to take on the most publicized flying challenge of the day—a first flight across the 22 miles of open water between Calais and Dover. True, a balloon had successfully made the crossing back in 1785, but in 1909 airplanes still had an annoying habit of coming back to earth after being in the air for a relatively short time, and few aviators were daring enough to risk a long flight over open water. Safety measures and instruments were still unknown, and to get a reading on the wind velocity a pilot used a simple gadget—a cigarette. He would light it, and if the smoke rose into the air in a fairly vertical line, then the wind was favorable for flying.

Latham and his fellow aviators had to reckon with the uncomforting knowledge that the English Channel was anything but an ordinary body of water. It was notorious for bad weather in all its forms, with rain, fog, and high winds taking turns at plaguing the boats that made the run between Calais and Dover. The weather was influenced by several factors, among them a peculiar counterclockwise movement of the Atlantic Ocean between Bristol Channel and Ireland, and the almost continual pressure of high tides. The prevailing winds were westerly, and a plane attempting to fly from France to England generally would have to battle a head wind to keep from being blown off course. This could end in disaster because, after all, England is only an island, a big one to be sure, but one that could quite easily be missed in the dark.

With the prevailing winds westerly, reason seemed to argue that a more practical course across the Channel would be the other way, from England to France, with a tail wind helping speed the plane along. So far, however, not a single English aviator had shown any serious desire to compete for the *Daily Mail* prize. By mid-July, only three contestants were in the running and all were French citizens, who, quite naturally, preferred to take off from La Belle France. And they wanted to prove that, despite all that talk about Britannia ruling the waves, it was only thin air that stood between France and England.

One was the Comte de Lambert, a flying aristocrat who was standing by on the Channel coast at Wissant where he had assembled two Wright biplanes. The distinguished-looking Comte was partial to Wright biplanes and had flown them in many demonstrations in Holland and elsewhere. Because of his presence and his announced intention to fly the Channel, the town of Wissant was rapidly filling with visitors, including the Comtesse de Lambert and her little daughter.

Meanwhile Hubert Latham had set up his flight headquarters back of the cliffs at Sangatte where he and his plane were in the midst of the Old Tunnel Works—the remnants of an unfinished project to bore a passage beneath the Channel to England. Lambert was a slender, sensitive young man of well-known artistic temperament whose pale face always seemed to have a tired, languid look—until he climbed into an airplane. Then his personality seemed to undergo a transformation, with his eyes sparkling and radiating a *joie de vivre*. The word around Paris was that he had taken up the adventuresome sport of flying because his doctors told him he had only one year to live.

Although his father was an Englishman from Lancashire, Latham was born in Paris and had become a French citizen, even to the extent of serving a hitch in the French Army. But he had so many English characteristics that the London newspapers always referred to him as "Mr. Latham" and not "Monsieur." Also, like a typical family-conscious Englishman, he had expressed a desire to land his plane in England at Folkestone because, as he put it, "I have cousins there and it would please them."

Throughout the previous month of June, Latham had flown his sleek, but fragile, Antoinette monoplane almost continually, trying to set new endurance records. On one flight he passed just above the heads of a crowd of Chalons, and astounded his viewers by taking both hands off the steering wheel, calmly rolling a cigarette, and then lighting it. This spectacular incident prompted one aero magazine to comment: "Mr. Latham has established a new record. He is undoubtedly the first man who has had the audacity to light and smoke a cigarette while in full flight!"

But as fliers of spectacular achievement, neither the Comte de Lambert nor Hubert Latham could match the exploits of Louis Blériot, the third contestant for the *Daily Mail* prize. At the age of thirty-seven, Blériot was a rather stern-looking, dark-complexioned Frenchman who sported a large red mustache. Non-confiding by nature, he adhered to an economy of words in his conversation, and was apt to become bored with anyone who made a practice of talking too much.

Blériot was trained at the Paris Central Engineering School, and early in his career became independently wealthy from the development and sale of a world-renowned motorcar headlight which bore his name. Married and the father of five children, he first experimented with airplanes in 1900, the same year the Wright Brothers began their flight studies.

Blériot's first plane was a flapping-wing model which found itself in extreme difficulty every time it became airborne even for a few feet, so he had the prudence to abandon it. He began building biplanes, and finally devoted his complete attention to monoplanes, the models which were to bring him his greatest successes. By the time he was ready to fly the Channel, Blériot had spent at least $150,000 on airplanes, and had become almost as famous for his crashes as for his flying. In fact, over a period of eight years, he crashed fifty times, with wings breaking in the air, tail assemblies collapsing, and with his planes sometimes going out of control and swooping violently down to earth. But the gods of flying were with him and he managed to escape death, or even serious injury. In one crash after another, when crowds would rush forward expecting to find him dead, Blériot would come crawling out of the wreckage, looking a bit annoyed and bewildered, but nursing only a few cuts and bruises. Staying alive, so Blériot concluded, was simply a trick. Acting on the principle that it was impossible to save both himself and the plane; he developed the acrobatic technique of throwing himself upon one of the wings just before the crash. Although this maneuver always broke the wing, it also succeeded in breaking his fall, and no sooner had one plane collapsed than he was back at the drawing board, designing another.

Blériot's name had become a synonym for perseverance by June of 1909, the month in which he became the first man to fly an airplane with two passengers aboard besides himself. This flight in a large and rather cumbersome flying machine was not a lengthy one, in fact only about a hundred feet in a straight line. But a few weeks later he established a new cross-country record by flying his new *No. 11* monoplane for 25 miles, all the way from Etampes to Orléans with only one stop along the way. It was this flight that made the infant world of aeronautics sit up and take notice of Blériot's *No. 11*, one of the smallest and lightest aircraft ever built.

It resembled a huge dragonfly. The fuselage was 25 feet long from propeller to tail, with the framework consisting of oak and poplar, spliced and reinforced with piano wire. The wings, with a 28-foot span, were covered with an opaque material like vellum, making them appear both light and fragile. Up front,

The exact replica of the 3-cylinder plane in which Louis Blériot made the historic first crossing of the English Channel, 1909. Blériot had been experimenting with airplanes and flight design since 1900, the year the Wright Brothers began their work. (*United Press International Photo*)

attached to a two-bladed wooden propeller, was a three-cylinder, 25-hp Anzani engine which could speed the plane along at 36 miles an hour. The rudder and elevating apparatus were on the tail, and the landing gear resembled two bicycle wheels. Without the pilot, the total weight was 484 pounds. When flying, Blériot sat in the open fuselage between the wings, where he operated the plane with a control stick and foot pedal.

Throughout the first weeks of July, Blériot kept the *No. 11* in the air almost constantly, sometimes flying at three different aerodromes on the same day. And he continually experimented with various ways of keeping the plane aloft for longer and longer periods, with the white cliffs of Dover his ultimate destination.

Then, suddenly, all his plans were nearly shelved indefinitely by another accident, this one inflicting perhaps the most serious injury of his flying career. While testing one of his planes, not the *No. 11*, the gasoline tank exploded, severely burning the foot he used for rudder control in flight. The foot developed an abscess, forcing him to resort to a pair of crutches as he hobbled to and from his airplanes. Even so, inspired by his sensational cross-country flight, he decided to ignore the injured foot and move quickly to seize the opportunity offered by Hubert Latham's failure.

On Tuesday, July 20, the day after Latham landed in the Channel, Blériot notified the Paris newspaper *Matin* that he would take off for England within the next few days, weather permitting. Even though the Channel flight was still a contest, Blériot knew it might well develop into a race if he gave Latham enough time to repair his plane or get a new one.

The following day, strollers on the streets of Calais paused to watch a horse-drawn cart slowly making its way through the town with Blériot's *No. 11* on board. The little plane, looking soiled and weather-beaten from so much test flying, was being towed out into the open sand dunes on the coast near Les Barraques where Blériot had decided to pitch his camp in front of the stately old castle of Calais. When the flying machine was unloaded, the horse turned and gave it one baffled look, then plodded off.

Unlike Latham who had chosen the cliffs for a takeoff point, Blériot was on flat land where the surrounding country was barely above sea level and protected from the Channel by a line of sand dunes. As soon as the plane was carefully rolled into a tent, Blériot limped along on his crutches, climbed into a motor car, and drove back to Calais to await weather reports at the Terminus Hotel.

The weather along the Channel that summer was particularly unsettled, and for the next three days high winds and near-gales made flying safe only for those who wanted to fly a kite. But down the coast of Sangatte, Latham was reported to be triumphantly ready for his second leap out over the water, and his spies were keeping in close touch with Blériot's movements in the same direction. At Wissant, however, the Comte de Lambert was taking an indifferent, if not disdainful, attitude toward flying the Channel first and winning the *Daily Mail* prize. His preparations were proceeding at a cautious pace, and he was making it emphatically clear that he would devote plenty of time to "practice spins" before starting out for England.

The first inkling that Blériot was ready to go came on Saturday night, and the hint was mysteriously dropped in Dover, not in Calais. The midnight Channel boat pulled into Dover Pier and among the passengers was M. Fontaine, a Paris newspaperman who was carrying a French tricolor neatly folded under his arm. Fontaine checked in at the Lord Warden Hotel, and casually told the desk clerk to rouse him early because he had "an appointment with Louis Blériot at 2 A.M." Outside on the Channel, a heavy sea was running with half-a-gale blowing, and the clerk dismissed Fontaine's remark as some kind of a Gaelic joke.

But Fontaine had been given the word. Even though the winds were still troublesome, the weather experts at Calais had informed Blériot that conditions over the Channel would moderate rapidly during the early morning hours. And that was all he needed for a decision—he would take off for England at dawn.

At 2:30 A.M., one of Blériot's friends, Alfred Le Blanc, went to the aviator's room in the Terminus Hotel and pounded on the door. Blériot hastily roused himself, got into a khaki flying suit with Le Blanc's help, and shambled downstairs on his crutches to have coffee with his wife who had loyally witnessed every flight he had made. Before sitting down, he dispatched a messenger to the French torpedo boat, the *Escopette*, which was standing by at Calais, ready to escort him across the Channel as a safety measure if and when he got underway.

Their coffee finished, Blériot gave his wife a farewell embrace, and she left to go aboard the *Escopette* which then weighed anchor and steamed out into the Channel. Blériot got into his motor car and drove as speedily as possible to Les Barraques, followed by a caravan of journalists, some of them Americans.

An eager band of helpers, including the engine designer, M. Anzani, rolled Blériot's plane from its tent and out to the flat grasslands behind the sand dunes along the coastline. In the distance an early morning fog was over the Channel, but the southwesterly wind had dropped off to about 15 miles per hour, leaving it still a bit risky for flying. Nevertheless, Blériot climbed into the cockpit and took the plane above the sand hills for a brief test flight, then came down and took off on another before deciding that the moment had arrived. Obviously, the Anzani was running smoothly and powerfully.

It was now 4:25 A.M., and even at that early hour, a large and enthusiastic crowd was gathering, attracted by the plane's droning engine during the test flying. The contest rules ordained that the flight must be made between sunrise and sunset, so Blériot was delaying his takeoff just a few minutes more until the sun could break the dawn. As he mounted the plane and climbed into the cockpit, he threw away his crutches, then looked over the crowd to say:

"If I cannot walk, I will show the world I can fly."

He adjusted a close-fitting cap around his head and standing up in the cockpit, peered out across the foggy Channel with a slightly puzzled expression on his face. He would carry with him neither a watch nor a compass, so he asked a pertinent navigational question.

"Where is Dover?"

Around him, about fifty hands flew up in the crowd, all pointing in the approximate direction. Even though the sea was foggy, Blériot's mission was clear. It was, of course, a matter of time, distance, and geography, but it had a curious geological twist.

Long, long before Blériot's time, the navigators and map makers of old had determined that the English Channel is 350 miles long, an arm of the Atlantic Ocean extending between France and England to the North Sea. The point of maximum width is on the west, a stretch of 150 miles between Saint-Malo and the inner shores of Lyme Bay. On the east near Calais, it narrows to 22 miles between Cape Gris-Nez and the cliffs of Dover, where the geological similarities on both sides of the Channel are obvious. It's entirely likely that in the dim prehistoric past, an isthmus once connected Calais and Dover, and the Channel was merely a gulf of the Atlantic until the sea cut through, probably in Pleistocene times. And now on Sunday morning, July 25, 1909, it was Blériot's intention to create a new kind of isthmus, an aeronautical isthmus, between France and England.

The sun came up behind Calais Castle at 4:35 A.M., and with a farewell wave, Blériot nodded instructions to start the engine. Anzani himself stepped forward to crank it up, and the crowd responded with much shouting and hand-clapping—while the nightgown-clad residents of nearby homes cheered from their doorways. Five men held down the tail of the straining plane, until Blériot gave the order to "Let go!"

Then it shot forward across the grassy flatlands, rolling rapidly toward the sand dunes and the open Channel beyond. It sped faster and faster until the wheels gradually left the ground, and Blériot eased back the stick to gain the altitude needed to zoom over a line of telegraph wires that skirted the coast ahead. The *No. 11* made the hurdle easily and sailed on over the water at a height of 180 feet. Blériot was on his way.

The crowd rushed to a waiting line of motor cars, cabs, and bicycles, then hurried along the shore road to the nearby crest of Blanc-Nez where the Marconi Company was in direct wireless communication with Dover. Any word of Blériot's progress

Spectators watch Louis Blériot's plane on its flight across the English Channel, 1909. Blériot had crashed fifty times before he made this trip. (*Culver Pictures, Inc.*)

was almost sure to come from there. And in all the excitement no one seemed to be thinking about the competition, for neither Hubert Latham nor his plane were anywhere to be seen. He was still asleep.

Standing several miles out to sea, the captain of the *Escopette* had been waiting and watching, while Madame Blériot and a group of journalists lined the rails, all anxiously scanning the sky above the French coast. Then, just as the sun rose, Madame Blériot gave a cry: "*Mon Dieu!* There he is!"

Still gaining altitude, Blériot was coming on fast. From the cockpit, he saw the *Escopette* galvanize itself into action and begin steaming full speed toward the English coast, rolling out

two huge waves as it cut through the water. The captain had
agreed to head his torpedo boat directly for Dover, so Blériot
might set his bearings on her course. By now he was up at the
dizzy height of 250 feet. But the wind was rising. Indeed, before
the takeoff, he had noticed a steady increase in the southwesterly
wind, and now it was blowing in sharp gusts. Still, the plane
remained on course and was rapidly coming up behind the
Escopette on the sea below.

For a moment it crossed Blériot's mind that the captain was
trying to race him to England. But clearly it would be no
contest, for the *No. 11*, breezing along at slightly more than
40 miles an hour, quickly overtook the escort and passed overhead. Down on the deck, Blériot could see his wife and the
journalists excitedly waving to him. And as he flew on he turned
to note that now the torpedo boat was following him, sending
up a great column of black smoke that concealed the rising sun.

By the time he reached mid-Channel, his escort was falling
far behind. Hoping that perhaps the French Navy could still
keep him in sight, Blériot marked time by flying in a wide circle,
then headed off toward Dover again. The *Escopette* could
travel no faster than 26 miles an hour, and he could no longer
count on any navigational aid. Behind him, the coast of France
had already faded from view, but straight ahead England must
be somewhere, though shrouded in fog. And below him was a
stormy sea.

Blériot, the crash expert, was not one to panic. His engine
was performing beautifully, and his parting glance at the
Escopette convinced him that he was still on a course to Dover.
But with the wind growing stronger, the little plane might be
veering eastward or northward and could easily wander off
course. With a wry smile, he recalled how he had boasted to a
friend that he planned to carry neither a compass nor a watch,
because he thought he would most likely come down in the sea,
and who wants to ruin a watch!

That had been his foolhardy decision, and now it was up to
him to do what airmen in succeeding years had to do—fly by

the seat of his pants. He relaxed his pressure on the controls, and the *No. 11* flew on and on, neither rising nor falling, nor turning right or left, he hoped. He would let the plane find its own way to England, or wherever it wanted to go.

While the minutes passed, Blériot had the strange impression that he wasn't moving at all. Surrounded as he was by fog with neither ships nor land in view, he had the bizarre feeling of being suspended motionlessly in the air. But suddenly he was jarred out of his fantasy by the airman's alarm bell—an unmistakable cough in the motor! Yes, for the first time the engine was running unevenly, obviously overheated by the high speed of such a long flight. It was losing power one moment, then picking up a little the next, while the wing was gradually dropping toward those rolling whitecaps. Was he to follow Latham into the water after all? Blériot looked hopefully toward the inflated rubber tube attached to the fuselage, to keep him afloat should an emergency arise. And to his right, a bright red flag was flapping from the wing to guide the *Escopette* his way should he splash into the sea.

But Blériot's luck in flying over land was not about to desert him over the water. The plane was still slipping downward when it ran into a sudden rainsquall, dousing the engine with cooling water and once more it began tooling along evenly again. Blériot quickly nosed the plane upward, regaining his lost altitude, and straining his eyes for a break in the fog.

His sense of elapsed time told him that at least 25 minutes had passed since the takeoff, that land had to be near—and he was correct. As the plane sped forward he could see a long gray line detaching itself from the sea. It was the coast of England and the fog was lifting, but it was not the landscape he had hoped to see. Instead of the chalk cliffs of Dover, the plane was headed toward Deal and St. Margaret's Bay, several miles east of Dover Castle where he had chosen to land. Obviously the southwest wind had taken him off course while he was flying through the fog.

Far to the west he could see Dover Lighthouse, England's

oldest, which had guided Roman ships into Dover Harbor. Hard by the lighthouse was Dover Castle, its fortifications rising from the cliff and commanding the approaches from the sea. Somewhere along those heights, Fontaine was supposed to be waiting, ready to signal him toward a suitable landing place. Blériot quickly made his decision—the flight had started out for Dover, and at Dover would end.

He gradually swung the plane to the left and headed directly into the wind, which was becoming even more of a problem because of tricky air currents along the shore. Remaining about a mile out at sea, he followed the coastline eastward for one, two, three miles. By now the gusts were slowing him down and his arms were beginning to ache from his efforts to keep the plane on an even keel. But happily, the fog had lifted, and he could see a fleet of battleships riding at anchor in Dover Harbor.

Turning toward the shore, he flew low above the masts of the ships and then headed out along the heights, looking for some sign of Fontaine. A moment later he saw him standing on the cliff, waving the French tricolor and shouting, "Bravo! Bravo!" as he signaled frantically toward a gap which opened into a spacious green meadow just below the heights of Dover Castle.

Blériot banked his plane into a half-circle out over the sea, and then came back to fly straight through the gap—and for the first time since the takeoff he was over dry land. He turned sharply to avoid a red building coming up on his right, and at that moment the plane went out of control.

Inside the cliffs, the *No. 11* had flown into a pocket of turbulence and it was whirling the plane around like a windmill, with Blériot desperately holding on to the cockpit. Three times the plane spun crazily, and Blériot, realizing that a normal landing was hopeless, cut off the motor. Powered now only by the law of gravity, the plane came swooping down from a height of 65 feet to whack the grassy meadow with a glancing blow that damaged the landing gear and propeller but, as usual, left Blériot an uninjured though rather exhausted French aviator.

As he sat there dazed in the cockpit, in the distance he saw figures running across the meadow toward the plane. It had taken him only 37 minutes to fly the Channel. The *Daily Mail* prize was his and the shrinking world would never again be the same. For, with this successful first long-distance flight over water, Louis Blériot had made history. A history to be enlivened by thousands, yes, tens of thousands of long-distance, even global, flights. And the ones that follow will go down in history as milestones in the annals of the human race.

Following Blériot there were many long-distance flights already rated as historic milestones in the annals of Man. One was the first non-stop crossing of the Atlantic by two airmen who for this feat were knighted by the King. And that brings us to the story of Alcock and Brown.

CHAPTER II

Alcock and Brown Fly the Atlantic

After Blériot's conquest of the English Channel, it was inevitable that the next major challenge for aviators of all nations would be a non-stop flight across the Atlantic. At first, the coming of World War I interfered with this, although as early as 1913 Lord Northcliffe and the London *Daily Mail* had offered £10,000 for a first non-stop aerial crossing in either direction. The flight had to be made in less than 72 hours, with the takeoff and landing points somewhere in the United States, Canada, or Newfoundland on one side, and the British Isles on the other.

When the First World War ended in 1918, commercial flying was still in its infancy, and the public, generally speaking, had a suspicion of airplanes whose job, first and foremost, had been to spread death and destruction throughout the four years of conflict. Thousands of wartime pilots found themselves with nothing to do, and many turned to other professions despite all the flying experience they had acquired during the war. Still, some were determined to pursue flying careers no matter what the odds, and their ambitions received quite a boost in the very month of the Armistice when Lord Northcliffe and the *Daily Mail* renewed that £10,000 prize offer for a first non-stop transatlantic flight.

By the spring of 1919, the island of Newfoundland off the

coast of Canada had become the busiest aviation center in the world. Airplanes were being crated in by freighter from England, landing fields and hangars were under construction, and aviators, mechanics, and navigators were arriving on every steamer. The intense preparations for flights across the English Channel in 1909 had been leisurely compared with the feverish activity that now gripped Newfoundland, the staging area for a far more spectacular and dangerous race.

At least four teams of British aviators had arrived by the middle of May and more were expected with each passing day. Two private fliers, Harry Hawker, an Australian, and Kenneth MacKenzie-Grieve, had pitched their camp at Mount Pearl Farm where they were running their Sopwith biplane through a series of tests. Captain Fred P. Raynham and his navigator, C. W. F. Morgan, were preparing their Martinsyde biplane on a landing strip at nearby Quidi Vidi, while at Harbor Grace, a third team, headed by Vice Admiral Mark Kerr, was assembling a huge four-engine Handley-Page biplane. With the bases, located within a 100-mile radius of each other, there was an air of competition, and all this was heightened by a growing international corps of newsmen who were sending out daily dispatches on the flight preparations. Naturally the Newfoundlanders were watching all these developments with intense interest and amazement.

Soon the Americans were in the running too, although their plans did not call for a non-stop flight to the British Isles, and therefore they would be ineligible for the *Daily Mail* prize. The United States Navy had decided to demonstrate the range and power of its new Curtiss Flying Boats by sending three of these planes on a flight from Newfoundland to the Azores, thence to Portugal and on to Plymouth, England. Even if only one of them made it to the Azores, America could claim the honor of first flying the Atlantic, although it would be over a shorter distance than the route from Newfoundland to the British Isles.

The Navy planes made their base at Trepassey, Newfoundland, and American warships were assigned areas all the way across the ocean to the Azores as standby vessels for refueling and rescue duties. Moving swiftly to get into the air ahead of the British, all three American planes, the *NC-1 NC-3*, and *NC-4*, took off from Trepassey late on the afternoon of May 16. First, the unlucky *NC-1* was forced down in the Atlantic within 200 miles of the Azores and the crew was rescued. Then, the hapless *NC-3* lost its bearings in a fog, came down at sea, and was missing for 52 hours. But it taxied through rough seas for 205 miles while riding out a gale and finally arrived safely in the Azores. Meanwhile, the *NC-4* under Lieutenant Commander Albert C. Read with a crew of four, including pilots Walter Hinton and E. F. Stone, did manage to fly all the way to the Azores, covering the 1380-mile distance in about 15 hours. Then several days later, the *NC-4* continued on to Portugal and arrived in England near the end of May, completing the entire journey from Newfoundland in about two weeks.

So the *NC-4* became the first heavier-than-air craft to cross the Atlantic and its crew won much temporary fame for the achievement. However, this still left unclaimed the *Daily Mail's* prize for a non-stop flight between North America and the British Isles in less than 72 hours. Moreover, flying the Atlantic without rescue ships deployed along the way remained a far bigger challenge in the eyes of a watching world.

On May 16, the day the American planes had taken off from Trepassey, the British aviators on Newfoundland were straining at the leash. And when the word came through that Commander Read and the *NC-4* had reached the Azores, Hawker and Grieve made a final inspection of their Sopwith, then roared out across the Atlantic heading for Ireland. Less than an hour later, Raynham and Morgan, not to be left behind, sent their Martinsyde down the runway at Quidi Vidi, but failed to get off the ground. In their haste to follow their rivals, they tried to take off in a cross wind and their plane crashed into a ravine, injuring Morgan so seriously that he had to give up flying.

For the next several hours, Hawker and Grieve flew on toward

Ireland, but loose solder in the radiator clogged the water-circulation system, forcing the plane down into the ocean a thousand miles east of Newfoundland. They were missing and given up for lost for the next seven days until the news came through that a Danish freighter had rescued them at sea, and a highly excited British public gave them a heroes' welcome when they reached London. Harry Hawker went on to become famous in aviation as one of the founders of Hawker Siddeley Aviation, Ltd.

Two British flying teams had failed in their attempts to cross the ocean while Admiral Kerr was still assembling his Handley-Page biplane at Harbor Grace, hopeful of getting away on his own flight by early June. But he was facing the threat of stiff competition from a pair of Royal Air Force fliers who had entered the race: their names—Captain John Alcock and Lieutenant Arthur Whitten-Brown. They had arrived at St. John's on May 13, but their airplane was stored in crates on board another vessel which wasn't due for another two weeks.

Who were these new entries? Some four months before, Arthur Whitten-Brown, a thirty-three-year-old World War I veteran born in Glasgow of American parents, had been looking for a job. He also had hopes of soon marrying Kathleen Kennedy, the beautiful red-haired daughter of a major in the British Ministry of Munitions. But the all-important question of a job had to be settled first.

During his early years, Brown attended school in England and, even though he possessed American citizenship, he had joined the British Army to fight the Germans. As a lieutenant, he led his men in battles at Ypres and along the Somme, then transferred to the Royal Flying Corps as an observer. Twice shot down, on the second time he was taken prisoner and spent fourteen months in a German POW camp before being repatriated.

During the war years Brown had made an intensive study of aerial navigation and after the Armistice he began making the rounds of aircraft firms that were showing an interest in transatlantic flying. One afternoon he visited the Vickers plant at Weybridge near London, and the superintendent, Maxwell Muller, listened quietly as Brown stated his qualifications. Then Muller asked:

"You are a navigator. But can you navigate a plane across the Atlantic?"

"Yes," Brown replied, apparently without misgivings.

"Then we have a job for you," Muller continued. "The *Daily Mail*, as you know, is offering a prize of £10,000 for the first plane to fly the Atlantic non-stop. We want our plane to be the first to do it, and Vickers doesn't care about the money. The men who fly the plane can have that. We have the pilot, and we have the plane, so come along and meet both."

A few moments later Brown was shaking hands with Captain John Alcock, a twenty-six-year-old British pilot who had come out of the war with seven enemy planes to his credit and a Distinguished Service Cross among his decorations. From the point of view of personality, the two were a study in contrasts, but they developed a liking for each other almost immediately. Brown, the Scottish-American, was slight of build, dark-haired, rather quiet and reserved. Alcock was sturdy, round-faced and blond, with a ready wit, a dry humor, and very British.

In fact, Alcock was a pioneer of British aviation, and had received his flying certificate at the age of twenty when he became an instructor in aerobatics. During the war he had flown bombing missions against the Turks, including one daring raid on Constantinople. Like Brown, he too had been taken prisoner after he was forced to ditch his plane in the Aegean off Gallipoli.

Together, Alcock and Brown looked over their transatlantic plane—a Vickers-Vimy biplane powered by two 350-hp Rolls-Royce engines. A converted bomber, it had been earmarked for raids on Berlin and had a cruising speed of about 90 miles per hour with a range of some 2400 miles. Considerable work remained before it would be ready for the flight, but by early May final tests were completed and the disassembled plane was placed in crates for the voyage to Newfoundland. The two fliers, aware of the hazards of their mission, put their personal affairs in order and Arthur Whitten-Brown told an understanding Kathleen Kennedy their marriage would have to be postponed until after the flight.

When they arrived at St. John's, Alcock and Brown took up residence at the Cochrane Hotel, the bustling headquarters of transatlantic aviators during that hectic spring of 1919. With their plane still en route from England, they spent the next few days trying to find a suitable landing strip, a task that wasn't so easy. Newfoundland was in the midst of a real estate boom, brought on by all this sudden demand for aerodromes, and property owners were asking sky-high prices for land that had even the remotest appearance of being level. Every day for a week, Alcock and Brown drove for miles over seemingly endless bad roads in an effort to find a suitable field, but it was a desperate search. The aerodrome at Mount Pearl Farm, recently vacated by Hawker and Grieve, would have been perfect, but the owner wanted $3000 rent until June 15 and $250 a day after that. Another likely area was found near Harbor Grace, but here Alcock was confronted with a demand for $25,000 when he approached the owner. The Newfoundlanders obviously were determined to make hay while they had the chance.

The Vickers-Vimy arrived and the tedious job of assembly began at Quidi Vidi where Captain Raynham generously offered the use of his aerodrome facilities, even though the runway there would not be long enough to permit the Vimy to take off with a full load of gasoline. Still looking for a landing field, Alcock and Brown divided their time between the plane and a search of the countryside until one afternoon their luck took a new turn. The owner of a large meadow near a place called Monday's Pool made them a reasonable offer. They promptly leased the land, and hired a labor force of thirty men who brought along picks and shovels to level the hillocks and remove the rocks and boulders. The work was completed on June 9 and Alcock flew the Vimy over from Quidi Vidi with a light load of gasoline.

For the next four days, Alcock and Brown virtually lived with their meteorological officers, but each day the weather reports were unfavorable, with high winds, fog, and rain continuing out over the North Atlantic. Coupled with their irritation over the delay was a growing apprehension that Admiral Kerr and his Handley-Page crew were almost ready to take off. But regardless of the weather, Alcock and Brown finally decided to wait no longer.

Early on the morning of Saturday, June 14, they showed up at the aerodrome in their electrically heated flying suits and, together with their mechanics, they began filling the tanks with a full complement of 870 gallons of gasoline and 40 gallons of oil. Their personal luggage was stored in a compartment near the single open cockpit. For food they took aboard sandwiches, chocolate, malted milk, and a thermos of coffee, along with a few small bottles of brandy and ale. Fitted into the area around the cockpit was a mail bag with three hundred private letters, and also their mascots, "Twinkletoes" and "Lucky Jim," two stuffed black cats which Kathleen Kennedy had given them before they left England.

At 4 A.M., they were again told that weather conditions were something less than perfect.

"Strong westerly wind. Conditions otherwise fairly favorable."

A few hours later, a cross wind was blowing from the west and the two fliers decided to wait a little longer in the hope that it would die down. But the morning hours gave way to the afternoon with the wind still blowing as furiously as ever.

Convinced that he could get the plane off the ground without a crash, Alcock made his decision. First, he asked the Vickers manager on the field for permission to take off, then he motioned Brown on board. Standing together in the cockpit, both fliers turned to say goodbye to their mechanics and a crowd of Newfoundlanders who had come down from St. John's to see them off.

Navigator Brown announced:

"Our objective is the Irish coast. We shall aim at the center of our target."

And Alcock, the blithe spirit, added:

"Yes, we shall hang our hats on the aerials of Clifden Wireless Station as we go by. So long."

At 4:10 P.M., the chocks were removed from the wheels—and the mechanics, hanging on the wings and tail, "let go" as Alcock gave both engines full throttle and the Vimy started across the turf. The two fliers were seated side by side in the cockpit as they headed over the slightly inclined runway into the westerly wind.

The plane lurched and lumbered forward for 300 yards before the wheels left the ground, and it was none too soon. A line of hills and treetops lay ahead, and gale-force winds were bedeviling Alcock's efforts to gain altitude as the Vimy slowly climbed to 800 feet and over the trees. With his machine now well under control, Alcock headed over the fishing fleet in Concepcion Bay and then on beyond Signal Hill to the open Atlantic.

It was at St. John's in 1901 that Signor Guglielmo Marconi received the first wireless signal ever sent across the Atlantic. And now, eighteen years later, the Marconi Station was flashing the news of the takeoff to every ship in the North Atlantic, asking them to be on the lookout and give the plane's position if sighted. Brown would be counting on this information to aid the navigation, and the moment the Vimy left the coastline he unstrung the wireless aerial to tap a message to the Marconi operator:

"All well and started."

Gradually, Alcock nosed the Vimy upward until they were at 3000 feet, while far beneath them the gray waters of the Atlantic were rolling and tossing in a gale-force wind. But the westerly wind which had been a problem on the takeoff, was now their friend, boosting them along at more than a hundred miles an hour. With both engines running smoothly and the getaway a success, Brown decided to run the wireless apparatus through a few tests, just to make sure it was working properly.

"Say, Jack," he said over the telephone, "I'm going to send St. John's a few words of greeting."

"Tell them we'll be across in sixteen hours," answered Alcock, "if this wind keeps us in its lap."

Brown began tapping out the Vimy's own call letters, D.K.G., but as he worked the key, the spark grew weaker and weaker until there was no flashing blue light at all. It was a difficult problem, for the wireless generator received its energy from a small, wind-driven propeller located under the forward fuselage and it couldn't be seen from the cockpit.

Brown told his companion about the trouble and, holding tightly to the struts, he climbed out on the wing for a close look at the four-bladed wireless propeller, despite Alcock's emphatic warning against taking such a risk. With the wind screaming around him, Brown crouched on the lower wing, and peering underneath the yellow fuselage, he saw a propeller with only one blade—the other three were gone, probably sheared away by the severe rocking of the plane on the takeoff. For the rest of the flight, their wireless would be out of commission and beyond hope of repair. They would have no way of sending or receiving messages, no way of getting their bearings from ships at sea, and all through the tense hours that lay ahead, they would be completely isolated from the world.

Throughout the early evening hours they flew between layers of clouds above and below, with the ocean completely shut off from view. Then, shortly after 7 P.M., more trouble. The starboard motor began coughing and stuttering so badly that both fliers were thoroughly alarmed as they leaned out to look at the motor. A large chunk of the exhaust pipe had split away, and, as they watched, it changed from red- to white-hot, then gradually crumpled as it grew softer in the intense heat. Three cylinders of the starboard engine were throwing their exhaust fumes straight into the air without benefit of the usual outlet, but throttling down the starboard motor was out of the question, and the exhaust problem was with them to stay.

Brown had brought along a small bubble sextant and was relying entirely on this for directional navigation. It was still evening, and he was taking sights on the stars and moon when suddenly the Vimy plowed into a thick bank of fog. Shouting into the intercom, he told Alcock to go higher, and when they reached 12,000 feet the stars once again were there to guide them.

The hours passed monotonously, and soon it was well past midnight with the moon still shining brightly above them, coloring the clouds with tinges of silver, gold, and red. Below, they could see the Vimy's shadow moving across the layer of clouds that covered the ocean. Twice during the night they polished off a quick sandwich along with a few shots of brandy, and they fought constantly to ignore the drone of the motors which almost lulled them to sleep.

Just as the sun was beginning to rise, the plane ran into another wall of fog, and they had the sensation of flying inside a bottle of milk. With nothing but the white mist around them, they lost their sense of balance and a glance at the instrument panel showed the plane was not on an even keel, and might even be flying upside down. Even worse, it was plunging rapidly through the clouds with the altimeter dropping to 2000 —1000—then 500 feet. And the tension was growing in the cockpit.

If the cloud layer reached all the way down to the ocean, Alcock would be unable to see the horizon in time to counter-act the spin and avoid a crash. Preparing for the worst, Brown loosened his safety belt and they were less than a hundred feet from the water when, in a moment of flashing light, the plane shot out of the cloud vapor into the clear atmosphere.

But the ocean did not appear below them!

The plane was tilted at an angle, and the line of the horizon seemed to be standing vertically to their view. But Alcock quickly regained his visual equilibrium, and the Vimy responded to the controls. At full throttle, he swung the plane back on a level course even though they were flying a mere 50 feet over the ocean. The danger was past, but they were lucky to be out of that one.

For the next three hours, the Vimy moved in and out of a

procession of clouds that enveloped the plane time and again, only to give way to patches of blue. But the clouds soon massed into a black wall and a driving rain began lashing the fuselage. Minutes later it turned to snow, and then to a heavy sleet. Trying to rise above the storm, they reached 9000 feet when Brown saw the glass face of the gasoline overflow gauge clotted with snow and ice. To guard against carburetor trouble, they had to read this gauge at any given moment, and clearing away the ice and snow would be no simple task. It was fixed to one of the center struts and Brown decided that, once more, it was up to him to climb out of the cockpit.

Holding on to a cross-bracing wire to keep the wind from blasting him off the side, he knelt on the wing and managed to reach up and wipe the sleet from the gauge. Time and again, Brown repeated the performance as the storm continued, and he implored Alcock to keep the plane on a level keel while he was out there on the fuselage.

They kept themselves warm by huddling as far down in the open cockpit as possible, while Alcock took the plane higher and higher, hoping to get above the sleet. And it was 6 A.M. when Brown saw the sun glinting through a gap in the clouds. Even though the horizon was shrouded in fog, he was able to get a reading that showed they were nearing the Irish coast and he scribbled Alcock a message:

"Better go lower; the air will be warmer and we may spot a steamer."

Once again, Alcock was feeling his way down through the clouds, knowing that at any moment the wheels might strike the surface of the sea. Then, the plane suddenly emerged from the cloud bank, and both engines responded as Alcock opened full throttle again. But there was no sign of a ship on the cold, gray ocean below as they roared on toward what they hoped would be the emerald coasts of Ireland.

It was exactly 8:15 A.M., and Brown had just finished screwing on the lid of the thermos flask when Alcock grabbed his shoulder, and pointed. There, looming through the mist, were two tiny specks of land—and Brown put both his charts and the thermos away. His navigation duties were over. They had spotted two islands off the Irish coast, and a moment later the mainland came clearly into view.

Still uncertain of their exact location, they crossed the coastline looking for a railway to follow. But when the masts of the Clifden Wireless Station pierced the sky ahead, they knew they were on the beam. It was time for a decision, and Brown asked a crucial question:

"Shall we land at London, or Clifden?"

Alcock was quick to answer, for he feared that Admiral Kerr and his Handley-Page might even then be roaring up somewhere behind them, anxious to beat them to the prize.

"I think we'd better make it Clifden," he said. "All we have to do to win is reach the British Isles, and it'll lengthen our flying time if we go on to London."

As they circled the wireless aerials of Clifden looking for a spot to land, Alcock saw what appeared to be a level stretch of ground. He brought the Vimy in for a perfect landing and it rolled for a hundred feet or so when—without warning—up it went on its nose.

Despite the benign appearance of their landing site, they had come down in an Irish bog. Brown was uninjured, but the soil of Ireland had risen up to give Alcock a black eye and a pair of badly bruised lips. Even so, as he climbed out of the wreckage a grin spread around his swollen mouth, and with a wink toward the Vimy he managed to say:

"She's a pretty fair old boat, eh what?"

The following morning the New York *Times* told the story in its page one headline:

ALCOCK AND BROWN FLY ACROSS THE ATLANTIC;
MAKE 1,980 MILES IN 16 HOURS, 12 MINUTES;
SOMETIMES UPSIDE DOWN IN DENSE, ICY FOG

King George V soon issued the orders making them Sir John Alcock and Sir Arthur Whitten-Brown, and Lord Northcliffe

Alcock and Brown's biplane lands in a bog in Ireland. It had left St. John's, Newfoundland, June 14, 1919, and arrived across the Atlantic on June 15. (*Brown Brothers*)

wrote the check for £10,000, shares of which the two fliers generously gave their mechanics.

Brown married his fiancée, Kathleen Kennedy, and he lived to the age of sixty-two. Sir John Alcock, however, was tragically killed in a plane crash in France only six months later.

Now, in the late 1960s, the trail Alcock and Brown blazed so long ago, against such great odds, is flown 1589 times weekly by huge planes that can speed at 600 miles an hour. But when Orville Wright, on the evening of June 15, 1919, heard about the first non-stop flight across the Atlantic, he couldn't believe his ears.

"What?" he asked with astonishment, "only sixteen hours! Are you sure?"

The Atlantic having been flown, aviators began tuning up for flights over parts of the planet where not even the shadow of an airplane had ever been seen. To fly from London to Australia, halfway round the world, this was regarded as sheer suicide. But there were young airmen eager to take the risk; once again with knighthood as one reward.

Captain Sir John Alcock (left) and Lieutenant Sir Arthur Whitten-Brown (right) two months after their historic transatlantic flight, 1919. Both men were World War I veterans with time heavy on their hands till the transatlantic flight project came along. (*The Bettman Archive*)

CHAPTER III

Halfway Round the World

(G—E A O U—God 'Elp All of Us!)

Early on the frosty morning of November 12, 1919, a big Vickers-Vimy twin-engined biplane rolled out of a hangar at London's Hounslow Aerodrome and taxied down the runway through a dense haze that covered the field. As the plane came to a stop, four young Australians, dressed in flying togs, jumped from the two open cockpits and began checking the propellers, ailerons, and engines, going about their routine with the air of men who knew their business. Three of them were wartime veterans of the Royal Flying Corps, and they were about to get underway with the greatest peacetime adventure of their lives.

The leader of the group was Captain Ross Smith, who had been an ace in the campaign against the Turks in Palestine. There was no second in command, but, for the record, Ross's brother, Lieutenant Keith Smith, was the co-pilot although he had just recently won his wings and had not seen active service with the Flying Corps. The other two were Vickers mechanics, Sergeants J. M. Bennett and W. H. Shiers, both of whom had served with Ross Smith in Palestine.

They soon completed their inspection of the sturdy plane which was similar in size and design to the one that Alcock and Brown had flown across the Atlantic. The two 350-hp Rolls-Royce engines were running smoothly, and all the necessary supplies and equipment were put on board, including 516 gallons of

The Vickers-Vimy Rolls bomber being inspected before the attempted flight to Australia from England, 1919. Brothers Ross (left) and Keith (center) Smith are the aviators in the cockpit. The marking on their plane was **G–EAOU** —God 'Elp All of Us. (*United Press International Photo*)

gasoline. But at 6:30 A.M., the ground haze had grown so thick that visibility was near zero, and the Air Ministry warned Ross Smith of bad weather extending from southeast England on across the north of France. Hoping for something better, the Australians waited until 8 A.M., but even then it was the same discouraging story—weather hopeless for flying.

Impatient with the delay, Ross called his mates into a conference on the snow-covered field, and the vote was unanimous —fair or foul, let's take off now. So they climbed aboard, and with the cheers of a small group of friends ringing in their ears, they gunned the big plane down the runway and up into the mist-laden skies. Far to the southeast was their goal—Australia. And painted across the wings and fuselage were the markings,

G–EAOU, letters by which the Air Ministry had officially designed the plane. But as far as the four fliers were concerned,
the alphabetical symbols meant–"God 'Elp All of Us!"

*   *   *   *   *

Within only a few months after Alcock and Brown had ended
their flight in an Irish bog, the eyes of the aviation world were
focused on Hounslow where the curtain was rising on the
Great London-to-Australia Air Derby–a grandiose adventure
that would carry devil-may-care aviators halfway around the
globe. Located in a London suburb about 12 miles southwest
of St. Paul's Cathedral, Hounslow had once been a hideout for
highwaymen, but by the autumn of 1919 it had become an aerie
for Australian airmen who were hell-bent on winning a new
cash prize. The government of Australia had offered £10,000
for the first successful flight from England to Australia, with
the aim of binding the Commonwealth closer to the Mother
Country through the air. A definite set of rules had been set for
the contest. For one, no plane could start before September 8,
1919, and the flight had to be completed within thirty days or
less. To be eligible for the prize, an airplane had to be of
British manufacture, and every man on board had to prove his
Australian citizenship.

Even though flying the Channel and the Atlantic had been
dangerous ventures, the problem had been the seemingly simple
one of remaining in the air long enough to get across an expanse of water. But a flight from England to Australia would
span not just one, but several oceans and seas. The land portions
of the journey would be over the rugged mountains of Europe,
the deserts of the Middle East, then on across the jungles and
islands of Southeast Asia–vast stretches that offered little in the
way of landing fields. True, the steeplechase courses at Rangoon
and Singapore could be used, but somebody would have to
stable the horses and clear away the hurdles before the planes
arrived. Equally hazardous would be the treacherous and constantly changing weather, with rain and fog over Europe giving
way to desert sandstorms, followed by the heat of the tropics
and the danger of sudden typhoons.

The perils of all this were obvious, but there was no shortage of eager Australian aviators whose Flying Corps had been one of the finest of all Allied combat outfits. And they had the enthusiastic backing of several aircraft firms and petroleum companies who were anxious to identify themselves with long-distance commercial flying. By October 1919, at least six teams of Australian airmen were preparing to take off from Hounslow whose rather drab-looking wartime buildings were the head-quarters for the big race. Mingled with the atmosphere of spirited rivalry, there was a sense of history-in-the-making. Only a few months before, in August, the first commercial flights had begun between London and Paris. Each day now a plane, carry-ing a pilot and a couple of passengers, was taking off from Hounslow and heading out across the Channel for Le Bourget.

Two other planes had begun the flight to Australia before Ross Smith and his crew took off on November 12. Even though they were ineligible for the prize because of their nationality, a team of two French fliers, Lieutenant Etienne Poulet and his mechanic, M. Benoist, got a head start on the others by leaving Paris on October 12, hoping to win the honor of being the first to fly from Europe to Australia. They made excellent time across Europe and the Middle East, but their progress slowed to a crawl in Asia where mechanical difficulties beset their twin-engined Caudron airplane.

Ten days after the French left Paris, the race officially be-gan when the first Australian team, Captain G. C. Matthews and his mechanic Sergeant Tom Kay, took off from Hounslow in their Sopwith "Wallaby." Captain Matthews was an old sailor who had an intimate knowledge of the Pacific Islands and he was counting on the hospitality of the natives, as well as his own ability as an expert navigator, to see the flight through. But almost immediately he ran into navigational problems over territory where there were no coconut trees or dreamy lagoons to guide the way. His plane wandered far off course in Ger-many, was forced to land, and became snowbound at an airfield in Alsace-Lorraine. So by the time Ross Smith and his crew left Hounslow on November 12, the box-score for the big race was: one plane in the air and on its way, two stalled en route, with at least four others hoping to get off. And it was still anybody's guess as to who would reach Australia first.

As he angled the Vimy slowly upward through the fog above Hounslow, Ross Smith listened to the smooth rhythm of the engines. There was no sign of trouble. At 2000 feet, the plane burst out of the fog into brilliant sunshine and he circled the airfield for ten minutes, giving the instrument panel a final check before setting off toward the cliffs of Dover. The start was perfect and in a moment of grateful reverie, the Australian ace imagined that already he was triumphantly shaking hands with the gentlemen of Vickers, Limited, who had agreed to sponsor the flight.

It seemed only minutes before they were over the English Channel, and through a break in the swirling fog beneath them they could see the white-maned waves crashing against the chalk headlands. Despite the Air Ministry's warning, the weather over England and the Channel was almost perfect, but in the distance, rising above the mainland of France, a mass of clouds was blocking their way. And the altimeter's needle was at 4000 feet when the Vimy plunged into rain, sleet, and snow.

A coat of half-frozen mush quickly covered the wings and fuselage, turning the Vimy into a white phantom as it sped through the mist. The icy slush clotted the windshield and clung to the goggles, turning the flight into a hazardous game of blindman's buff until Ross Smith nosed the plane sharply upward in a determined effort to get above the storm. Climbing steadily in a wide-ranging spiral, the Vimy reached a height of 9000 feet and once again there were blue skies above, while below the vast sea of clouds resembled a polar landscape. In consultation with his brother Keith, Ross took a compass reading, setting a course toward Lyon in south-central France, and for the next three hours they flew above the storm, hoping for an opening that would give them a glimpse of land.

The late afternoon sun was beginning to wane when a break came, with the clouds opening up below them like a crater in a vast white volcano to reveal the French terrain through a

shaft of falling snow. Smith swung the Vimy into a wide
arc as the descent began, and they spiraled slowly downward
until the snow-covered buildings of a town came beneath the
wings.

Keith Smith turned to his maps, and in a moment the town
had a name.

"It's Roanne," he told his brother, "and Lyon is only forty
miles away."

After landing at Lyon and taking on more fuel, the Vimy
pounded down the runway at 10 o'clock the following morning
and headed for Rome, another 560 miles away. As they crossed
the Italian border, a strong head wind cut the plane's speed to
a mere 50 miles an hour, and they came down at Pisa with
insufficient gas to continue. That night, heavy rain turned the
airfield into a sea of mud, causing a delay of two days before
they could get the Vimy unstuck and into the air again for
the short flight to Rome.

The skies were cloudy on the morning of November 16 when
the Smiths left the Eternal City and headed east across the
Apennines, but the ceiling was so low they were forced to fly
just above the valleys where the atmosphere was clear. With a
tail wind helping them along and the altimeter's needle juggling
between 400 and 1000 feet, the Vimy soared down the Italian
coast to the seaport of Taranto where they landed at one of
the busier aerodromes on the route from London to Cairo.

The story of flight was an old one in Taranto, for it was there
in the year 400 B.C. that Archytas, the learned geometer, constructed a wooden dove and carried out man's first recorded experiments with flying. In trying to explain how the wooden
dove sustained itself in flight, Archytas and his colleagues noted
only one irritating difficulty: "If it fell, it could not raise itself
up any more." Archytas thus came close to preceding Sir Isaac
Newton in discovering the law of gravity, the difference being
an apple and a wooden dove.

The following morning the Anzac airmen were up with the
rising sun and the Vimy was off again, flying eastward to the
heel of Italy and on across the Ionian Sea toward the Greek

coast. But the weather once more had turned foul, with fog and rain forcing them down to 800 feet as they flew southward above the rocky shorelines, then out over the Mediterranean to the island of Crete.

After refueling and another overnight stay, they took off from Crete on the long 650-mile stretch to Cairo, and it was there they learned the shocking details of the first tragedy to strike the Great London-to-Australia Air Derby. Another team of Australians, Lieutenants Roger Douglas and Leslie Ross, had taken off from Hounslow on November 13 in their single-engined Alliance P-2. After only a few minutes of flight the plane emerged from a cloud above Surbiton and nose-dived to a crash, killing both fliers. So now the box-score read: one plane crashed with two dead, two planes stalled en route, one in the air and on its way, and three others still trying to get off from Hounslow.

The next day, a telegraphic report from Palestine issued a clear warning: WEATHER CONDITIONS UNSUITED FOR FLYING. With rain falling in Cairo and the prospects none too good for the 450-mile flight to Damascus, they talked it over and decided that, with one day already lost at Pisa, they'd better keep moving if they were to reach Australia within the contest limit of thirty days. So despite the rain, they headed for the "oldest city in the world," flying eastward over Tel-el-Kebir, a famous battlefield of 1882, then El-Arish, Rafa, and Gaza. When they reached the skies above Ramleh, where Ross Smith had flown with Allenby's army, the rain was coming down in torrents, lashing their faces and drenching their plane. But the sun broke through above the Sea of Galilee and Ross took the Vimy to 5000 feet as they sped on across Syria to a safe landing at ancient Damascus.

The next morning it was still raining, so heavily that the Vimy's wheels were gradually sinking into the aerodrome mire. Threatened with a crippling delay, they climbed into the cockpits and, to their relief, the plane rolled through the muck with just enough speed to become airborne even though it had to rise through a whirling curtain of water. Two hours later the rain ended, and they were flying low over a desert dotted with black tents and more camels than they had ever seen. The sudden and unexpected appearance of the Vimy sent the dromedaries stampeding in all directions, while their Bedouin masters ran from their tents, wondering at the strange uproar. The sun was calling it a day as they flew on down the Euphrates and descended to Ramadie, rather than risk a night landing at Baghdad only another 40 miles away.

That night a windstorm threatened their plane, and fifty men from a nearby camp of the 10th Indian Lancers helped them save the Vimy from destruction. Four struts were torn loose in the gale, but with the engines going full blast, they managed to swing the grounded plane around into the wind and hold it firmly until the gales died down at dawn.

For the first time since leaving Hounslow, the fliers were greeted by clear skies and, after repairing the broken struts and shoveling sand from the fuselage, they took off with enough petrol to carry them on to Baghdad and Basra, some 350 miles to the southeast. Then, almost before they could say "Ali Baba and the Forty Thieves," the Magic City of Baghdad was beneath the Vimy's wings, and soon they were over the Tigris and Euphrates, flying. on to the Persian Gulf.

Basra, home of Sindbad the Sailor, was reached on November 21 and that same day back at Hounslow another team of four Australians roared down the runway in a twin-engined Blackburn "Kangaroo" to join the race. Heading the crew of the big biplane was George Hubert Wilkins, a thirty-one-year-old explorer who had spent two years in the Arctic with Vilhjalmur Stefansson. During World War I, Wilkins had been in the thick of the battle on the Western Front and his motion pictures were the first ever made of actual combat. Now he was commander and navigator on an Australian flight, with a three-man crew consisting of Lieutenant Valdemar Rendle as the pilot, and Lieutenants Reg Williams and Garnsey Potts as assistant pilots.

Trouble plagued their flight almost from the moment they left Hounslow. The "Kangaroo's" controls froze in a rainstorm over the Maritime Alps, forcing them to land in Italy on a field surrounded by Roman ruins and they narrowly missed crashing into an ancient aqueduct. The next day engine trouble forced them to land again, and they made the startling discovery that someone had tampered with the machines by disconnecting an ignition wire. And when the plane finally reached Crete and took off for Cairo, an oil leak developed, compelling them to turn back and come in for a crash landing near an insane asylum. Nobody was injured, but so much time had elapsed that Wilkins decided it would be futile to continue the race.

So now the box-score stood: one plane crashed with two dead, another plane down and out of the race, two planes stalled en route, one in the air and on its way, and two others still hoping to start. Across the Atlantic in America, the editors of the New York *Times* were shaking their heads and making the gloomy comment that "Columbus did not take one-tenth the risk these bold air pioneers are facing—they are throwing dice with Death."

On the morning of November 23, the Vickers-Vimy rose into a sky flooded with sunshine and a few hours later landed safely at the little known Persian city of Bundar Abbas, where a delegation of Persian Moslems objected strenuously to the presence of a vehicle "not mentioned in the Koran." Facing them now was the longest leg of the entire journey, the 730 miles across the deserts and barren mountains of Baluchistan to Karachi on the Arabian Sea, and they knew this part of the flight would have to be made non-stop if they valued their lives. Aware of one danger facing the fliers, the British Consul at Bundar Abbas gave them a letter written in Arabic, commanding all natives to treat them hospitably if the "big bird" should come down to land. But with perfect weather all the way and the Vimy's engines performing beautifully, they arrived safely at Karachi, their gateway to India, after a flight of eight and a half hours.

The Royal Air Force officers who greeted them had some unexpected news—their French competitor, Lieutenant Poulet, was at Delhi, only a day's flight away, and he was still determined to beat them to Australia. So the race had now become truly an international one, and the following morning the Australians took up the chase as they headed the Vimy into the rising sun.

But that same morning Lieutenant Poulet had taken off for Allahabad, and he was still a jump ahead of the Aussies even though the Vimy was gradually closing the gap. Confident of eventually overtaking the Frenchman, they spent a day of rest at Delhi, then on November 27 the Vimy ascended through the Indian dawn and headed across the vast plains to Allahabad. But when they arrived, again there was no sign of Poulet. Like a jack-in-the-box, he had bounced into the air once more and was on his way to Calcutta.

Ross Smith was tempted to take out after Poulet immediately, but decided against it because the afternoon was so far advanced. The next day saw the Vimy early on the wing, following the course of the Jumna River as far as Benares, and then turning southeast along the railroad to Calcutta. Their landing site there was a race course on the far side of the city, but when they arrived, mobs of Indian natives swarmed across the infield, threatening to engulf the Vimy as it rolled to a stop. The police quickly formed a barricade to save the plane, while the fliers struggled through the surging crowds looking for Poulet, only to learn he had eluded them again. Still showing a clean pair of heels to his pursuers, he had left Calcutta several hours before and was flying on to the Burmese port of Akyab, 420 miles to the east.

Even though Calcutta was the halfway mark, perhaps the most hazardous part of the journey still lay ahead. And it was another mob scene the next morning when thousands of natives came down to the race course to see the Vimy depart. The takeoff was perfect, but the wheels were barely off the ground when, without warning, two hawks circled out of the sky and crashed head-on into the plane. In those days even a cigarette butt could smash a whirling blade to pieces, and one of the big birds slammed into a propeller, with the feathers scattering in all directions. For a moment, Ross Smith had the impression that the blade was broken with the plane on a collision course toward a grove of tall trees. But the propeller miraculously survived the blow, and the Vimy moved steadily upwards to a thousand feet where it was safe from the belligerent hawks.

Moving down the Burmese coast, the Vimy arrived over the airfield at Akyab and Smith was circling to come in for a landing when his brother Keith grabbed his arm, pointing to the runway below. There, standing beside his small Caudron airplane, was the elusive Poulet with his mechanic, M. Benoist, and they were the first to greet the Australians when the Vimy's propellers came to rest. Sitting on the field side by side, the Vimy and the Caudron were like the eagle and the humming-bird, and the Australians found it hard to believe that Poulet's frail machine could withstand the rigors of such a long flight. They agreed to fly on to Rangoon together, but the next morning the Vimy was delayed by some needed repairs and Poulet took off without their company.

The Frenchman had been gone an hour when the Aussies finally got away, but the Vimy's powerful motors followed the sky trail with ease and soon they were flying across the Ir-rawaddy River and on to Rangoon. The steeplechase course there was not difficult to find for, seen from miles away, it was an oval of green, encompassed by a hand-waving mass of Bur-mese. And when the Vimy came down to land they were greeted by the lieutenant-governor of Burma, Sir Reginald Craddock, who assured them that never in the history of Rangoon had any race meeting been so well attended.

It was the first time an airplane had ever landed at Rangoon, and the vast assemblage of natives staged a wild celebration of joy. Then, the bedlam rose to a crescendo when Poulet's plane came circling out of the sky only an hour behind the Australians, although he had had the same time advantage at the start.

That night, the fliers enjoyed the hospitality of Sir Reginald and Lady Craddock who graciously entertained them, but also urged them to get to bed early. It was then that Ross Smith remembered the strange lizard of the East which made a weird sound like, "tuk-too," and the superstitious belief that if one hears this sound repeated seven times, good luck lies ahead. Just before taking to their beds, the fliers heard their lizard, and they counted on their fingers as it "tuk-tooed" seven times. Then they went to sleep.

Even though the idea hadn't worked out so well on the flight from Akyab to Rangoon, Smith and Poulet agreed to keep company on the next leg of the journey to Bangkok in Siam. The route would carry them across 400 miles of mountains and uncharted jungles, and obviously they could help one another in an emergency. So the Vimy and the Caudron were taxied out together on the morning of December 1, ready for the takeoff, but this time it was Poulet who was delayed by engine trouble. Anxious to start, Captain Smith decided to get the Vimy into the air and circle the race course until Poulet was ready to leave. But twenty minutes later the Caudron was still on the ground, so with reluctance Ross shrugged his shoulders and pointed the Vimy's nose to the east. Straight ahead now, somewhere across the Gulf of Martaban, was the city of Moulmein where temple bells were chiming along Rudyard Kipling's all-weather route, *The Road to Mandalay*.

The day was crystal clear as they looked down upon the pagodas of Moulmein, but far to the southwest a barrier of clouds stood between the plane and the purple mountains. Keeping the Vimy just below the cloud ceiling of 4000 feet, they flew through a deep valley where the visibility was good. Eventually the plane would have to get across mountains that rose to 7000 feet with their summits buried in clouds, and Ross decided the safest flying altitude would be 9000 feet. But when they reached those heights, another wall of clouds blocked their way, and this one towered even several thousand feet higher.

Smith had no choice but to continue climbing, even though at 11,000 feet the clouds still rose above them, and this was as high as the Vimy could go. Leveling off, he guided the plane straight into the cloud bank and for the first time they were flying blind. Far below and hidden from view were mountains, and they would have to stay above them for at least another fifty miles with only a compass to guide the way.

An hour passed and they felt sure they must be over the range, but it could only be a guess because they were still boxed in by the clouds. As Smith nosed the Vimy down to take a look, the altimeter dropped from 11,000 feet to 8000, and as they approached the 7000-foot mark they braced themselves for a crash.

But nothing happened. For a brief moment, they saw a dark spot far below through a gap in the clouds. This gave Ross the confidence to descend even lower to 4000 feet . . . 3000 . . . 2000 . . . and then, they were under the overcast, flying over the rice fields and a winding river that led them to Bangkok where they landed safely, but with a set of badly frayed nerves.

What had happened to the French team? They finally took off from Rangoon and reached a point above the mountains east of Moulmein where they faced a combat problem far different from any they had faced in the war. Poulet and Benoist were flying above the peaks at a height of about a thousand feet when they saw a huge vulture circling overhead. Perhaps annoyed by the mechanical intruder, the bird plunged straight toward them, crashing into the right propeller and rendering it useless.

Further flight being impossible, Poulet scanned the terrain for a landing place, and managed to bring the plane down on a mountain plateau. But a vulture had delivered the *coup de grâce* to France's hopes of reaching Australia first.

With the competition virtually eliminated and the finish line only 3000 miles away, the Australians left Bangkok on December 2 and headed down the Malay Peninsula toward Singora. But soon they were flying through a tropical rainstorm, and Smith took the plane down to the thousand-foot level where the visibility was fair. When they reached Singora, half the "aerodrome" was flooded with water, and even worse, it was also studded with tree stumps! His field of choice was a slim one, but Smith picked a spot that looked the driest and down they came with the plane losing its tail-skid when it struck one of the stumps.

Repairs and refueling kept them grounded for a day. But on December 4 off they sped again and flew on down the peninsula to Singapore. The race course there was so small that Smith was worried about the landing room, but just before the wheels touched the ground, Bennett climbed out on the tail assembly and his weight forced the plane's rear end to the ground. The big Vimy then rolled to a stop after traveling only about a hundred yards.

Tragedy struck the air derby for the second time during the first days of December. Captain Cedric E. Howell and his mechanic, Henry Fraser, had left Hounslow and reached the Italian port of Taranto a few days later. But on the flight across the Ionian Sea, their single-engined Martinsyde crashed near the Greek island of Corfu and both airmen were drowned. So the death toll of the race had risen to four. Of all the entries, only Ross Smith and his companions had a chance to win. In fact, there was only one team left—Lieutenants Raymond Parer and John McIntosh—and they hadn't even taken off.

Flying over the open sea after leaving Singapore, Smith steered the Vimy through dark columns of rain, with the clouds above almost continually illuminated by lurid flashes of lightning. But as they pushed on beyond the storm and outran a few rainsqualls, the Vimy crossed the Equator and at long last they were in the Southern Hemisphere. Beneath them now were the jungle-clad islands and the mangrove swamps. Then they were over the mountains of western Java, and far beyond they could see other islands with hundreds of tiny white-sailed fishing boats moving through the channels between. The scene was a far cry from the snow-covered aerodrome at Hounslow, and it held them almost spellbound until they turned their eyes away to concentrate on the landing at Batavia.

When the Vimy touched down on the Dutch Flying School runway at nearby Kalidjati, they were greeted by His Excel-

lency Count Van Limburg Stirum, Governor-General of the
Netherlands Indies. And the Count had good news for the
Australians. His government had constructed several new aerodromes in the Indies, especially for their use along the remainder
of the route to Port Darwin. Overjoyed with this unexpected
development, the fliers expressed their gratitude, knowing that
with any kind of luck now, the prize would be theirs.

The weather was a poet's dream on the morning of December 7 when the Vimy took off for the next port of call—
Surabaya, some 350 miles to the east. Before long they were
flying over the "paddy" country of the Indies, miles and miles
of irrigated land that extended across the plains and on up the
green mountainsides. But the sight of so much inundated terrain was an omen of ill luck, for when the Vimy came down
to land at Surabaya, the wheels began to drag and they were
bogged down in mud. The Dutch had built their aerodrome on
a stretch of land which had been reclaimed from the sea. The
weather was broiling hot, the plane was stuck, and even worse,
they had to reach Australia within the next four days to stay
within the 30-day limit set for the race.

This situation became really grim when thousands of natives
broke through the police lines and rushed toward the plane.
The combined weight of so many people broke the sun-dried
crust on the field and great globs of mud began oozing through.
But the Dutch hospitality went beyond the governor-general's
formal words of greeting. A Netherlands engineer arrived on
the scene with a hundred or more hired laborers who set to
work, digging out the wheels. A strip of bamboo matting was
placed across the runway, then the big plane was hauled out of
the quagmire and up on the mats.

Even so, this failed to provide a final answer because in trying to take off, the Vimy would have to roll beyond the matting
and back into the mud again. But Keith Smith had a suggestion:
Why not cover the entire length of the runway with bamboo?
The Dutch engineer threw up his hands, pleading that it would
be impossible to collect so much bamboo in so short a time,
but he agreed to give it a try.

The following morning as the sun came up over the Flores Sea, hundreds of natives began converging on the field, bearing large sheets of bamboo on their backs. During the night the genial Dutch engineer had sent out a call to all nearby districts, and some of the natives had even torn down their homes to contribute to the cause. By 9 A.M., some 300 yards of matting covered the runway and the airmen gunned the Vimy for the takeoff. At first, all went well as it rolled across the bamboo with increasing speed. Then, just as the wheels were about to leave the ground, some of the mats flew up and lodged themselves in the tail assembly, swerving the plane off the track and into the mud again. It took three more hours of tugging and hauling to pull the big plane back onto the matting, and Ross Smith opened the throttles wide for another attempt. This time, the Vimy sped across the bamboo and rose into the air, with strips of matting flying in all directions.

Skirting the coasts of Bali and Lombok, they leveled the plane off at 3000 feet for the flight to Bima on the island of Sumbawa. As they flew on eastward, the Flores Sea below them was a mirror of blue, broken only by the glint of silvery wings wherever the flying fish came up to play. After an overnight stay at Bima, they were off again for Atamboea on the island of Timor, hopefully their last stop before the final flight to Australia. The aerodome at Atamboea was one of those especially constructed for them, and when they landed the Dutch were eager to help the plane get away on the 470-mile flight across the Sea of Arafura to Port Darwin.

A fog had settled over Timor, but on the morning of December 10 the fliers proceeded as though nothing could stop them now. Realizing that when a plane comes down at sea the forward fuselage sinks first, Ross Smith took the precaution of placing an extra supply of food and water in the tail. He also had the reassurance of knowing the Australian government had ordered a warship to patrol that empty sea between Timor and Darwin.

At 8:35 A.M., the fog began to lift and propellers whirled into action, with the sudden blast of air sending a row of

natives toppling from their perch astride a fence. As the coast
of Timor disappeared over the horizon, they saw the smoke
rising from the stacks of H.M.A.S. *Sydney*, and Smith came
down low to salute the sailors who were cheering them on
from the deck.

Soaring on across the sea at a speed of 75 miles an hour—
which seems incredibly slow today—they soon caught their
first glimpse of the Australian coast. And precisely at 3 P.M.,
they landed at Port Darwin on a field that appeared thronged
with all the Australians in Capricornia! So, on December 10,
exactly twenty-seven days and twenty hours after leaving Hounslow, they had reached the Land Down Under and the prize
was theirs. And so were the thousands of cables and telegrams
of congratulations that descended on Darwin from all parts of
the world. They flew on to Melbourne and then to their home
in Adelaide, and a few days before Christmas, King George V
conferred knighthood on both Ross Smith and his brother,
Keith, just as he had honored Alcock and Brown.

Although the Smiths and their companions had won the race,
and the prize, the story of the Great London-to-Australia Air

(From left to right) Keith Smith, Ross Smith, and Lieutenant J. M. Bennett,
planners of the flight from London to Australia, 1919. Keith and Ross Smith
were the aviators. Both brothers were knighted by King George V. (*International News Photos*)

Derby doesn't end there. Early in January of 1920, the final team of contestants, Parer and McIntosh, took off from Hounslow in a war surplus DeHavilland-9. In fact, they eventually became the only other team to finish the race. But it took them six times as long to fly halfway round the world as it had Sir Ross, Sir Keith, and their two fellow crewmen. Even though they were not dubbed Sir Ray and Sir John, Parer and McIntosh became involved in an aerial odyssey full of hair-raising adventures. And their trials and tribulations added so much drama, and comedy, to the Great London-to-Australia Air Derby that they were given the wildest welcome of all when they finally reached Melbourne. The story of their rousing adventures is told in the epilogue of this book.

Blériot had spanned the Channel, Alcock and Brown had flown the North Atlantic, Ross Smith had spanned half the globe, from London to Australia, but what were American airmen doing to maintain the prestige of the country where the airplane had been invented? So far they hadn't even been able to fly non-stop from coast to coast. However a young airman from Nome, Alaska, was about to show them how to do it, and two of his Army flying pals pulled it off with the help of a "Hudson Bay High."

CHAPTER IV

Kelly and Macready
Ride a Hudson Bay High

After Louis Blériot made his sensational flight across the English Channel in 1909, the growing ranks of American airmen had joined the rest of the world in hailing his achievement. But there may have been a tinge of chagrin along with the cheers. After all, only six years before, America's Wright Brothers had been the first to successfully fly an airplane, and now a French-man had made the first major point-to-point flight in history. Lord Northcliffe and his London *Daily Mail* had won a place in aviation annals by offering the prize for the Channel flight, the first to link France and England by air. Naturally, the American newspaper publisher William Randolph Hearst thought he should get in on all this publicity. So it came as no great surprise on October 10, 1910, when the Hearst papers announced a prize of $50,000 for the first flight across the U.S.A. from coast-to-coast within a time limit of thirty days.

It may seem odd now but nearly a year passed before there were any entries. The first to compete was twenty-six-year-old Robert G. Fowler, who took off from San Francisco on September 11, 1911, and headed east across the continent. But a series of accidents forced him to give up the attempt. A few days later, on September 17, Calbraith P. Rodgers left New York City heading for Pasadena, California, but fifty days had elapsed when he finally arrived so he couldn't claim Hearst's award.

Rodgers had rambled 3390 miles across the country in a Wright biplane, making sixty-eight short flights, the longest of these being for 133 miles.

Although Hearst withdrew his prize offer, young Bob Fowler decided to try again. On October 19, he left Los Angeles in a Wright biplane intending to fly to New York, but he changed his itinerary along the way to finally land at Jacksonville, Florida, after 122 days.

Both Rodgers and Fowler had crashes and other hardships along the way—in fact, so much trouble that ten years passed before anyone seriously tried it again. Even then the next attempt hardly got off the ground before it came to a rather ludicrous end. In February 1921, an Army flier, Lieutenant Alexander Pearson, Jr., decided to fly across the continent from east to west. But on the flight from Texas to Jacksonville, his official takeoff point, he became lost over the Big Bend of the Rio Grande and drifted across the border to land in Mexico. Pearson was listed as missing until he showed up a few days later, riding into the village of Sanderson, Texas, on a mule. In March of the same year another Army airman, Lieutenant William D. Coney, took off from Florida on what he hoped would be a one-stop flight to the West Coast. But his plane crashed in Louisiana, and Coney died of his injuries a few days later.

Both of these efforts to fly the continent in 1921 were closely watched by another Army flier, on whom Dame Fortune was destined to bestow many laurels. He was Lieutenant James H. Doolittle, who many years later was to become a national hero by leading American bombers in their first raid on Tokyo during World War II. He went on to win almost every aviation honor and rose to the rank of lieutenant general, and then became a top national figure in science and industry. Even at the age of twenty-five, Jimmy Doolittle already had a reputation of being one of the Army Air Service's most daring and skillful fliers.

In 1922, he asked Generals Mason Patrick and Billy Mitchell for permission to make a coast-to-coast flight, and perhaps was just a little surprised when it was granted, in view of the ill luck which had befallen Pearson and Coney. The Doolittle plan was to fly the continent from Jacksonville to San Diego in less than twenty-four hours, making only one stop to refuel at Kelly Field, Texas. For the task, Doolittle chose a World War I DeHavilland observation plane, outfitted with a Liberty engine and an extra-large gasoline tank, and by the evening of August 6, he was ready for the takeoff from Pablo Beach near Jacksonville.

The newspapers had given the flight big headlines, and a crowd of a thousand or so was on hand to give him a send-off. When the big moment came, the DH roared down the beach in the moonlight, but Doolittle's "one-stop" came much sooner than he expected! As he gathered speed, the wheels struck a soft spot in the sand, causing the plane to turn-turtle out into the ocean and bury its nose in the surf. Doolittle didn't have his safety belt fastened, and was thrown clear of the plane with his flying helmet down over his eyes and his goggles across his nose. Floundering in the water with his vision cut off, he thought he was drowning and threshed wildly in an effort to surface. But on finally getting to his feet, he found himself in only two feet of ocean. Soaking wet and embarrassed, he stood there while the cheers of the crowd turned to gales of laughter. Nor could he derive any consolation from the insignia on the plane's fuselage—a pair of dice, with the "lucky seven" turned up.

The plane sustained only minor damage, and four weeks later on the night of September 4, Doolittle was back at Pablo Beach ready for another try. This time he wanted no publicity and kept his plans more or less a secret, so much so that only a few friends and his mechanics were present when he took off and headed west across the Florida Peninsula. Flying through a rainstorm over Louisiana, he landed at Kelly Field in the early morning hours. After pausing for an hour to refuel, he was off again on the final lap to San Diego and landed at Rockwell Field where he had received his early training during the war. He completed a coast-to-coast flight of 2275 miles in an elapsed time of 22 hours and 35 minutes—a transcontinental record that brought him fame and, eventually, a Distinguished Flying Cross, one of the first of many, many decorations that would be pinned on the Doolittle tunic.

While Rodgers and Fowler had to land many times in their flights across the continent, Doolittle had now shown that it could be done with one stop alone. However, the biggest challenge yet remained, and airmen were asking: How about a *non-stop* flight from the Atlantic to the Pacific? Within only a month after Doolittle landed there, Rockwell Field became the takeoff point for the first serious attempt to fly the continent without stopping along the way.

It was appropriate that Rockwell Field should be either the takeoff or the terminal point for the Army's first efforts to send its planes on transcontinental flights. Situated on North Island at San Diego, the field had been named for Lieutenant Louis C. Rockwell, an Army flier killed in a crash in 1912. Known as the "Cradle of the Air Force," it was the home of the Army's first regularly organized aviation school, and during World War I many of our combat fliers were trained there. Rockwell was also the scene of the first successful refueling in mid-air, with buckets of gasoline being lowered from one plane to another—a routine soon to be replaced by a far simpler method that employed a long flexible tube invented by Sir Alan Cobham.

Early on the morning of October 4, 1922, Lieutenants Oakley G. Kelly and John A. Macready rolled their huge single-engined Fokker transport out to the runway at Rockwell Field, for an attempt to fly to New York, non-stop. Their plane, known as the T-2, had a 450-hp Liberty engine and carried an overall load of 10,850 pounds, including more than 700 gallons of gasoline. They took off in cloudy weather, and within only a few hours a fog forced them to turn back to Rockwell. Four weeks later in early November, they headed east again and all went well until a cracked water cylinder forced them down in Indiana. They landed on the famed Indianapolis Speedway, and

The Fokker T-2 in which Americans Macready and Kelly were to make their record non-stop flight from New York to San Diego, May 2–3, 1923. (*Brown Brothers*)

Macready promptly went to a telegraph office and wired his mother:

LANDED SAFELY; BROKE ENGINE; PILOTS UNINJURED.

Newspapermen got a bit confused and sent out the report: "The first thing Macready did on landing was to send a wire to his wife." Inasmuch as he was unmarried at the time, Macready said he had a lot of explaining to do about this "wife" whom none of his friends had ever heard of, and no matter how hard he tried, his explanations never seemed to be satisfactory. Even later when he did get married, he said his friends ribbed him about being a bigamist.

Discouraged, the two fliers vowed to give up their plans for good and yield the non-stop project to others. But a few days later at Dayton's McCook Field, they were poring over a map, planning a new route across the continent.

It was Kelly who had first approached his friend, Macready, with the proposal for a non-stop flight across the nation. A thirty-two-year-old Pennsylvanian, Kelly had entered the Army as a flying cadet in 1917 and he saw his share of active service during the War.

Macready was a thirty-five-year-old Californian with a rather colorful civilian background. After graduation from Stanford University in 1913, he made his residence in the frontier town of Searchlight, Nevada, where he served as justice of the peace and pursued such varied occupations as mining and cattle-raising. Even while still a young man in his twenties, Macready held the scales of justice in Searchlight for four years, and performed marriage ceremonies with all the brevity of frontier tradition, such as: "Stand up. Join hands. You are married! The fee is $2.50."

Like Kelly, Macready entered military service as an Army flying cadet in 1917, and years later, by the time they got down to hard planning for their cross-country flights, both men had logged many hours in the air. The main reason they had decided to fly from California eastward to New York on their first non-stop attempts was simply a matter of favorable winds. Over a period of years the weather maps had shown that, during the month of October, the prevailing west winds across the nation had an average velocity of 22 miles per hour. This would be a very helpful tail wind while flying eastward, for it would increase their ground speed by 22 miles an hour, even though there was still the problem of rising above the California mountains with a heavy load of yet unused gasoline.

From a geographical point of view, they realized the logical way to fly across the country would be westward from New York to California. For one thing, there were no extremely high mountains around New York to provide climbing problems for a plane heavily loaded with gasoline on the takeoff. With each passing mile the fuel load would grow lighter, and by the time they reached the towering mountains of the Far West, getting across them would be much easier. On the other hand, the prevailing winds blew from west to east, and a flight from New York to California would most likely mean bucking a head wind. Kelly and Macready knew the ideal answer. If they could only fly on a rare day when the prevailing winds blew in the opposite direction, from east to west, they would obviously have both a tail wind and the topography on their side.

They learned from Weather Bureau experts in Washington that each year, during April and early May, an unusual high pressure weather condition often developed in the Hudson Bay region of Canada, causing the winds to change direction and blow from east to west across the United States. This unusual condition, when it occurred, was known as a "Hudson Bay High."

That was all Kelly and Macready wanted to know and by the latter part of April 1923, their Fokker T-2, equipped with a new engine and a full load of fuel, was parked on the runway at New York's Roosevelt Field, waiting for a "Hudson Bay High." For nearly two weeks they studied weather reports day and night, seeing no indication that the winds were ever going to reverse direction and blow the other way. Then, at 11 A.M. on May 2, this report came through from the Weather Bureau:

"New York to Dayton, Ohio, northeast and east winds, clear sky; Dayton to Kansas-Missouri line, low clouds and rain, east winds; Kansas-Missouri line to San Diego, clear sky, variable winds."

To the waiting airmen this seemed to be it. Kelly and Macready first had lunch at the home of Major Walter Weaver, commanding officer of nearby Mitchel Field. Then, with a thermos full of hot coffee from Mrs. Weaver's kitchen, they drove to Roosevelt Field, and at 12:36 P.M. the Fokker rolled sluggishly down the runway.

Kelly was at the controls and even after lumbering forward for about a mile, the plane had not left the runway. Roosevelt Field was on a slight plateau, the edge of which dropped away about 20 feet to the level of adjacent Mitchel Field. When the T-2 rolled across the drop-off point, its wheels at least were off the ground, even though Kelly had to nose the plane up sharply to get above a row of hangars just ahead. Maintaining a steady climb across Brooklyn, they cleared the Ferris wheel and roller-coaster at Coney Island at a height of 350 feet.

As they flew across New York Harbor, the silver pinnacles of Manhattan swept by to their right, and soon they were over New Jersey with Kelly maintaining a steady altitude of 400 feet. It was a shaky start, but they were on their way and there was no hint of trouble until Kelly unexpectedly signaled Macready to take over the alternate controls in the rear cabin. Because of obstructed visibility, flying this type of plane from the rear cabin was a difficult task, and Macready thought Kelly only wanted a moment to consult his map. But thirty minutes passed with no sign of Kelly resuming his duties as pilot. Macready, puzzled, was becoming a bit provoked, until he learned that something had gone wrong with the voltage regulator and Kelly was busy replacing a defective switch.

Before long they were over the Delaware River and, as time passed, they crossed the Allegheny Mountains. Navigation over Pennsylvania was a continuing problem, with the rivers, roads, and railways winding in all directions and the cities shrouded in smoke or hidden in the hills. Far to the west, perhaps a hundred miles away, they saw a great pall of gray smoke rising above the Monongahela Valley, blotting out the sky. It was the city of Pittsburgh, and as they drew nearer they could smell the acrid fumes rising from the coke ovens in the mills.

According to the prearranged plan, Macready took over again when they looked down on Dayton at 6 P.M., well ahead of schedule. The easterly tail wind was still their friend, but at dusk a drizzle warned them of bad weather ahead. As they flew over Dayton's McCook Field, Kelly dropped a message, optimistically announcing that they would land at San Diego before noon the next day. Then, only a short distance beyond Dayton, the visibility became increasingly bad, but they found their way to Indianapolis by watching the automobile headlights moving along a highway. After they crossed the Wabash River into Illinois, the mist became so heavy they could no longer chart their course by the automobile lights.

Flying blind with only a compass as a guide, Macready suddenly saw a shaft of light in the distance. He turned the plane toward it, and within minutes they were over Belleville and the 450-candlepower searchlight that was sweeping the sky from nearby Scott Field. With this checkpoint in the darkness, they swung south toward St. Louis, and dimly through the fog they made out the red and green lights strung along the five bridges over the Mississippi. On west they flew across the Ozark foothills, moving now through a light rain that kept Macready wiping his goggles as he peered over the cockpit, seeking some guiding light in the rugged country below. Before long they passed south of Jefferson City whose lights were barely distinguishable in the gloom. But at midnight they crossed the Missouri–Kansas line to emerge into bright moonlight, and once again Kelly took over the controls.

The moon was riding high as the T-2 sped on westward across the wheatfields of the Great Plains. Then, as the moonglow gave way to the approach of dawn, Kelly looked over the cockpit and gave out with a yelp of joy. Below them were the familiar adobe huts of Tucumcari, New Mexico, and they knew they were right on their course westward with San Diego now less than 900 miles away.

When they reached the small settlement of Santa Rosa, Macready again moved into the pilot's seat and picked up a railway line that soon brought them above the muddy Rio Grande. Rising in the distance were the Rockies, and as they crossed the border into Arizona, the landscape was ascending faster than the plane could climb.

By now the friendly east wind had given way to a stubborn cross wind that challenged the plane's efforts to gain altitude. With the T-2 rapidly reaching its point of maximum height, Macready changed course in the hope of finding a pass through the mountains. He spotted a canyon to the northwest and headed into it, only to find himself weaving through a maze of ravines and valleys that seemed to have no end. It was a losing battle, and soon the towering wall of a mountainside blocked their way, forcing Macready to swing round and find a way out of the labyrinth. The minutes passed like hours until they finally shot through a pass that led to the Colorado River, and California's Imperial Valley lay just beyond.

The T-2 responded like a songbird as Macready nosed her upward to climb the last range between them and the coast. With the altimeter at 8000 feet, in the distance they saw their goal, San Diego. As they began the long descent and the buildings grew closer, they could see thousands of people on rooftops, and atop the U. S. Grant Hotel, some were even waving sheets. Diving down to within a hundred feet, the T-2 roared the length of Main Street, then took one turn around North Island before coming in to land at Rockwell Field. Kelly, with a wide grin on his face, had the cabin door open and one foot on the ground even before the plane rolled to a stop. The clock read exactly 11:26 A.M. As they had promised them back at Dayton, they had made it—before noon.

Lieutenants John A. Macready and Oakley G. Kelly after landing in San Diego, non-stop from New York, May 3, 1923. An unusual east-to-west tail wind had aided in the success of their flight. (*United Press International Photo*)

The commanding officer who greeted them was none other than Major H. H. "Hap" Arnold who, years later, was to become Chief of the U. S. Air Force. As the two fliers stepped down to the runway, even the combined shrieks of every boat whistle in San Diego Harbor failed to drown out the cheers of the base personnel. They had flown 2516 non-stop miles in 26 hours and 50 minutes, and the coffee was still hot in that thermos bottle they had taken aboard at Mitchel Field!

Within only a few minutes, a telegram arrived from President Warren G. Harding, reading: YOU HAVE WRITTEN A NEW CHAPTER IN THE TRIUMPH OF AMERICAN AVIATION. When reporters gathered around and asked Kelly if he had encountered favorable winds, he replied, quite truthfully:

"We did not encounter favorable winds. We picked them. We made it thanks to the Hudson Bay High!"

Within months of the day Kelly and Macready touched down at San Diego, eight U. S. Army fliers were off on the greatest aerial adventure of the age—an attempt to be the first to circle the globe. Two crashed in Alaska. Two lost their plane between the Faeroes and Iceland. However, four of the eight made it all the way, and won the accolade "Magellans of the Air."

CHAPTER V

The Magellans of the Air

One of the world's most majestic mountains had its serenity disturbed by four airplanes on the morning of April 6, 1924. They were "World Cruisers," setting forth on one of the great adventures of all time. Snowcapped Mount Rainier, monarch of the Pacific Northwest, was the backdrop for the four biplanes on pontoons as they roared up from the waters of Lake Washington, heading into the northern sky on an attempt to be the first to circumnavigate the globe.

As they circled the 14,000-foot cone of Rainier and flew toward the Juan de Fuca Strait, residents of the islands in Puget Sound and along the Washington coast easily could see that the planes were of identical shape and design. All four had 450-hp, 12-cylinder Liberty engines, open cockpits, and were designed for interchangeable landing gear—either pontoons or wheels. For months before the takeoff they had been under construction in the plant of a young, and until then, almost unknown aircraft engineer named Donald Douglas, who had set up shop at Santa Monica in a former movie studio.

The round-the-world air race actually had been in progress for several years. Immediately after the Smith brothers' Vickers-Vimy arrived at Melbourne in 1919, halfway round the world, airmen of many countries started planning to circle the globe by air. Some crashed before getting far. Sir Ross Smith himself had been killed while testing a new round-the-world "Vimy" at Brooklands, England. Even when America entered the race, only one plane had made it more than halfway around.

The United States, slow in getting involved, finally entered because of the persistence of the irrepressible General Billy Mitchell. Then, after Washington made its decision, it took months for a special U. S. Army Air Committee to conclude arrangements for the flight. Donald Douglas was awarded a contract to design and build the planes, advance men were sent out to set up supply bases around the world, and officers assigned to key points along the route. At least twenty-two countries were asked for permission to fly over their territories and use their landing fields, if any.

Spurred on by the knowledge that would-be aerial Magellans of at least five other countries were ahead of them, the Army Air Service was finally ready to enter the greatest air race of all time. The planes had been flown from Santa Monica up the coast to their point of departure from the U.S.A.

Although it was a hazy morning, with visibility only fair, the fliers were impatient because of many delays, and the squadron leader decided it was time to get going. Their first

Douglas World Cruisers after christening, lined up and ready for the start of the "round-the-world" flight, 1924. These planes brought fame to Donald Douglas. (*Air Force Museum, Wright-Patterson*)

foreign port of call was to be Prince Rupert, British Columbia, 650 miles to the north.

Those chosen for this global odyssey were, of course, among the most experienced fliers in our Army Air Service. All had clocked many hundreds of hours in either cross-country or endurance flying. Some were also aviation engineers.

Leading the formation was the flagship *Seattle* piloted by Major Frederick L. Martin, head of a U. S. Army Signal Corps aerial technical school. In his rear cockpit rode Sergeant Alva Harvey, mechanic and experienced pilot, a flier destined to become a World War II general officer and see more years of service than any of the others.

Following close by was the *New Orleans*, with veteran Lieutenant Erik Nelson as pilot, and Lieutenant John ("Smiling Jack") Harding of Nashville, Tennessee, as his Number Two. At the age of thirty-six, Swedish-born Erik was the oldest man of the group and the only naturalized citizen. Nelson had left Stockholm to see the world when he was only sixteen, and, before he wound up in our Air Service, his career had carried him through a variety of experiences on land and sea. For a time he was even a masseur and swimming instructor at a Turkish bath on 42nd Street in New York.

Then came the *Chicago*, with taciturn Lieutenant Lowell Smith at the controls and Lieutenant Leslie Arnold as his co-pilot. "Smitty," a thirty-two-year-old Californian and a direct descendant of Daniel Boone, was something of a soldier of fortune. As a civilian he had flown in Mexico for the rebel chieftain, Pancho Villa. His most recent aerial achievement had been to fly the first plane ever refueled in mid-air. He had decided to be his own mechanic on the flight, and rightly thought that Les Arnold might be an important addition to their group in other ways.

Arnold, a thirty-year-old native of New Haven, Connecticut, had once toured New England as an actor in summer stock, and later sold pianos to farmers' wives. After joining the Air Service, on one occasion he was ordered to Dresden, Tennessee, to do exhibition flying at a country fair. The assignment was a memorable one, for on the takeoff his engine stalled and he nose-dived the plane into the roof of a chicken house to avoid crashing into a line of trees. However, he crawled out of the cackling bedlam of feathers and flapping wings, uninjured.

Plane number four, the *Boston*, was so overloaded that Lieutenant Leigh Wade and Sergeant Henry Ogden had been unable to join the other three in formation at the start. But on getting rid of a few cargo items, they soon were in pursuit of the *Seattle, Chicago,* and *New Orleans.*

Crossing the International Border, they flew north over the Strait of Georgia, with Vancouver Island on their left and the skyscrapers of Vancouver city silhouetted against the rising sun to the right. Ahead, the haze was growing more and more dense, like smoke from a forest fire. This forced them to fly so low they soon were just off the water, weaving in and out of passageways between the heavily wooded islands that line the British Columbia coast and the Alaskan Panhandle. Here and there a break in the fog would reveal an Indian paddling his canoe, a waterfall plunging over a cliff, or the green forest of the mountainsides.

Still skimming just above the water near the upper end of Vancouver Island, they found themselves on a collision course with an excursion steamer! There was near-panic on the vessel when the passengers saw the on-coming planes, but Major Martin swerved the *Seattle* to the right and the formation flew safely past, waving a "hello" as they vanished in the fog.

When they sought the shelter of the "Inside Passage," the forecast of bad weather was fulfilled with rain, snow, sleet, and hail belting them as they proceeded north. Fighting a stiff head wind in a driving snowstorm, they finally reached Prince Rupert and circled for a landing at Seal Cove.

Blinded by the snow, Martin and Harvey felt their plane side-slipping from a height of 30 feet, and the left pontoon dug into the sea with a crash. No one was hurt, but the *Seattle* was sitting cockeyed on the water with a number of broken struts and wires. Harvey, in disgust, took the rabbit's foot someone had given him in Sacramento and threw it into the sea. Unfortunately, he was soon to learn that even though he had gotten rid of the rabbit's foot he hadn't gotten rid of the jinx.

"Gentlemen," said the Mayor of Prince Rupert, "you have arrived on the worst day in ten years."

Three days later after repairs were made, the planes took off under rainy skies and headed toward Sitka, the old Russian capital of Alaska. The last of the Canadian coastline had passed beneath as they flew over Ketchikan with its wooden streets, totem poles, and canneries. Word of their coming had been wired ahead to this metropolis of southern Alaska, and a throng of American, Chinese, and Indian salmon packers were waving from the wharves as the planes swooped down to 50 feet above the water. The roaring motors joined an earsplitting din of cannery whistles chat welcomed them to Alaska.

It was noon when the fog lifted, and for the first time they had bright skies as they flew over the open sea to land on the picturesque harbor at Sitka with its old-world Russian church, great forests, and snowcapped mountains in the background.

For the next twenty-four hours, they worked on their planes, getting ready for an open sea flight to Seward, 625 miles to the northwest. Tumbling out of their beds at dawn they found a gale blowing, and by noon it was obvious there would be no flying that day. To while away the time they wandered along the streets to a photographer's shop. An Indian walked in and stood by silently for some minutes, until the proprietor asked him if he wanted anything. Then, in a casual unhurried way, he replied: "Yes, I just wanted to let these men know that one of their planes is adrift."

The fliers nearly fell over one another in a dash for the door. They sprinted through the streets, and sure enough, the *Boston*, torn loose from its moorings, was heading toward the *New Orleans*. A Forestry Service motorboat came to the rescue and for hours they battled the gale in a successful effort to keep the planes apart. Then the next day, they flew on through snow squalls across the stormy Gulf of Alaska to Seward on Resurrection Bay, one of the most magnificent fjords in the world.

Here at Seward, southern terminus of the new government railroad built to open up the interior of Alaska, were the rugged, colorful fishermen—"Humpbacked Jake," "Whiskey Nels," and others—all preparing for the "silver horde," the annual salmon run.

In a hurry now to reach clear weather somewhere, the round-the-world fliers took off between the two rows of extinct snow-crowned volcanoes that line Resurrection Bay, heading for the Aleutian Islands and nearby Asia. Erik Nelson and the *New Orleans* led on this leg, bound for Chignik on the Alaskan Peninsula, 425 miles to the southwest. Over the stormy waters of Shelikof Strait, the *Seattle* began to lag behind, often losing sight of the others in the sudden snow squalls. Five hours out of Seward, Harvey informed Flight Commander Martin their oil pressure had dropped to zero, whereupon they quickly landed in a sheltered cove called Portage Bay.

Examining their Liberty engine, they discovered a hole in a now-dry crankcase; also, their self-starter would no longer work. With night coming on they had no choice but to stay aboard the plane out there in the ice-choked bay, hoping that by morning help would arrive.

Meanwhile, the others had reached Chignik and radioed two American naval destroyers in the vicinity to start a search for the *Seattle*. At dawn, the commander of the USS *Hull* saw three rockets streak into the sky, set off by the stranded airmen, and soon the vessel was alongside the *Seattle* and had Martin and Harvey on board.

The plane was towed to the nearby village of Kanatak where Major Martin radioed the other fliers to continue on to Dutch Harbor in the Aleutians where he and Harvey would join them. At the same time, a new Liberty motor was ordered from the nearest supply base, and by April 25 they were ready to fly on.

Despite bad weather, Major Martin reached Chignik but more snow and high winds kept them immobile for another four days. On April 30 they started for Dutch Harbor, hoping to rejoin the squadron, but almost immediately they were in trouble again. While flying through a fog they swerved to avoid what looked like a mountain. It wasn't. A moment later they slammed into the ground with the right pontoon striking first. Major Martin, who was at the controls, suffered a few minor cuts on his face though Harvey escaped unhurt. But the grim truth was, for them—the world flight had come to an end.

For days they tried to find their way out of an uninhabited part of the Alaskan Peninsula. Wearing their fur-lined flying suits for protection against the cold, they wandered through the fog and deep snow hoping to reach the coast. Their compass proved of little help, and once they came within inches of stepping off a precipice. Emergency rations from the wrecked plane kept them from starving although they supplemented their food supply by killing two ptarmigan with an Army pistol. The nights were bitter cold, with sleep almost impossible when they sought shelter in alder thickets. Then early on the morning of May 6, they made their way over a frozen marsh and found themselves near a cabin on the shore of Moller Bay. They had crossed the Alaskan Peninsula, all the way to the Bering Sea. In the cabin they found a small cache of food including flour, salted salmon, bacon fat, baking powder, dried peaches, condensed milk, and coffee—just about everything two marooned men might need for survival.

Continuing snowstorms plus their own weakened condition held them up for the next three days, and it was May 9 before they managed to walk around the bay to a fishing village where smoke was rising from a cannery. Soon they were greeted by friendly Alaskans who, as Major Martin put it, "seemed as overjoyed at seeing us, as we were at meeting them."

In the meantime, the other three planes had been waiting at Dutch Harbor, and on May 2 a message arrived from Major General Mason M. Patrick in Washington, ordering them to continue on to Japan. He also designated Lowell Smith as the new flight commander, with the *Chicago* henceforth to be the flagship. In spite of more stormy weather for which the Aleutian Islands are notorious, the three planes made their way to Atka, flying almost "on the deck" through fog, sleet, and snow. They remained there for five more days of dirty weather, suffering from "cabin fever" and wondering about the fate of Martin and Harvey. Said Jack Harding to a fisherman: "Say, when do your seasons change up here? When does winter end, and spring begin?"

"Don't be funny, young fellow," the chap drawled. "We have only two seasons. This winter, and next winter."

The next hop took them 555 miles over long stretches of open water to Attu, on the far end of the Aleutian chain. Here, where the Arctic Ocean meets the vast Pacific, they rounded a smoking volcano and descended to our farthest west harbor of Chichagof, at that time the home of fifty-nine Aleuts.

One-sixth of the global flight was now behind them, and they were knocking at Asia's door. Also, they were preparing for an historic first aerial crossing of the Pacific—a feat no other airman had ever even attempted. Of course, the distance between continents—or rather from our Alaskan islands to those belonging to Russia—is not so great up where the Pacific Ocean is called Bering Sea. The nearest land to the west was the Russian Komandorskies, barren masses of rock off the coast of Siberia. Since the United States had not yet recognized the Soviet Union, they planned to fly all the way from Attu to Japan and, if possible, bypass the Komandorskies.

When they finally took off from Attu and headed for Japan, a storm forced them to change their course. With no choice but to head for the Komandorskies, they landed there in the late afternoon, three miles offshore. And the moment the planes taxied to a stop, a boatload of Russians came out from the islands.

Meanwhile, an Alaskan Fisheries Bureau boat, the *Eider,* had arrived on the scene and one of its sailors, a Lithuanian from Chicago, served as an interpreter when the Russians came along-

side. Some were in uniform, and all were sporting shaggy beards.
Lowell Smith saluted them coolly and explained they were
merely birds of passage flying around the world, intending to
remain on the *Eider* overnight—then take off at dawn.

The Russians left, promising to return after getting an official
decision on what should be done about the unexpected visitors.
When they did show up at dawn with word from Moscow that
the Americans must leave, the fliers were already set to fly on
to Japan. "Smitty" merely asked the Russians to move their
boat a bit, and off they went.

Two hours later they crossed the Gulf of Kronotski and flew
over a headland that was a part of the continent of Asia. So,
for the first time, an airplane had successfully made it across
the Pacific. Then, they flew on through more fog, mist, rain,
and snow, to the southern Kuriles. They landed on a lake near
Hitokappu Bay, where several hundred Japanese school children
were waiting to greet them. And they asked the Americans how
they could fly without flapping their wings!

Two days passed before they could "flap their wings" again
and head for Lake Kasumigaura, near Tokyo. On a perfect
afternoon in May, they flew over dozens of fishing villages
and endless rice fields, forests and mountains. Here and there,
teahouses and rustic bridges dotted the landscape like a stage
setting from Gilbert and Sullivan's *The Mikado*. Sometimes they
could see the shadows of their planes moving over the clear
sea below, blending with the white and yellow sails of the fishing junks.

Awaiting them at Lake Kasumigaura was a crowd of some
25,000 Japanese, including admirals, generals, and U. S. Embassy
officials, as well as representatives of the Imperial Japanese
government. As the fliers approached the shore in small boats,
the throng was almost hidden by a waving mass of Japanese
and American flags. After they overhauled their planes, changed
the pontoons and engines, a special train took them in triumph
to Tokyo where a crowd of 100,000 or more was assembled at
the station to shout more "banzais."

On Sunday morning while they were still in Tokyo, word

arrived that the British round-the-world flier, Major Stuart Mac-Laren, had crashed at Akyab in Burma with he and his companions escaping serious injury. Colonel L. E. Broome, advance officer for the British flight, was in Tokyo and told the Americans about MacLaren's misfortune. Whereupon Lowell Smith asked our Navy people to rush an American destroyer to Hakodate Harbor, 500 miles north of Tokyo, to take on board a spare British airplane which was stored there, and steam with it all the way to Akyab where MacLaren was waiting to resume his flight. The British Navy, at the time, had no vessel available for this mission.

Bidding sayonara to geisha girls and Tokyo, the Americans returned to Lake Kasumigaura for six more days of work on their planes. Word had just arrived that another rival, the French round-the-world flier, Captain Pelletier D'Oisy, had crashed while trying to land on a golf course near Shanghai. Even so, there was no time to lose. With MacLaren back in the running, and with Portugal, Italy, and Argentina also involved, it was still a wide open race.

While in Tokyo Lowell Smith had performed still another good deed. He wired General Patrick in Washington, asking him to promote Leigh Wade's companion, Henry Ogden, from sergeant to lieutenant and the request was granted. Now, all six world fliers were lieutenants as they flew on south to Kagoshima Bay on the lower end of Kyushu Island.

On June 2 they took off on the flight across the China Sea. Upon reaching the mainland of China, they were over the mouth of the Yangtze River, looking down on thousands of junks, sampans, and steamers. For a moment they wondered where they could drop their planes in that teeming harbor, but the harbormaster had been thoughtful enough to clear all river traffic along several miles of waterfront. As the planes came in they were greeted by scores of Chinese officials, as well as foreign notables, diplomats, and journalists.

Even though the harbormaster had cleared the traffic for their arrival, he didn't do quite so well on the morning of June 7 when the flight departed for Amoy. The junks and sampans were so numerous and jam-packed that very little open water was available for taking off, and on their first attempt, the planes nearly collided with rivercraft. Even on the second try, the *Boston* had to swerve to avoid a sampan, then went roaring up the Yangtze at 60 miles an hour, dodging traffic and coming within inches of a collision.

As usual, they flew low along the coast over scores of villages —the streets and roads bustling with Chinese, and chickens and pigs by the thousands. When they tired of watching the villages, they would swing out over the sea to play leapfrog with fishing junks as they dived toward them at full speed just over the tops of their masts—relieving the monotony of life for themselves as well as for those on board the junks!

On reaching Hongkong they paused a day for refueling and repairs, then took off on a 490-mile flight to the French Indochinese city of Haiphong—now the main port for North Vietnam. The sun had just gone down behind the mouth of the Red River when they descended to Haiphong Harbor, and French officials greeted them with the news that the Portuguese round-the-world fliers, Major Brito Paes and Major Sarmento Beires, had arrived at Rangoon in Burma. The Portuguese, like the British, were flying on an eastward course around the globe.

On hearing this news, the Americans excused themselves from an official reception and hurried aboard a destroyer for a good night's sleep. The following morning, with the temple bells of Haiphong almost drowning out the roar of their engines, they took off, hoping to reach Saigon by nightfall. First, however, the planes headed for Tourane, a seaport halfway between Haiphong and Saigon. Soon they were passing over a vast area of flooded rice fields where the Annamite farmers were at work with their water buffaloes. Then, on farther south, there were dense jungles with rarely a sign of habitation. About 2 o'clock in the afternoon, the *Chicago*'s motor began to overheat, and Smith brought the plane down on a lagoon, filled the radiator with salt water, then rose to rejoin the other two planes circling above.

Still, the *Chicago* was in real trouble. The radiator had developed a leak with water splashing back into the cockpits in a steady stream. Even worse, the engine was pounding badly, growing red-hot and showing signs of bursting into flames. With jungle everywhere below them they spotted a lagoon none too soon, for just as the *Chicago* glided toward the water, a connecting rod broke loose to punch a hole in the crankcase, and the engine began falling apart.

The other two planes came down beside them, gave Smith and Arnold their supply of drinking water, and then continued on to Tourane where arrangements were made for an American destroyer to bring the *Chicago* a new engine from Saigon. An oil company agent, M. Chevalier, was the flight's contact man in Tourane. After looking over a few maps, he told Nelson, Harding, Wade, and Ogden that the *Chicago* had come down not far from the old city of Hue. Figuring the stranded fliers would soon need more food and water, Nelson drove to Hue with Chevalier, leaving the others to look after the planes.

From Hue they headed along the coast in search of the *Chicago*. Following winding jungle paths with the aid of flashlights, they finally found a native fisherman who said, yes, there is a "flying monster" in a nearby lagoon. Beating their way on through the jungle, they kept waving their flashlights and shouting until, suddenly, they heard Lowell Smith's answering call.

At dawn, Chevalier and Nelson went to the nearest village, roused the natives and arranged to have three large war sampans tow the *Chicago* out of the lagoon and some 25 miles down the coast to Hue. It must have been a strange procession for each of the sampans was propelled by ten naked paddlers, while in the bow of the leading boat sat a patriarch, beating a tom-tom as the paddles dipped to its rhythm. The chieftain, making the trip to Hue in his own royal sampan, reclined under a sun-shade with his junior wives doing the paddling. Beside him sat his favorite concubine, rolling and lighting his cigarettes. Behind all this came the *Chicago*, moving majestically through the jungle lagoons with the aviators perched on the lower wings where it was shady and cool.

The following day, Nelson and Chevalier drove back to Tourane to make certain the new Liberty-12 engine was delivered to Hue as quickly as possible. Ogden, with the help of four American sailors, loaded the motor in a truck and began the journey, with an Annamite driving. Up and down the jungle mountains they went like a roller-coaster at a speed of 45 miles an hour, rounding curves on two wheels, so it seemed, and once nearly plunging over a precipice. When the truck came to a railroad crossing, the driver made a sharp turn to the left and went bounding along the ties. Whereupon it took them half an hour to push and pull the vehicle back to the road again.

But miracles do happen. The new engine finally reached Hue undamaged, though the same couldn't be said for Ogden's jangled nerves. Then, seventy-one hours after the forced landing in the jungle lagoon, the *Chicago* was ready to fly again.

Their ordeal over, Smith and Arnold made the short flight to Tourane and at dawn on June 16 all three planes took off for Saigon, the *Paris of the Orient*. Flying on westward over the Mekong Delta and the rain forest of the upper Malay Peninsula, the planes came down to land on the Irrawaddy at Rangoon. Here, they were again delayed and it was five days before they could leave on the flight to India. On their very first night in Burma a river boat plowed into the *New Orleans*, smashing the bottom left wing. Also, Lowell Smith came down with a case of dysentery, probably from some bad drinking water back in that lagoon.

They received more news about their competition. The Portuguese, Majors Paes and Beires, had reached Macao off the China coast but their machine was wrecked while they were preparing to take off again. As for the British flier, Major MacLaren, rainy weather still had him pinned down on the Burma coast at Akyab even though the American destroyer had arrived with his new plane.

As soon as Smith recovered from his illness and the *New Orleans* was shipshape again, the planes taxied into midstream and were off across the wide Irrawaddy delta—next goal, Calcutta. A refueling stop was scheduled at Akyab where they looked forward to meeting Major MacLaren at the "jinx seaport" where he had crashed only recently, and where, in 1919, one of Ross Smith's supply ships had blown up.

As it turned out, they were not destined to meet MacLaren. Instead, they were to pass each other in the rain. That day, June 25, the Britisher had decided to resume his flight and was winging toward Rangoon while the Americans were flying to Akyab. It was raining so hard MacLaren decided to take no chances with his new plane, coming down in a little bay to wait out the storm. While there, he heard the roar of the World Cruisers and looked up just in time to see them flash by. MacLaren later resumed his round-the-world flight and eventually reached the North China coast where he crashed in a fog. Again, an American destroyer hastened to his assistance with a new plane, but by then the season was considered too far advanced for safe flying across the Pacific to Alaska.

After refueling stops at Akyab and Chittagong, the planes continued on to Calcutta, only a short distance across the Bay of Bengal to the west. This route was across the deltas of two great rivers, the Ganges and the Brahmaputra, a region of swamps and jungle known as the Sundarbans, haunt of tigers and crocodiles. With the visibility perfect, they got across the Sundarbans and by mid-afternoon saw the smoke rising from the factories of Calcutta—second largest city in the British Empire. Upon landing, they found the summer heat so oppressive they took out their maps to calculate how many more days would pass before they reached Iceland!

By now they had flown nearly halfway round the world, a total distance of 11,232 miles, all with pontoons. Now, they would change to wheels for the long journey across Asia and Europe. Using a giant British crane, they hoisted the planes out of the Hooghli River and over into the Maidan, the famous common along the river in the heart of Calcutta.

Great crowds gathered to watch them convert from pontoons to wheels, with turbaned Indian police holding back the mobs.

The changeover was completed in about three hours despite the sacred cows that wandered over to enjoy the shade of the wings.

Before the fliers could leave the city, Lowell Smith had a slight accident. Returning from a reception, he stepped into a hole in the dark and fractured a rib.

A British doctor strapped him up, then on the morning of July 1 the planes arose from the Maidan to head for the city of Allahabad, 450 miles away. After six hours, they landed near Allahabad on the sun-baked plain of central India at the junction of the Ganges and the Brahmaputra. Moments later, while unfastening their safety belts and climbing out of the cockpits, Wade and Ogden received what they have always maintained was the shock of their lives.

They saw a stowaway, casually crawling out of the *Boston's* baggage compartment. This was none other than Linton Wells, an Associated Press newsman who had followed them by boat and train ever since they had left the Kurile Islands in northern Japan. Intead of bawling him out, they greeted him with much enthusiastic backslapping. Presumably—though no one would admit anything—while still in Calcutta, Linton Wells had discovered that the substitution of wheels for pontoons would make the plane's overall weight considerably lighter, since pontoons weigh more than half a ton. Convinced that his own 140 pounds would not be an overload, he awaited an opportune moment (so they said) and slipped unobserved into the *Boston's* baggage compartment just before takeoff—carrying only a toothbrush and a pencil.

The world fliers decided to change Wells's status from "stowaway" to "passenger" and take him along on at least part of the flight. Also, they put him to work carrying cans of high-test gas to and from the planes, as well as performing other chores in the heat of the Indian sun. Just to make things official, Flight Commander Smith cabled Washington, asking General Patrick whether it would be okay to take Wells along. There was no immediate reply and Wells squeezed himself into the rear cockpit of the *Boston* with Henry Ogden when the planes left the following morning. For the next six hours, all the way to Ambala, they sat jammed together like a pair of Siamese twins.

Leaving Ambala on the morning of July 3, they headed across the great Sind Desert on a 360-mile hop to Multan, one of the hottest places in Asia. On the way, a sandstorm gave them a little trouble, but nothing to compare with what happened the next day.

The planes were about an hour out of Multan when white smoke began spurting from the *New Orleans'* engine. Two of the cylinders went to pieces, with chunks of metal tearing a hole in one wing. Nelson, looking for a place to land, could see nothing but one vast desert of baked mud filled with open seams that would surely wreck the plane. So he kept the *New Orleans* flying all the way to Karachi, with the motor spewing oil into his and Harding's faces. Nelson's skill as an aviator became the deciding factor, and when he brought the plane safely into Karachi, it was covered with oil from nose to tail—some of it soaked into their hair.

A large crowd greeted them, and the American Consul stepped forward to hand Lowell Smith a cablegram from General Patrick in Washington. In reference to Linton Wells, the message read: REQUEST DISAPPROVED. But that only "locked the barn door after the horse had been stolen," for Wells, by then, had completed a unique joyride across India. Now, he merely looked forward to the inconvenience of losing his AP job with a sigh of, "Oh well, it was worth it."

The fliers remained in Karachi just long enough to install new engines before heading west across the empty desert of Baluchistan. After reaching the Persian port of Bandar Abbas, the actual halfway mark of their global flight, they flew on to Bushire. This Persian seaport looked very much like an oriental Manhattan Island—a long narrow neck of land with almost every square yard covered with streets, buildings and squares. Late on the afternoon of July 8, the planes followed the trail of the Tigris, and soon they were above the minarets and domes of ancient Baghdad. Like Caliphs of old, they arrived on their magic carpets, coming down to land on the outskirts of the City of the Arabian Nights.

Heading next for Aleppo in northern Syria, the World Cruisers climbed to 6000 feet while crossing the North Arabian Desert to avoid a sandstorm that was moving toward them like the "mountain coming to Mohammed." On leaving Aleppo they crossed the Taurus Mountains, following the line of the Berlin-Baghdad Railway until they saw the blue waters of the Sea of Marmora and the gleaming spires of Constantinople where, for the first time, the planes landed on European soil.

The fliers were anxious to reach Paris by Bastille Day, July 14 —now only a few days off. So they limited their Sublime Porte stopover in Constantinople to a single day and left on a flight to Bucharest which carried them over Dracula country, the brooding Transylvanian Alps.

From Bucharest they flew up the Danube Valley past Belgrade and on across the Hungarian plain to Budapest, which was still there despite what the history books say about the city being destroyed by the Mongols in 1241. Less than four hours later they landed at Vienna where, to their great surprise, they were greeted by a large crowd of American tourists with their cameras clicking away.

Leaving Vienna at dawn, they soon plunged into a driving rain —the first bad weather since leaving Burma. A stiff head wind reduced their speed to 50 miles an hour over the mountains of Austria and Bavaria and when they landed at Strasbourg, the fuel tanks were almost dry. As they neared Paris, the weather cleared and from 50 miles away they could see a squadron of French planes coming out to meet them. It was July the 14th and the boulevards below were jammed with cheering, flag-waving Parisians as the World Cruisers circled the Eiffel Tower, then dipped their wings above the Arc de Triomphe in a salute to the Unknown Soldier.

Landing at Le Bourget Field, they spent a full hour shaking hands with scores of French officials, generals, foreign diplomats and celebrities who were out to greet them. Finally, when they did get a moment to look after their planes, their preoccupation was noted by one Paris newspaper:

"There are cries of *Vive la France!* And *Vive l'Amérique!* But where are the heroes? They have vanished. 'Feeding their horses,' someone explains. And, in fact, the fliers have left the throng, and, with a gesture that is as simple as it is symbolic, they are wiping down the engines to which they owe a part of their glory."

After refueling, the fliers were driven to a hotel in special staff cars and later endured the usual "ordeal" of a night at the Folies Bergeres. Exhausted from more than ten hours of flying, they made themselves comfortable in their seats only to drop off to sleep and miss all the girls. Again, a Paris newspaper remarked:

"If the Folies Bergeres won't keep these American airmen awake, we wonder what will?"

Paris was a delight that had to end, and on the morning of July 16 a group of not-too-wide-awake world fliers climbed into their cockpits, said *au revoir*, and took off for London. They crossed the Channel at 7000 feet with the clouds parting just long enough to reveal the heavy seas between Calais and Dover, and they thought of Louis Blériot's Channel flight only fifteen years before.

London, to their surprise, was not shrouded in fog. Here they came down at Croydon Aerodrome, not far from Brooklands where Sir Ross Smith had been killed two years before while testing his round-the-world plane. None of the American world fliers had ever met the Smith brothers from Australia. The stay in London was brief, though they took the time to attend a glittering official dinner atop the Criterion in Piccadilly as guests of the British Air Ministry. No sooner had they seated themselves at the table than Leigh Wade fell asleep, with a knife in one hand and a fork in the other—snoring!

Next morning they hurried north to Brough, near the seaport of Hull on the Humber where their landing gear was converted back to pontoons. From the British Isles they were to attempt the most hazardous stretch of all—the foggy North Atlantic by way of Iceland, Greenland, and Labrador. Since they were well ahead of schedule, General Patrick had ample time to arrange for the stationing of Navy destroyers along the route for possible relief duty. The fliers remained in Brough for thirteen days, enjoying English hospitality and overhauling their planes while the naval ships got into position. Their devotion to the job forced them to turn down an invitation to attend a garden party at Buckingham Palace as guests of the King and Queen.

There were more delays when a crane cable broke in the Blackburn aircraft plant, sending the *Chicago* crashing to the floor and damaging a pontoon. On the same day Argentina's round-the-world fliers, Major Pedro Zanni and his mechanic Felipe Beltrame, left Holland heading southeast across Europe. So it was still a race to the swift, and no one knew it better than "Smitty" and his pals when they finally reached Kirkwall in the Orkney Islands, north of Scotland.

Heavy fog kept them grounded for two more days until the weather cleared a bit, so it seemed, and they began the 555-mile flight to Iceland. Barely ten minutes later they found themselves flying through fog so thick it forced them almost down to the rolling whitecaps. The *Chicago* and *Boston* climbed to 2500 feet and were in the clear again, but the *New Orleans* had disappeared. The two planes circled, hoping to catch sight of their missing companion, but with no luck. Fearing that Nelson and Harding had been forced down in the heavy seas, Smith and Wade turned their planes around and flew back to Kirkwall where they radioed the American Navy vessels to begin a search.

The *New Orleans*, meanwhile, was still very much in the air although Nelson and Harding did have a close call. Flying blindly through the fog, the plane got caught in "propeller wash" from one of the other aircraft and went into a spin. With his plane spiraling downward through the clouds, Nelson tried everything in the book to pull out and finally succeeded— with only seconds to spare. The waves were lunging at the pontoons when he straightened out to climb above the fog and continue on to safely land in Iceland at the village of Hornafjord.

Back at Kirkwall that night, the other fliers received Nelson's happy message, and the following morning the *Chicago* and *Boston* again took off for Iceland. Visibility was good and a stiff tail wind kept them moving at a hundred miles an hour, even though heavy seas were kicking up mountainous waves.

The flight had been underway about an hour with everything going smoothly when, suddenly, Wade saw an alarming indication on the *Boston*'s instrument panel. The oil pressure was falling and before he could think about it twice, it had dropped to zero. It was a rough sea for a landing, but Leigh brought the plane down perfectly, even though the impact nearly wrapped the left pontoon around a wing. A quick check revealed that something had gone wrong with the oil pump, and this meant repairs could not be made at sea. So Wade threw out the anchor, and signaled to the *Chicago*.

Circling overhead, Smith and Arnold got the message. They should continue on and summon help as soon as possible. Reluctantly, Lowell Smith decided this would be the best course, so he headed for Iceland, scanning the sea for a destroyer.

Just north of the Faeroe Islands they spotted the USS *Billingsby*, then flew low over her deck to drop a message bag that missed the ship by several yards. Arnold took his one and only life preserver and tied it to another message, giving the exact location of the imperiled *Boston*. It also missed the target and fell into the sea, but this time a sailor dived overboard and brought it back. The captain quickly read the note and gave three blasts on the ship's whistle, indicating he would go to the rescue immediately. Whereupon, the *Chicago* continued on and came down a few hours later at Hornafjord, alongside the *New Orleans*.

It was 11 A.M. when the *Boston* landed on the water, with Wade and Ogden doing everything possible to keep the plane from capsizing in the rolling sea. After floating around for about three hours, Wade saw smoke far off on the horizon. Scrambling out on the top wing, they began waving a piece of canvas and setting off flares with their Very pistol. For half an hour the ship remained in sight, then vanished over the horizon without even seeing them.

The fliers were growing disheartened now, with fog and rain closing in and the wind whistling through the struts. They began to wonder what the end result would be. Hours passed, until later in the afternoon they saw more smoke on the horizon. Climbing back on the wings they repeated their signaling, wigwagging, and firing their Very pistol even more frantically. This time the ship headed straight toward them and, as it came closer, it turned out to be a trawler—the *Rugby-Ramsey*. Wade and Ogden were a bit startled when the skipper leaned over the rail and shouted:

"Do you want any help?"

"Well, I should say we do!" Wade shouted in reply, after recovering from the question.

A towline was thrown out and the trawler tried to pull the *Boston* back toward the Faeroes, but could make no headway because of the huge waves. When the destroyer *Billingsby* arrived on the scene, followed by the USS cruiser *Richmond*, it was decided the best plan would be to hoist the plane to the deck of the *Richmond* and return to Kirkwall for repairs. A sling was lowered from the ship's crane, and the *Boston* was slowly rising from the water when the crash came. The tackle broke loose from the main mast, and the plane slammed back into the water, crushing the pontoons.

Now it would be a problem of keeping the aircraft afloat while it was being towed to the Faeroes. It was well past midnight with a gale blowing as the cruiser approached the islands, slowly pulling the battered plane through the waves. It was a losing battle for shortly past 5 A.M. the *Boston* capsized and sank to the bottom of the Atlantic. With heavy hearts, Wade and Ogden now headed on to Iceland aboard a destroyer.

After receiving Wade's wireless that the *Boston* was lost, the other fliers continued on across Iceland to its capital, Reykjavik, to await the arrival of the *Richmond*. The remaining world fliers—Smith, Arnold, Nelson, and Harding—now faced the longest single flight of all: From Reykjavik, 830 miles across the North Atlantic to Fredricksdal near the southern tip of Greenland, all of it over water. No shorter route was possible because the harbors along Greenland's east coast were clogged with ice. Still, it would be nearly three weeks before the *New Orleans* and the *Chicago* could take off, mainly because of advance supply problems, work to be done on the planes, and as always—the weather.

During this period, the Italian round-the-world entry, piloted by Lieutenant Antonio Locatelli with three companions, arrived over Reykjavik and dropped their Dornier-Wal super-flying boat into the harbor. They had begun their flight at Pisa three weeks before and, like the Americans, were following a westward course around the globe. Two days later, word arrived from the Far East that the Argentine flier, Major Zanni, had crashed while taking off from Hanoi in French Indochina.

The American airmen entertained the Italian fliers one evening and Lowell Smith invited them to join the flight to Greenland so they, too, could have the added support of American naval vessels across the Atlantic. Locatelli, much pleased at this show of sportsmanship, promptly accepted the offer.

When a report of better weather over the North Atlantic came through the two American planes, accompanied by the Locatelli flying boat, headed for Greenland at dawn on August 21. The skies were blue and visibility excellent, so they left hoping there would be no need to call on the Navy for help, even though there were five cruisers and destroyers stationed across the ocean at intervals of 125 miles.

The Italian plane was not only bigger but it was faster than the *Chicago* and *New Orleans*. Although he did his best to fly in formation, Locatelli sometimes would get far ahead and have to circle until the Americans caught up. Finally, weary of this or possibly impatient, Locatelli turned on the speed and vanished over the western horizon.

Iceland was 500 miles astern when the *Chicago* and *New Orleans* passed over the destroyer *Barry*, headed for Nova

Scotia with Lieutenants Wade and Ogden as passengers. As he flew low over the vessel, Smith noticed two flags on display from her yard—a warning of bad weather ahead. It was too late to turn back now. Within minutes they were flying through fog, rain, and high winds that seemed to grow worse with every mile.

Mountainous white shapes rose out of the ocean—icebergs! —looming up all around. Down near the water and traveling at 90 miles an hour, neither Smith nor Nelson could see these white menaces until they were almost upon them. Then they could only make a fast calculation, swerving right or left to avoid a berg, and, if no time for that, zooming up over it.

The *New Orleans* was flying close behind the *Chicago* when a particularly big one appeared ahead. This time a crash seemed inevitable. Smith heard Arnold saying his prayers, and said one himself as he swung the *Chicago* sharply to the right, the wings almost grazing the tall iceberg as they roared past. At the same time, the *New Orleans* swung the opposite way—a maneuver that left them separated in the fog, and from then on they were each alone.

For another hour, Smith dodged around bergs until the dark shores of Greenland appeared through the mist. Following his chart, he skirted the coast until he reached a point where he figured Fredricksdal ought to be. Then, they came down in a fjord between snowy mountains. There was still no sign of the *New Orleans*, but forty minutes later they heard the familiar hum, and in came Erik Nelson with his plane.

Still, the mystery was: what had become of Locatelli and his big Dornier-Wal? Hurrying ashore, Smith sent a wire to Admiral Magruder on the cruiser *Richmond*, informing him that nothing had been seen or heard of the Italians. Whereupon the admiral ordered all ships to search the ocean between Greenland and Iceland, knowing there was still a chance that Locatelli may have crashed or landed on Greenland itself.

The search was still underway on the morning of August 24 when the *Chicago* and *New Orleans* left Fredricksdal for the

short flight up Greenland's west coast to Ivigtut, the last stop
before crossing Davis Strait to Labrador. Here, the USS cruiser
Milwaukee was standing by with supplies and new engines.

The following morning word came that Locatelli and his
companions had been found, floating on their plane in the ocean
120 miles east of Greenland. The huge waves had battered
their flying boat into a useless wreck, and after boarding a
cruiser, Locatelli decided to set his plane afire and sent it to the
bottom.

He told his rescuers he landed in the sea to avoid crashing
into the same icebergs that had been such a hazard to the Americans. He planned to wait for the weather to clear, then take off
again. The waves made this impossible, and for three days and
nights they were tossed about, hoping someone would find
them.

On August 31, the *Chicago* and *New Orleans* swept out of the
fjord and headed for North America, with their immediate
destination a Labrador cape with the improbable name of Icy
Tickle. What a glorious feeling, sailing along in perfect weather
with America now a mere matter of hours away! Alas, it wasn't
as easy as all that. Two hundred miles off Labrador the *Chicago*'s
gasoline pump went out, forcing Smith and Arnold to turn on
their reserve tank and rely on a hand operated emergency
"wobble-pump." Les Arnold, stripped to the waist, began pumping for all he was worth.

For three hours he pumped and pumped with his sweat and
sinew supplying the engine with its lifeblood. Meanwhile, Smith
kept an eye on the instrument panel, hoping nothing else would
go wrong now that they were so near their goal. Arnold's task
became even more rugged when they encountered a 40-mile-an-
hour head wind. By now, his shoulders and arms were so numb
he couldn't feel the pain, and when Icy Tickle finally came into
view, Lee said he felt as though he had crossed the Atlantic with
the *Chicago* on his shoulders.

Once again repairs were made, then at dawn on September 2
they started south for Pictou, Nova Scotia, where Wade and

Ogden were waiting to rejoin them with a new plane—*Boston II*. General Patrick had sent the plane north after deciding the hard-luck team should be included in all the homecoming thrills.

Over Belle Isle Strait, called "the foggiest stretch of water in the world," the World Cruisers flew only a few feet above the sea and nearly crashed head-on into a steamer. Landing at Hawkes Bay to refuel, they continued on to Pictou where they saw the *Boston II* sitting in the harbor below them. Every steam whistle in Pictou was going full blast and the shores were lined with cheering Canadians when the two planes taxied to their moorings.

Once again it was a three-plane formation that roared across Nova Scotia, over the Bay of Fundy and on to Boston. When they reached open water south of Saint John, New Brunswick, they encountered their old adversary—fog, with the visibility dropping to zero as they crossed the International Border into the U.S.A. This was no time for taking chances, so Lowell Smith led them down to land in Casco Bay, a sheltered cove on the coast of Maine.

Following an evening with hospitable New Englanders, they were ready to leave next morning when an aerial squadron appeared, roaring up from the south. It was a flight of ten U. S. Army planes and each in turn broke formation, diving in salute. In the lead plane was their commander-in-chief, Major General Mason M. Patrick, who had ordered the squadron up the coast to escort the world fliers on their triumphal return.

Bedlam greeted them in Boston. Geysers of water spouting from the fireboats, the piercing scream of steam whistles, the roaring boom of naval cannon with their 21-gun salutes— such was the scene when the World Cruisers came out of the clouds and glided down into the harbor. Not since the midnight ride of Paul Revere had so many Bostonians been aroused. A wildly cheering crowd of some 50,000 waved from the shore as six oil-smeared, aerial Magellans were brought to a landing-float to stand at attention while a band played "The Star-Spangled Banner."

September 8, 1924. Crowds greet American "round-the-world" fliers at Mitchel Field, New York. (*Wide World Photos*)

The rest of the flight on across the United States to Santa Monica and finally Seattle, was a series of triumphs such as America had never before seen. For the last time, the landing gear was converted to wheels, and on September 8 the cruisers took off for New York with General Patrick and the escort planes leading the way. At Mitchel Field, Long Island, the young Prince of Wales emerged from the crowd to shake hands and say:

"Great show, boys! Well done!"

For three hours, President Calvin Coolidge waited in the rain at Bolling Field to greet them—the first time in history a President had left the White House to welcome an American citizen to Washington. In Chicago, they were guests at a mammoth banquet where each flier received a box crammed with five-dollar gold pieces and a card reading: *May this box never be empty. Enclosed is the wherewithal to keep it filled.*

Arriving in Omaha, they were entertained by a "Queen" and her five ladies-in-waiting. Instead of merely shaking hands, they held hands all evening. At Santa Monica, they came down to land on a field strewn with roses. And when they reached San Francisco, Flight Commander Lowell Smith received a kiss from "Miss San Francisco" while the other five fliers stood by, nervously awaiting their turns. Then, one more brief flight and they were back at their official starting point—Seattle—where a crowd of 50,000 gave them a tumultuous welcome. They had flown 26,345 miles around the globe, and their actual flying time was 363 hours, 7 minutes.

The Great Adventure was over and another page of aviation history had been written in red, white, and blue ink. As a Navy admiral eloquently summed it up:

"Other men will fly around the earth, but never again will anybody fly around it first."

What they had done meant the dawn of a new era—the era of round-the-world flying in which we now live, with huge airliners circumnavigating the globe every day.

The most widely read pundit of that day, Arthur Brisbane, whose column appeared in papers from coast-to-coast, had this to say about our Magellans of the Air:

Many centuries from now when the names of all the Presidents of the United States, with possibly the exception of Washington and Lincoln, have vanished from the pages of history, the names of these airmen will still be there, for the simple reason that their achievement marks one of the major milestones in the History of. Man.

If he was a prophet who really could see into the future, how will we ever know?

Although Americans had circled the globe by air, the distinction of flying the length of the Dark Continent of Africa now went to a "Flying Taximan of London," who, cockney accent and all, was soon dubbed "Sir Knight" by the King.

CHAPTER VI

Mr. Cobham Flies to Cape Town

It was a sunny afternoon in the summer of 1919 and anyone driving by the big open field on the outskirts of Swindon surely must have thought a local ladies club was holding an outdoor meeting. A crowd of fashionably dressed women, of ages ranging from twenty to forty, was gathered around a rather garrulous young Englishman in flying togs, and they were listening with rapt attention to what he had to say. But it wasn't exactly a formal club meeting, although the ladies did have one thing in common—they were all excited over the prospect of having Mr. Alan Cobham take them up for a ride in his airplane.

All this was strictly a business routine for Cobham who only recently had been demobilized from the Royal Flying Corps, and now was barnstorming around the English countryside, specializing in taking air-minded females for "joy" rides in his three-seater plane. His fee for a spin over Swindon was one pound sterling, and being a promotion-minded fellow, he had hit upon the idea of staging a foot race to keep his customers amused while they awaited their turns to go aloft.

"Ladies," said he, pointing to a Casper Milquetoast type of an elderly gentleman standing nearby, "I want you to meet Mr. 'Arris, who supplies this 'ere aeroplane with bloomin' petrol. Now, I will give free flights to the first two girls who succeed

Sir Alan Cobham, who flew 20,000 miles from England to Africa and then back, 1925. He was knighted by the King for his record flight. (*Wide World Photos*)

in kissing Mr. 'Arris." Cobham was a cockney, and even years later when he became Sir Alan and a wealthy man due to his inventions, he never lost his accent.

Harris, who hadn't been consulted about this ahead of time, heard every word Cobham said, and he took off across the field at a speed that belied his age. The ladies followed in hot pursuit, their ribbons and bows flying in the wind, and even though he had a good start on the pack, he was overtaken by two swift-footed damsels after a chase of 50 yards or so. The first to reach Harris grabbed his arm, threw a half-Nelson on him, and both went tumbling to the grass. A moment later, the second contestant came puffing up and threw herself on top of the two. A wild scramble followed, and then the two ladies arose from the gasoline agent's prostrate form, adjusted their dresses, and strode triumphantly toward the plane where the dashing Mr. Cobham was already in the pilot's seat, waiting to give them their free ride.

Six months before, Cobham had been one of 22,000 British combat pilots who received their discharge papers. But when he looked around for employment in commercial aviation, he discovered that in all of England there were only about twenty-two civil pilots' jobs to be filled. So he formed a partnership with the Holmes brothers, Jack and Fred, and went into the "joy flight" business with a remodeled Avro 504K. As the firm's chief pilot, Cobham flew most of the passengers, and from time to time he also entertained the gaping crowds with a series of loops, rolls and spins. For several months now, the town criers all around England had been ringing their bells at the aerodrome gates, shouting, "Mr. Alan Cobham, late of the Royal Air Force," and then going into a spiel about his "amazing" career.

In the interest of accuracy, it should be pointed out that 'til now there had been nothing really amazing about Cobham's career. Alan was not a World War I ace, although it wasn't long before he was living up to the "amazing" billing, with something to spare. In 1920 he landed a regular job as an aerial photographer with the DeHavilland Company. And a year later, when he discovered that many of his wartime flying comrades were taxicab drivers and chauffeurs, the thought occurred to him—why not be a taxi-driver of the air? He started an "air flivver" service and among his first customers were various wealthy Americans whom he flew to Paris, Berlin, Vienna, Constantinople, and other capitals of Europe, or on short hauls to Scotland, Ireland, and Wales.

One day he met a Mr. Lucien Sharpe, an American millionaire from Providence, Rhode Island, who enjoyed flying so much that he hired Cobham as his aerial chauffeur. Together they flew some thousands of miles around Europe, the Middle East, and North Africa, often landing at places where the local populace had never seen an airplane before. Once, on a flight to Italy, while they were approaching Naples and could see the smoke belching from Mount Vesuvius in the distance, Sharpe casually suggested, "Let's fly over Vesuvius."

Cobham stole a sidelong glance at his passenger, believing he was only jesting, but when Sharpe repeated the suggestion in all seriousness, Cobham replied: "Why not!" Whether they were the first to do this, we don't know. People don't normally go out of their way to gaze into a smoking volcano, but Cobham took the plane up to what seemed to be a safe altitude and set his course across the top of the crater. As they neared the wide, gaping bowl and its fulminations of poison gases, he flew just a bit too close to the rim and a sudden updraft sent the plane a thousand feet higher. Cobham's head began to swim when he inhaled some of the sulphurous fumes, and for a moment he lost control, while below them the molten lava hissed and sizzled. But he recovered in time to level off, and they got away as fast as the plane would carry them.

Cobham soon expanded his flying taxi service to include such diversified chores as the delivery of London newspapers to nearby towns and villages, also long flights into Europe to pick up exclusive photographs and speed them back to London newspaper offices for the early editions. Hard working and willing to take chances to accomplish a mission, he rapidly gained recognition as Britain's leading commercial flier.

In 1925, when Imperial Airways decided to pioneer a few aerial routes, Cobham was assigned the important task of surveying the wilderness between Amman and Iraq in the Middle East. That same year, while on still another mission, he completed a round-trip flight between London and Rangoon, a distance of more than 17,000 miles, and for this achievement he was awarded the Royal Aero Club's Britannia Trophy. By the time he was thirty-one years old, Cobham's name had become a household word in England.

As early as 1922, Cobham had dreams of taking off from London and flying south over Africa all the way to Cape Town. But his talents as a promoter notwithstanding, he was never able to sell the idea to any of England's patrons of aeronautics—he just couldn't convince them it was a sound proposition. Arguing that aerial communications were non-

existent in Africa, and that it was time to open up the Dark
Continent to long-distance air transportation, he met one rebuff
after another. Cobham had the vision and others didn't, for even
as late as the mid-twenties some still believed the only form of
transportation Africa needed was a jungle vine to swing from
tree to tree.

The African continent includes an area of 11,600,000 square
miles, and some idea of its immense size can be gained by re-
lating it to distances in the United States. On a north-south
line from the Mediterranean to Cape Town, the distance is
more than 5000 miles, and it's 4600 miles from east to west.
By comparison, the distance from New York to San Francisco
is about 3000 miles.

After World War I the Royal Air Force tackled the task of
building landing fields in Africa, although the problems seemed
insurmountable. Hundreds of natives would work for weeks,
leveling a runway and stomping it dry and hard, only to see it
washed away by one night of tropical rain. Work crews were
constantly badgered by everything from poisonous insects to
herds of stampeding elephants, and in some areas unfriendly
natives were a constant problem. Even when an aerodrome
was completed, the enormous and rapid growth of vegetation
often made it necessary to start work all over again. African
grass could grow as high as an elephant's eye within a few
weeks, and the removal of trees often became an exercise in
futility. If roots remained less than two feet beneath the ground,
a tree could throw out suckers and replant itself within a month
after the start of heavy rains. Despite all these obstacles, within
a year the men of the RAF had established a chain of twenty-
three "so so" aerodromes and nineteen emergency fields from
Cairo to the Cape. But twice in 1920, planes tried to fly the
entire 5000-mile route and failed.

Cobham, who had made a study of these early flights, was
confident he could succeed where they had failed. In planning
a long journey, he always ran a careful check on the weather
reports, and the size and facilities of possible landing fields.

Above all, he was meticulous about the condition of his planes and engines. This painstaking attention to detail had made him a familiar figure at Stag Lane Aerodrome which, by 1925, had become one of the busiest airfields in England. It was also headquarters of the London Aeroplane Club which maintained a small hangar at the southeast corner of the field. The building was just large enough to house two tiny Moth airplanes, and when empty it served as a club room for members.

After some months, Cobham finally succeeded in arranging financial backing for his flight. He used his promotional talents to line up support from the infant Imperial Airways, and an imposing array of twenty-one business firms which were directly or indirectly connected with aviation. And on November 15, 1925, when he rolled his DeHavilland-50 out to the runway at Stag Lane, no one was surprised to see the fuselage covered with the neatly lettered names of the sponsoring firms. As one newsman remarked: "They have left out only the names of Mr. Cobham's fountain pen and toothpaste."

Almost anything Cobham said or did had long since come to

November 16, 1925. The DH-50 biplane Sir Alan Cobham was flying on his 8000 mile trip from England to Africa. The time spent in the air on this historic journey was 90 hours. (*United Press International Photo*)

be regarded as "a good story" by the newspapermen of Fleet Street and they were not averse to "pulling his leg." But Cobham, with his heavy cockney accent, was amiable enough in the face of it all, and once was heard to say that he didn't mind having his leg pulled, so long as the pulling left him a little taller at the finish.

Cobham's blue and silver plane, the same one that had carried him to Rangoon and back the previous winter, now had a new and more powerful engine—a 385-hp Siddeley Jaguar. The DH-50 biplane was constructed of paneled plywood, with a preparation known as "Titanine Dope" applied to the wings to help them withstand the heavy rains and heat of the tropics. Cobham chose two crewmen for the flight. One was his veteran engineer, A. B. Elliott, who had been with him on many aerial journeys including the flight to Rangoon. The other was B. W. G. Emmott, a motion picture cameraman who would make a film record of the Sudan, Uganda, Kenya, Tanganyika, Rhodesia, and South Africa, all in the vast region to be visited.

Our "Taximan of the Air" and his two companions made final preparations for the takeoff, going about it with all the casualness of a trio setting out on a holiday. Two suitcases full of tropical clothing were placed on board along with some emergency food supplies, the motion picture camera and film, a spare propeller, a couple of rifles and a light camping outfit, just in case they were forced down in the jungle. Then, on the morning of Monday, November 16, the DeHavilland took off from Stag Lane on a brief flight to London's Croydon Aerodrome where the journey would officially begin.

The trip normally required only fifteen minutes, but they ran into fog over London, and had to circle for a half hour before even finding Croydon. When the plane taxied up to the runway platform, a crowd of well-wishers met them, including Mrs. Cobham, who was struggling with a leash as she tried to keep her Alsatian wolfhound from jumping on board. Friends and relatives crowded around for the final farewells. Then, with a rather formal British cheer ringing in his ears,

Cobham climbed into the cockpit and the DH-50 was off for Africa.

After stopping at Paris, they set their course down the Mediterranean coast where the atmosphere became so bumpy Emmott was forced to hold onto his camera to keep it from being dashed against the cabin. In an effort to get away from the tricky air currents, Cobham flew out over the open sea and swooped low over a fishing fleet, much to the excitement of the fishermen who dropped their nets and waved so vigorously two fell overboard. Flying on southward, they landed at Grottaglie on the "Heel of Italy," where the local commandant greeted them with wine and brandy. Feeling no pain, they went on across the Ionian Sea to Corfu, then along the Greek coast to Athens, where they faced a 480-mile flight across the Mediterranean to Africa. They crossed the African coast at Sollum on December 7, and as they neared Cairo, Cobham decided the time had arrived for Emmott to take some motion pictures. Both Elliott and Emmott were seated in the cabin space just behind the engine, while Cobham's cockpit was located even farther to the rear and connected to the cabin by a small window. As they approached the Nile Delta, Cobham banked the plane into what he thought was a proper picture-taking angle and yelled to Emmott, telling him to start cranking the camera. But for some reason, Emmott failed to get the message, and the Delta soon passed out of view without a single foot of exposed film to prove that it was even there.

It was a hot day, and Cobham was getting just a bit exasperated as he throttled the engine down and shouted more instructions through the window. Still, neither Elliott nor Emmott seemed to comprehend. As they were approaching the Pyramids, always important to anyone with a camera, Cobham again banked the plane—and shouted his head off. Even then, Emmott gazed vacantly out over the desert, just as though he had given up the idea of aerial photography. So Cobham concluded it was all his fault for failing to give the proper instructions beforehand. After the plane came down at Heliopolis, the

RAF aerodrome outside Cairo, they spent several days getting their signals straight on the matter of photography, and also taking on more fuel. Then on December 16, the long flight over the length of Africa began. With Emmott now faithfully grinding away on his camera, they flew up the Valley of the Nile and reached Malakal in the southern Sudan where the natives welcomed them with a ceremonial war dance.

The modern airplane provided a startling contrast in the background, as the primitive Shulluk warriors, dressed in leopard skins, formed a long line across one end of the field. Then, to the beat of the tom-toms, the Shulluks began a slow advance forward, chanting a war song and waving their spears and shields as they approached the Englishmen and their flying machine. They continued their steady progress, jumping a few paces at a time, and stomping the ground so hard that clouds of dust arose around them.

For a third time the Shulluks advanced with a mighty shout, and finally they rushed headlong toward the fliers who, by this time, were afraid the situation was getting out of control. When the line of warriors came to a halt, the spear points were quivering only inches away from the uneasy English faces. But it was all in fun, and when the tom-toms ceased, the fliers continued their journey on southward across the great Sud swamps to Jinja on the shores of Lake Victoria, one of the largest bodies of fresh water in the world.

Located in the East African highlands, the aerodrome at Jinja was 4000 feet above sea level and Cobham momentarily forgot the difference the high rarefied atmosphere would make in the landing maneuver. As the plane came in low over a banana grove, several natives scampered across the runway and Cobham decreased the speed in a side-slipping maneuver to avoid crashing into them. But in the high altitudes speed was needed to maintain flight, and instead of floating down gently, the plane slammed into the ground, damaging the landing gear. When he climbed from the cockpit to survey the results, Cobham made a mental note that from now on, even with natives, cattle or elephants in the way, he'd land straight ahead.

The repairs were made, and thousands of natives gathered at the Jinja aerodrome to see them off—a spectacle that inspired Cobham to entertain the crowd with a series of loops and rolls before heading southward over the mountains. He soon picked up the trail of the Northern Rhodesian Railway which led him to the city of N'Dola, where the landing strip was surrounded by a thick forest. First, Cobham made one pass over the airfield to get his wind bearings, and then he brought the plane down. The moment he set foot on the runway, a Rhodesian official came running up, quite out of breath.

"I say, old chap," the official asked, "could you see the landing ground all right?"

"Perfectly," Cobham assured him.

"By gad," the Rhodesian replied, obviously relieved, "when you flew by I thought you'd missed it. Did you see me wave my hat?"

By now, it was late in January and a few hours after resuming flight, Cobham was following the railway line south of Broken Hill when he first saw the clouds of smoke that appeared to be rising from a gigantic forest fire. But as the plane drew nearer, he discovered it wasn't smoke at all. It was the perpetual cloud of vapor that rises from the incomparable Victoria Falls.

As every English schoolboy knows, David Livingstone became the first Westerner ever to see the Victoria Falls in 1855, and of course he named them for Queen Victoria. The natives had their own name for this natural wonder of the world on the Zambesi River. They called it "Mosi-oa-Tunya," which means "the smoke that thunders." More than a mile wide, 420 feet high, the falls can be heard for miles and the mist from the spray can be seen from afar if you are in a plane. More than 60,000,000 gallons of water plunge over the brink every minute, night and day, and the raging river below crashes through a gorge barely a hundred feet wide. All of which I hope you saw in our Cinerama production, *The Seven Wonders of the World*, and, as we shall see, Cobham's cameraman also made a few brief "shots" for their black-and-white film.

As he approached the falls from the north, Cobham could see a crowd waiting to greet them on the airfield at Livingstone, but he decided to give Emmott a chance to bring the camera into action before coming in to land. The brink of the falls was barely 50 feet beneath the wings, and Emmott was cranking away when the heavy mist and spray rose up to envelop them. Suddenly, the engine began to sputter, and Cobham put on full power to climb quickly away from the falls. The air-intake pipes had sucked spray into the carburetor, causing the engine to misfire, but the condition soon cleared itself and the plane came down to land at Livingstone.

The biggest reception of their Cairo-to-the-Cape flight was at Bulwayo on January 31 and, for the first time, Alan Cobham had the pleasant feeling that his flight was receiving even more attention than he had anticipated. Then, when they reached Pretoria, the Union of South Africa ordered six of its Air Force planes to escort the explorers on the 30-mile flight to Johannesburg. It was the first indication that the flight was being regarded as something more than a mere "stunt." Any lingering doubts about this were completely dispelled at Johannesburg where the South African Parliament adjourned its session early so its members could join a welcoming throng of thousands at the airport.

For the next several days, Cobham was besieged with invitations and had to hire two secretaries to handle his emergency correspondence. He also found himself making four or five speeches a day on the future of trans-African aviation. So the rest of the flight seemed almost an anticlimax. They landed at Cape Town on February 17 after zigzagging across Europe and Africa for more than 8000 miles—the actual air time being only ninety hours. The return flight to London was made over virtually the same route, with the plane landing at Croydon on March 13 after only eighty hours in the air. As part of a tumultuous welcome home, King George V received Cobham at Buckingham Palace that very evening, and it came as no surprise when the "Taximan of the Air" was dubbed "Knight of the Air"—Sir Alan Cobham. With modesty hardly becoming a promoter, Sir Alan made the following statement:

"I don't want you to think the flight was very daring. It wasn't really, you know. The main thing was organization and tenacity of purpose. Apart from that, it was an everyday affair. Most of all, it seems to have stimulated public interest in aviation and I hope proved that, after all, flying is not a fool's game."

And from there Sir Alan Cobham went on to further fame—and fortune too.

With the world still at peace in the mid-'20s, the aerial achievements of France, England, Australia, and the United States spurred airmen of other nations to seek international acclaim in this new realm of high adventure. In Spain a swashbuckler who would have made a popular bullfighter decided to be the Columbus of the Air. In so doing he left us with one of the epic aerial narratives of all time.

CHAPTER VII

A Spaniard Flies the South Atlantic

From the Pyrenees to Gibraltar, and from the Portuguese frontier to the Gulf of Valencia, an epidemic of "aviation fever" was sweeping all of Spain on the afternoon of January 21, 1926. For at least once, the airdromes had replaced the *plaza de toros* as the centers of rampant enthusiasm, with cheering crowds surging through the magnificent flag-lined avenues of Barcelona, Valencia, and Madrid in a thundering farewell to a national hero—Major Ramón Franco of the Spanish Military Air Service. And while the emotions of patriotism were running full tide, a twin-motored seaplane circled above the southern coastal town of Palos, then came in for a landing on the Domingo Rubio Canal at the very spot where Christopher Columbus had weighed anchor on his voyage of discovery 434 years before. Standing only a few yards from the wings of the plane were the ancient ruins of the Franciscan Convent of Santa Maria la Rabida whose prior, Fray Juan Pérez, had persuaded Queen Isabella to give Columbus royal encouragement and support in his plans to sail the unknown seas to the West.

Major Ramón Franco, resplendent in a Spanish Air Force uniform, climbed out of the cockpit and saluted a group of ficials who hurried from the Convent and came forward to ome him. Moments later, he was escorted inside the build- umbling walls where members of the Columbia Society were meeting to solemnly memorialize a new voyage for the glory of Spain—an airplane flight across thousands of miles of the South Atlantic Ocean to the shores of Brazil.

Writing with a flourish, Franco signed the Columbus Book which rested on an ornate lectern just inside the doorway, then he turned to receive the embrace of the Society's president, Marchena Colombo, who fervently told him:

"May God be your guide in your noble and patriotic enterprise."

Franco silently nodded his appreciation and replied:

"This place which once gave Columbus all aid for the discovery of the New World, now gives wings to the aviators who are about to mark out a new route to the West with their seaplane. We will be the bearers of salutations from this historic region to the people of the Americas."

All through the night excitement prevailed, and the following morning, as Franco and his crew of four made their final preparations, a fleet of military planes rose into the skies above Madrid and headed southward to Palos to give the transatlantic flight an aerial umbrella at the moment of takeoff. Spanish warships, having left their port in the Canary Islands, were steaming southward across the Atlantic, ready to provide assistance anywhere along the route. And from the four corners of Spain, thousands of men, women, and children were streaming into Palos well before the scheduled takeoff time.

For years, the leaders of Spain had hopefully predicted that someday a Spanish aviator would follow the seapaths of Columbus in an unprecedented flight to establish an aerial bond with South America, and Ramón Franco had delegated himself for the task. At the age of thirty, he was Spain's most noted aviator, having won his wings throughout the early 1920s in the military campaigns against the rebellious Riffs in Spanish Morocco. He was the younger brother of Colonel Francisco Franco who, ten years later, would lead the Nationalist Army to victory in the Spanish Civil War and then become the nation's Chief of State.

Both Ramón Franco and his older brother were natives of the port of Ferrol in northern Spain where their father had been a naval paymaster. But they spurned a naval career for the Army, and Ramon became one of the first Spanish soldiers to receive training with the military air arm. He was ordered to Morocco for aerial combat duty against the forces of Abd-el-Krim, the Riff leader who was trying to drive the Spanish out of North Africa. Within only a few years Ramón's face was rough and reddened from the Sahara sun and desert, while the shaggy coonskin coat he wore when the nights were cool had earned him the nickname of "Jackal."

Among his fellow fliers of the Spanish Foreign Legion, "Jackal" Franco was known as a quiet, reserved hombre who liked to put a sandwich or two in his pocket, fly behind the Riff lines for lunch, and then return before dark. If, on a clear afternoon, a plane was seen going through a series of acrobatics in the sky somewhere over North Africa, the Spanish Legionnaires took it for granted that "Jackal" was in the cockpit. He crashed on several occasions but always escaped serious injury, and during his eight years of service in Morocco he seldom returned to Spain, although he did make a speedy trip in 1924 to take a Spanish girl as his bride.

That same year, Ramón first broke into the news in a big way by taking part in a flight of Spanish planes from Melilla around the northwest coast of Africa to the Canary Islands, a route that had never been flown before. To Franco went most of the credit for the flight's success, and it did much to increase his popularity. Then, before the limelight of newly found recognition had time to dim, he sought support for a transatlantic flight to commemorate the military victories in Morocco. He succeeded and late in 1925 his plans were approved by Premier Primo de Rivera, who was then political head of the Spanish government.

A sea-trail across the Atlantic had been flown—or almost flown—once before, but the achievement was something less than sensational. In March 1922, a pair of Portuguese Navy officers, Rear Admiral Gago Coutinho and Captain Saccadura Cabral, started out from Lisbon, but twice they crashed along the way and had to wait for new planes to arrive before continuing their journey. They were even forced to travel part of the way on a steamship before they finally reached the Brazilian coast more than three months later, in June. Franco's flight plan called for four separate hops in traversing the 3683 miles across the South Atlantic from Spain to Brazil. The first leg would carry him to the Spanish-owned Canary Islands, a distance of 872 miles. Next, he would fly 1100 miles to the Portuguese Cape Verde Islands, and then would come the longest and most perilous part of the journey, a distance of 1432 miles across the open Atlantic to Fernando de Noronha Island—a penal colony known as "The Isle of Murderers." Once Noronha was attained, the remainder of the distance would be a mere 279 miles to Pernambuco on the coast of Brazil. Then would follow a triumphal flight down the coast to Rio de Janeiro, Buenos Aires, and other capitals of South America. Franco was even talking of expanding the project into a flight around the world or, short of that, a return trip to Spain by way of New York, London, and Paris. Clearly, it would be Spain's all-out bid for world aviation honors.

In choosing a crew, Franco had carefully screened a large number of volunteers in order to make certain their professional efficiency would be exceeded only by their unswerving loyalty to him. As relief pilot and navigator, he chose El Capitan de Artilleria Ruiz de Alda, who had also won some recognition as a military flier. The important post of flight mechanic went to Pablo Rada who, as Franco well knew, liked nothing better than climbing out on a wing to repair a motor, even while a plane was in mid-air. Two additional crew members were chosen even though it was uncertain whether they would remain on board throughout the entire flight. One was Ensign Durán of the Spanish Navy who would serve as a military observer. The other was Señor Alonso, a motion picture cameraman who, of course, would try to record the flight on film.

Major Ramón Franco (center) and two of the crew for his 1926 South Atlantic flight. (Left) Navy Lieutenant Durán and (right) Captain Ruiz de Alda. They received a Papal blessing before they took off. (*United Press International Photo*)

As the moment of departure drew near, Franco's plane, the *Plus Ultra*, was riding calmly on its moorings in the Domingo Rubio Canal, its tanks loaded with fuel and its two British-made engines pronounced in the cutting edge of perfection. The 450-hp Napier Lion engines were in tandem position, one placed forward with its propeller pointed outward, and the other directly behind the wing with its propeller directed toward the tail. Franco had ruled that the plane's name would be "without limitations," and there were certainly none in the Latin term *Plus Ultra*, which, translated into idiomatic English, can be construed to mean "even more than the most." It was a Dornier-Wal flying boat, the same type Roald Amundsen and Lincoln Ellsworth had flown in their unsuccessful attempt to reach the North Pole the year before. Designed by the famed German aircrafts-man Claude Dornier, the *Plus Ultra* had been especially built in Pisa, Italy, where Franco had insisted on carrying out the test flights himself, rather than allow someone else the privilege of being the first to handle its controls.

The skies above Palos were clear as eager hands went busily about the task of loading the final items of cargo on the plane, including 400 pounds of mail from the officials of countless towns and cities throughout Spain who were sending their greetings to the people of South America. Then came the food supplies—barley, ham, sugar, coffee, biscuits, chocolate, and last, but by no means least important to the Spanish menu, *una botella de coñac y una de vino de Jérez*. It was an insufficient amount of food, and drink, to provide for five persons through-out the flight—another indication that Franco intended to leave part of his crew somewhere along the route. Loaded on board also was a special distilling machine, capable of producing a pint of water every hour and guaranteed against accident, an assurance which no one was prepared to give for the plane.

As Franco and his crewmen prepared to climb aboard a messenger arrived from the Vatican, bringing Pope Pius XI's special blessings for the flight's safety. A high mass was cele-brated on the banks of the Canal in the shadow of the plane, and then a Franciscan monk came forward in his heavy brown robes to pin the medal of Our Lady of Loretto, the patron saint of aviators, upon Franco's breast just before he mounted to the cockpit. The cheers and shouts swelled to a crescendo as the two propellers whirled into action, and the *Plus Ultra* began to move slowly across the Canal toward the open sea. Seated in his cockpit above the forward fuselage, Franco waved a farewell as he gave both engines full throttle and the plane skimmed across the waves to take off at 8 A.M.—the exact hour the caravels of Columbus had unfurled their sails more than four centuries before. Before heading on southward toward the Canaries, he swung into a wide bank and circled the statue of

Columbus, while overhead roared a parting escort of fifty military planes.

For the first two hours, Franco maintained a steady altitude of about 330 feet, but soon he ran into a blustery rainstorm that forced him to climb another 3000 to get above it. Then, the rain was far below, but the crest of the clouds continued to close in around them, and Franco nosed the plane upward another 1500 feet to emerge into sunshine with blue skies above. Four hours passed as the *Plus Ultra* soared on across a limitless field of white clouds that blotted the sea from view and kept Alda from using his wind drift indicator. Cramped into the small radio cabin at the rear, Alda was following Franco's orders by sticking to his post, making no effort to stretch his legs and talk with the others. Durán, whose duties as observer permitted some freedom of movement, spent his time handing out bars of chocolate, while the chain-smoking Alonso remained cooped up in the photographer's cabin, looking for something to film besides a sea of clouds. As for Franco, he was in the cockpit, gazing straight ahead with the expression of a contented bird sitting on his favorite limb in the tree. Little did he realize that over his shoulder far to the northwest, one of the worst storms in recent years was smashing freight steamers in the North Atlantic, and tossing huge ocean liners about like toys.

At 3 P.M. Alda's navigational report placed them within a hundred miles of Las Palmas, and ten minutes later a break in the clouds revealed a thin dark line in the distance. Franco plunged the *Plus Ultra* through the opening and came above Fuerteventura, one of the northernmost Canary Islands. Striving for better visibility, he roller-coasted the plane through the sky, flying just above the water and then zooming sharply upward above the clouds, until at 3:30 P.M. the radio signals told him that Las Palmas was less than 45 miles away. Within a few minutes, the plane flew through another gap in the billowy white mass and Las Palmas lay beneath the wings. Franco circled the city once, then came down in full view of the wildly cheering crowds along the waterfront. Precisely on schedule, he had arrived in the Canaries—where the geographers of ancient Greece and Rome had once drawn a meridian to mark the western limit of the known world.

Franco, elated over his progress so far, had planned to leave Las Palmas on the very next morning, but for four straight days extremely high winds churned the seas, making a takeoff impossible. Facing him now was the long leap southward to the Portuguese Cape Verde Islands, a distance of 1100 miles that could place heavy demands on the plane's gasoline supply. To make room for more drums of fuel, Franco decided to remove some 800 pounds of spare parts from the cabin and send the entire lot on ahead to South America by boat. Still pushing his weight reduction drive, he informed Alonso, the cameraman, that he would have to dispense with his services and leave him behind in Las Palmas. When the *Plus Ultra* finally raced across calmer seas to take off on the morning of January 26, Alonso was so upset and disgusted that he could hardly turn the crank to film the event.

The skies were hazy but for the most part clear as they sped southward, moving on a course roughly parallel with the African coast which lay just beyond the eastern horizon. Shortly after 9 A.M., the luxury liner *San Carlos* crossed the sea lanes beneath them, and the radio crackled with an exchange of greetings and bearings. Ensign Durán, apparently becoming bored with his job of "observing," made a raid on the pantry and emerged with a handful of hardboiled eggs and sandwiches, only to be challenged by Rada, the mechanic, who harangued and gesticulated, demanding his share. But Franco remained such an inflexible part of the machine that even when an egg was placed within reach of his mouth, he glanced at it disdainfully as if to say: "Bah! Who needs food?" Finally, after much persuasion, he was prevailed upon to take at least one small bite, although he had to be hand-fed because his hands never left the controls.

A strong tail wind was speeding the plane along when they arrived above the Spanish gunboat *Infanta Isabel* which was maintaining constant radio contact with Alda all along the route.

After getting a correction on his bearings, Alda took a "break" to join Durán and Rada for a smoke. All three were tobacco addicts and they had discovered a small compartment in the plane's tail where a cigarette could be enjoyed at a safe distance from the gasoline drums. But their "smoking salon" was so small that Alda and Durán had to strain themselves mightily to squeeze inside, though Rada had no such trouble since he was as slender and lithe as an *hombre reptil.*

As the plane neared the Cape Verdes, Franco, seeing a grayish-black wall moving across the southern horizon, braced himself for another encounter with a rainstorm. But as the ominous-looking barrier came closer, he realized that it wasn't rain at all. It was an African sandstorm, a dense wall of sand propelled from the desert by whirlwinds and carried far out into the Atlantic. Franco needed no reminder that the flight would be finished if even a tiny portion of this airborne dirt should find its way into the engines. The plane had just passed over Boa Vista and Mayo Islands, and through the dusty haze he could see the dim outlines of San Thiago, another landfall in the Cape Verdes. The immediate goal of Porto Praya lay just beyond, but Franco swung the *Plus Ultra* off course to the west, hoping to fly around the dust cloud and land in the harbor with his engines undefiled by all that sand.

After flying due west for several miles, he looked over his shoulder to see that he had outflanked the unusual storm. Then, just as he was turning the plane back east again, he felt someone tapping his arm. It was Rada, with trouble to report.

"It's a loose cable, rubbing against the outer tail assembly and causing some electricial friction," he told Franco. "Should I climb out and set it straight?"

"No!" shouted Franco, as he swung the Dornier-Wal around Point Bicudas to come above the harbor at Porto Praya. A strong wind was blowing across the bay, whipping up waves and tide, but he made a masterful landing and taxied over to a buoy that was already in place for the anchoring.

High tides and rough seas were forecast for the next several days, but Franco had already planned a Porto Praya stay of at least three or four days before starting the longest leg—the 1432 miles over water to Fernando de Noronha Island. Time was needed as well to consider a problem that lay ahead. The Cape Verdes, at 23 degrees, West Longitude, marked the point where the real crossing of the Atlantic would begin. And Franco faced the question of whether to fly this mid-ocean distance by day or by night. He didn't like the idea of risking a landing in the seas off Fernando de Noronha in the dark, and that could be avoided only by leaving Porto Praya in the early evening and arriving in daylight. But it would present the problem of flying on through the night, and the danger of being forced down in a possibly stormy sea. On the other hand, if he left Porto Praya at dawn, there was still a question as to whether they could make it before nightfall.

The high seas continued for three days with no sign of a letup and Franco's humor was growing even worse than the weather. In order to increase the fuel capacity, he swung the personnel axe again by dropping Ensign Durán from the crew and sending him on ahead to Noronha Island aboard the Spanish cruiser *Alsedo*. Then shortly after midnight on January 30, another cruiser, the *Blas de Lezo*, began towing the plane from the turbulent waters of the bay out into the open sea, for the takeoff would require a long run across the water. The impatient Spaniard had decided to leave during the early morning hours and push the plane to the limit in an effort to make the Atlantic crossing before sundown. The towline broke once and there were a couple of false starts, but finally the *Plus Ultra*'s pontoons plowed through the waves to take the air at 6:10 A.M. The long flight westward was underway—the first non-stop over the South Atlantic.

The visibility was foul, but a steady stream of radio signals from the *Blas de Lezo*, steaming through the sea beneath them, enabled Alda to plot his course for the first three hours after the takeoff. By 10 A.M., visibility had improved from poor to hazy, but strangely, the cruiser's signals had ceased. Shortly after noon, Franco took his first ten-minute "break" and Alda slipped into the pilot's seat. Another hour passed with the west-

ern skies rapidly growing dark with rain and Franco, back at
the controls again, began the gas-consuming routine of circling
in a never-ending search for better visibility. As they crossed
the Equator, rain was lashing the fuselage and, try as he might,
Franco found it impossible to climb out of the storm. For nearly
two hours the downpour continued, until suddenly the clouds
opened up on both sides to form, as Franco described it, "a
guard of honor" through the sky.

When the rain ceased, Alda began receiving signals loud and
clear from Pernambuco far away on the Brazilian coast, assuring
him the plane was on course. But Alda accepted this news with
little enthusiasm because, by now, the long flight was beginning
to wear on his nerves. Even worse, the radio telephones of that
era were like sharp forks in his ears. Encouraged by the weather
and confident of his fuel supply, Franco notified the radio station
on Fernando de Noronha that he would probably try to make
it all the way to the South American mainland without stopping,
and not to worry if no plane was heard flying over the island.

But just before 7 P.M., when the sun was dropping into the
western sea, Franco caught a glimpse of Noronha some 60 miles
away, and he discarded his plan to fly non-stop to the bulge of
Brazil. Instead, he opened the engines full throttle in a race
with the sun, hoping to reach the island before nightfall. However, he didn't have the luck of Joshua who made the sun stand
still. When the plane arrived over Fernando de Noronha the stars
were out and a cross wind was kicking up a rough sea. Circling
in the darkness, he flew to a point some 25 miles offshore and
then came down to a safe but bumpy landing on the waves.

Darkness descends rapidly near the Equator, and their only
guide now was the blinking beam of a lighthouse that was dis-
appearing and reappearing with the rising and falling of the sea.
The waves were crashing against the fuselage, sending floods of
water into the cabin and soaking the uniforms, food and charts.
Hoping to find shelter from the winds, Franco turned on the
engines and taxied through the swells to the western end of the
island. But when Alda set off a few flares, signaling for as-

sistance, the Noronha radio flashed them the message: "Don't come closer. Reefs!"

Dimly in the distance they saw a series of twinkling lights that seemed to be mysteriously floating on the sea. Franco swung the plane in that direction and, on coming closer, they found the lights attached to a raft-like platform that remained stationary, despite a constant battering from the waves. Ropes were thrown out and the *Plus Ultra* was made fast to the strange platform which, they reasoned, might very well be a deep-sea fishing pier. For nearly half an hour, they peered hopefully into the darkness, and soon a rowboat came out from the island and pulled alongside. The oarsmen were common laborers, probably convicts from the penal colony, but the coxswain was a well-dressed gentleman who identified himself as the island governor's secretary. And alas, he brought the sad news that the seas were so rough it would be impossible to get them ashore that night.

In spite of this edict, Franco and his crewmen insisted on going to the island. So the boat started out with them, only to turn around and come back again after nearly being swamped in the waves. By this time, the water was ankle-deep in the plane's cabin, and the wary fliers were having trouble finding a dry place to sleep. Alda settled down in the pilot's chair, while Rada climbed up on the motor and soon was snoring away. As for Franco, he got into a pair of bathing trunks and fashioned a makeshift bed in the tail assembly, where he fell asleep with a bottle of cognac in his arms.

All through the night, the rain came down in cataracts, but at daybreak the cruiser *Alsedo* arrived and took the fliers aboard where they enjoyed the luxuries of a bath, some fresh clothing and a ship's breakfast. Ensign Durán removed his handbag from the warship and placed it in the plane's cabin for he would rejoin the crew for the remainder of the flight to Brazil. The distance to Pernambuco was only 279 miles and, once again, Franco loaded the cabin with all the tools and spare parts the *Alsedo* had carried across the ocean from Porto Praya. Next, they spent the morning hours inspecting the plane, and were relieved to find the engines in excellent condition despite the night-long battering from wind and waves. A cross wind was blowing and it was still raining when Franco revved up the motors, but the *Plus Ultra* showed no strain as it glided across the sea and took off into the western sky.

Flying at around 450 feet just below the clouds, they were soon bucking an increasingly strong cross wind, forcing Franco to correct his course several times even though the radio signals from Pernambuco were perfectly clear. Two hours passed with the engines running smoothly and there was no sign of trouble until they reached a point about a hundred miles from the Brazilian coast. Just as Alda routinely checked his bearings with the Pernambuco radio, the plane began shaking and vibrating as though a giant pair of hands was trying to tear it apart. Not even the rough air was strong enough to cause such convulsions, and Franco knew that something must have gone wrong with one of the propellers. But the question was, which one? He quickly throttled down both engines and the instrument panel pinpointed the trouble to the rear. The back propeller was turning listlessly in its socket.

Faced with no alternative, Franco shut off the rear motor, and now the front engine would have to carry them to the Brazilian coast—if they were to get there at all. Little by little with its one good motor straining, the *Plus Ultra* began to lose altitude, and when the pontoons were 60 feet above the water Franco ordered the crew to throw out all their cargo to lighten the plane for a possible landing in the sea. All the while, the plane dropped lower and lower until the pontoons were barely above the waves, with great curtains of spray rising to douse the fuselage.

Then, like a heaven-sent dispensation, the sun broke through the clouds and far in the distance Franco could see the shadowy outline of the South American coast. Alda and Durán, having cast overboard virtually everything that wasn't nailed down, came forward to ask Franco whether they should jettison the radio and navigation equipment as well—and maybe Ensign Durán, too!

"No, we'll keep them," Franco told them wryly, "if only to be humane."

Wafted on the winds like a glider, the plane finally reached the coast and Franco swung southward, following the shore toward Pernambuco. With the rolling surf never more than 30 feet beneath the wings, the *Plus Ultra* limped its way down the coast, flying at half the normal speed.

When the buildings of Pernambuco gradually appeared on the horizon, Franco reluctantly abandoned his original plan to fly triumphantly around the city before landing in the harbor. The buildings seemed much too tall, and it was even doubtful whether the plane could climb high enough to clear the seawall that bordered the waterfront. Gradually easing the plane down into the bay, he taxied slowly toward a pier where they were welcomed by thousands of cheering Brazilians who lined the quay for miles. Our Lady of Loretto indeed had remained faithfully on their side.

The fliers had hardly reached the Palace Hotel when a cablegram of congratulations arrived from King Alfonso who had declared a national holiday throughout all of Spain. Political crises were forgotten, and the Spanish government celebrated the achievement by reducing the sentences of all criminals who were being held. Schoolteachers were ordered to give their pupils special instruction on the scientific significance of the flight and, quite unexpectedly, Franco received a favor from the Crown. Two years before he had married against the wishes of his mother and, for this reason, had failed to obtain a royal license. Now King Alfonso was setting the record straight by sending a special messenger to Bilboa to deliver the license to Franco's wife!

From Pernambuco, they flew on down the coast to receive tumultuous welcomes in Rio de Janeiro, Montevideo, and Buenos Aires, with dark-eyed señoritas coming forward with roses and kisses at every city along the way. Good things should not

Major Ramón Franco's Dornier-Wal flying boat, the *Plus Ultra,* arrives at Buenos Aires from Spain, 1926. This was the first aerial crossing of the South Atlantic. (*United Press International Photo*)

end too quickly, and Franco notified the Spanish government that he intended to fly up the west coast of South America, then to New York City on his return trip to Spain. But he was stunned a few days later to learn that his plans were disapproved. Instead, he was instructed to give the plane to the Argentine government as a token of good-will, and return to Spain by steamer.

"By steamer!" Franco roared in protest. "I'll give up flying if I have to do that."

For days, the transatlantic dialogue exploded in expressions of Spanish temperament until finally Franco bowed to his government's commands, although he didn't suffer the indignity of returning to Spain by steamer. An Argentine cruiser took him home.

Some four years after he flew the South Atlantic, Major Franco became involved in a revolutionary plot against the Spanish government. He dropped Republican propaganda pamphlets from a plane over Madrid, and was reported to have been, with difficulty, restrained from dropping bombs on the Royal Palace itself. Franco was forced to flee the country in 1930 and was later held in Portugal when he sought refuge there. He died in 1938 while the Spanish Civil War was at its height.

In 1926, the North Pole seemed as remote as the planet Mars. Nevertheless aviators of many nations were jostling one another at the starting line in a race to be the first to reach the Ultimate North. Whereupon we come to the first installment of the story of the "glamour boy" of aerial exploration.

CHAPTER VIII

The Race to the North Pole

When the sun rises over Spitsbergen during the first week of April, it doesn't seem to behave in a normal way. In fact, it remains in the sky most of the next five months before again sliding below the horizon. To put it another way, the Spitsbergen Archipelago, situated as it is well above the Arctic Circle some 500 miles north of Norway, is geographically a part of that polar region known poetically as the "Land of the Midnight Sun."

So on the afternoon of April 29, 1926, when he stood on a snow-covered bluff overlooking the fjord at King's Bay, it wasn't the glory of the setting sun that caused Captain Roald Amundsen to pull the visor of his ski cap back from his shaggy eyebrows and gaze intently at the western horizon. And the famed explorer, then Norway's national hero, was not alone as he leaned on his ski poles and stared out across the ice. Standing in groups along the bluff, watching the horizon with him, were other Norwegians, members of his latest polar expedition who were there for one purpose—to help their leader achieve his dream to be the first to fly across the North Pole.

Far away and approaching the entrance to the fjord was a thin plume of black smoke. Amundsen and all his weather-beaten men said nothing, but they knew who was coming. For weeks they had been expecting a visitor, and now here he was—coming to upset their plans.

The smoke was from an American ship, the *Chantier*, with Commander Richard E. Byrd and his polar party. Also on board was a tri-motored Fokker, for Byrd had announced his intention of being the first to make a flight to the North Pole. The Norwegians realized that, in his Fokker, Byrd would be able to fly twice as fast as Amundsen and the Italians in a dirigible. To make matters even more discouraging, the airship *Norge* had not even reached Spitsbergen, and was yet standing by in Russia at Leningrad, awaiting favorable weather for the flight across the Barents Sea.

Still standing motionlessly, the rugged Amundsen seemed deep in thought as he watched the ship moving toward him through the floating ice. The scene was taking him back in time, back to 1911 when, at the age of thirty-nine, he became the first man to reach the South Pole. There, he had planted the Norwegian flag after a dash across the high Antarctic plateau, on skis and with a team of dogs.

That was fifteen years ago, and now, here in the Far North was a new challenge. Commander Robert E. Peary of the U. S. Navy had been the first to reach the North Pole in 1909 after painfully crossing the Arctic pack ice on dog sleds with a party of Eskimos. Though no one had reached the North Pole by air, there was still some question in Amundsen's mind as to whether that, in itself, was really important. Only a few weeks before, he had told the New York *Times:* "Our main purpose will be to find land, if it exists in the polar region. We expect to fly a dirigible from Spitsbergen to Alaska. This will take us in a straight line across the North Pole through the center of the unexplored part of the Arctic. We have one main purpose—to get across. Flying over the Pole itself, that will be incidental."

But, despite anything he might say to the contrary, Amundsen realized that the world at large and even the men of his own expedition, could not shake off the notion that he and Byrd were making a race of it.

It would take the *Chantier* another two hours to reach King's

Bay, and Amundsen's Viking face with its arched nose, was impassive as he turned his skis and headed back toward his expedition's headquarters.

* * * * *

Plans for the voyage of the *Chantier* had been set in motion several months before when Secretary of the Navy Curtis D. Wilbur, carrying an armful of maps, had called at the White House to keep an appointment with President Calvin Coolidge. Wilbur wanted to tell the President about Commander Byrd's ambition to reach the North Pole by air. Coolidge listened silently as the secretary cited Byrd's record with the Navy, and pointed out the advantages the United States might derive from aerial exploration of the Arctic. Then, spreading a map over the President's desk, Wilbur pressed his argument.

"You can see there is a lot of unexplored white space on the map. Don't you think we ought to let Byrd go?"

In what was reported to have been one of Coolidge's longer statements, the President replied:

"Why not?"

Armed with this rather oblique but full approval, Secretary Wilbur promised Dick Byrd that he would give him an indefinite leave of absence to organize his expedition. A few weeks later, in December 1925, Byrd walked into Edsel Ford's office in Detroit, and, when he left, in his pocket he had a check for $20,000 which Ford had given him with no strings attached. In a matter of a few more weeks, Byrd received similar amounts from John D. Rockefeller, Jr., and other men of wealth who were willing to back the handsome and persuasive young Virginian. The epitome of a Southern gentleman, Byrd moved with ease into the presence of some of the nation's richest men who, perhaps, stood a little in awe of the Virginia aristocracy. At any rate, they were sold on Byrd's enthusiasm and alleged devotion to the expansion of scientific knowledge through exploration.

At the age of thirty-seven, Richard Evelyn Byrd had come a long way toward realizing his boyhood dream of helping draw the curtain from some of the little known areas of the earth. Born in Winchester, Virginia, he was a member of one of the nation's most distinguished families whose lineal ancestor was Colonel William Byrd, the aristocratic planter and North America's "first man of letters." With his two brothers, he was a part of Virginia's famous trio of Tom, Dick, and Harry—Harry, a governor of Virginia who became a United States senator of great influence.

As for Dick's career as an explorer, it began at the age of twelve when he traveled alone around the world, not as a runaway but with his parents' consent. Boarding a ship in San Francisco, he sailed first to the Philippines where, for a while, he was guest of a U.S. circuit court judge, a friend of his father's. On the voyage to Manila, crossing the China Sea, the ship encountered a typhoon that swept away the smokestack and most of the lifeboats. The letters young Byrd sent home indicated that, even while the storm was at its height, he spent most of his time on the bridge with the captain.

On being appointed to the U. S. Naval Academy in 1908, he immediately went out for football, only to discover that he was accident-prone. His ankle was smashed in a game with Princeton and a year later, when he was captain of the Annapolis gym team, he broke it over again. The fall came as he was changing from one pair of flying rings to another in mid-air—a maneuver which, years afterwards, he painfully recalled as his "first aerial adventure."

On the day Byrd arrived at the Pensacola (Florida) Naval Air Station to begin flight training, he had hardly unloaded his baggage before he saw a training plane crash into the sea, killing both the student pilot and the instructor. Despite this disheartening beginning, he went on to receive his wings and was commissioned a naval aviator in 1917. His father, a Virginia attorney, tried to persuade him to give up flying. Said the senior Byrd: "You are undertaking a dangerous and inconsequential career."

Two years later, Byrd attracted considerable attention in the

Navy's navigational section by working on the development of two new instruments for ocean flight. One was a highly efficient wind drift indicator, and the other was a bubble horizon sextant which bore his name. Recognizing his special talent, the Navy assigned Byrd to duty with the department that dealt with the navigational problems of the NC transatlantic flying boats in 1919.

Promotions came rapidly for Byrd, and by 1925 he was a lieutenant commander with an assignment that was to launch him on his career as an explorer. Donald B. MacMillan, then a professor of anthropology at Bowdoin College, was planning an aerial survey expedition over the vast unknown area between Canada's Hudson Bay and the North Pole. The U. S. Navy decided to supply MacMillan with an aviation unit, and Byrd was placed in command with the authorization to choose eight

Commander Richard Byrd and his pilot, Floyd Bennett, on their polar flight. One of Byrd's planes on a later mission was named for Bennett. (*Wide World Photos*)

men for his crew. On May 20 one of the men he interviewed and selected was Navy Aviation Pilot Floyd Bennett who, as Byrd's companion, was to become one of the best known fliers of his time.

Byrd had acted upon the recommendation of a fellow officer under whom Bennett had served while testing catapults on one of the Navy's first aircraft carriers. Born in 1890 in an old-fashioned farmhouse in western New York State, Bennett, at the age of thirty-five, was still something of a gawky country boy whose predominant trait was rugged, straightforward simplicity. Fearlessness was another. When he was only ten, Floyd talked the owner of a circus into giving him the job of driving a gaily painted wagon full of shaggy lions through his home town of Warrensburg. As he grew older, automobiles fascinated him and, after pursuing an auto mechanic's career for a time, he enlisted in the Navy during World War I, then went on to take flight training and win his wings at Pensacola.

The MacMillan Expedition got underway in June 1925 with Etah, Greenland, as the main base. And for the next five months three Navy amphibian planes flew a total of 6000 miles, surveying and mapping the rugged islands and waterways of the Canadian Far North under Byrd's direction. It was while he was on this assignment, serving under the magnetic and versatile MacMillan, that Byrd decided to make a try for the North Pole.

He set out to raise $140,000 to finance a polar flight but even with the generous contributions already made by Ford, Rockefeller, and others, he was far short of what he needed. It was late in January of 1926 before he finally had time to organize the expedition, and by then some eight other North Pole expeditions had already reached the formative stage. In addition to Amundsen's plans, the Australian explorer, Captain George Wilkins, was preparing to fly across the polar sea from Alaska to Spitsbergen in a search for the mythical Arctic Continent. Speed, consequently, had became important to Byrd who felt the prime point of his flight would be lost if someone else flew across the Pole ahead of him.

One afternoon in New York, Floyd Bennett looked up from his newspaper and remarked:

"Our north polar axis is going to crack under sheer weight of explorers by the time we get there, if we don't get a move on."

"Don't worry," Byrd replied. "Well be there, first."

Still, Byrd had only about three months to acquire a plane, assemble a group of about fifty men, train them for their tasks in the Arctic, and find a ship to ferry the expedition, airplane and all, across 5000 miles of ocean to Spitsbergen. Should there be any delays, they might be too late—trapped by the Arctic winter.

For his plane Byrd had decided on a tri-motored Fokker with the new and revolutionary 200-hp Wright Whirlwind engines which had emerged as by far the most advanced and efficient aeronautical motors of the day. Ever since that Sunday morning in July when Blériot flew the Channel, the tendency to over-heat had been a major problem for "in-line" engines whose cylinders were placed one behind the other, the same manner as the automobile motor of that period. In designing the Whirl-wind, engineer Charles Lawrence of the Wright Corporation had placed the cylinders in a circle, outside and around the motor, leaving space between so as to expose the cylinders to the cooling effect of the airstream in flight. It was the first of the so-called "radials."

The problem of an oceangoing vessel to carry the expedition north was also quickly solved. The United States Shipping Board had its World War I "mothball fleet" off Staten Island, New York, ready for the auction block. Dick Byrd had friends on the Shipping Board and prevailed upon them to loan him the 3000-ton steamer *Chantier* for the duration of the expedition with veteran Captain Mike Brennan as her skipper.

Byrd next tackled the long task of interviewing hundreds of candidates for the jobs of rank-and-file seamen. They came from all walks of life and every social strata, sons of millionaires, dishwashers, plumbers, West Point graduates, adventuresome merchants, doctors, lawyers, college students with horn-rimmed glasses, and even husbands who frankly admitted they wanted to get away from their wives. For weeks they flocked to the Brooklyn Navy Yard where the *Chantier* was anchored. After screening them all, Byrd chose fifty for the expedition. There were also some attractive feminine applicants who wanted to go along. These were, reluctantly, turned down although one pretty young lady, a real eyeball-turner, even brought along her baggage when she arrived at the Navy Yard for an interview. Her plan was to write a history of the expedition, and it took all of Byrd's well-known tact and persuasion to convince her that she couldn't be included among the ship's company.

By mid-March, supplies were arriving at the Navy Yard from all parts of the country, and the expedition was gradually emerging as a streamlined organization. Byrd, with his gifts for promotion and preparation, seemed to leave nothing to chance. In a ceaseless effort to insure success, he studied oils, for instance, being aware of the tendency of poor quality lubricants to freeze or congeal at extremely low temperatures. He outfitted his men with heavy boots, furs and gloves from Alaska. From the Yukon he ordered the tried and tested foods of the Arctic, like pemmican—a concentrated lean, dried meat, pounded fine and mixed with melted fat, which the North American Indians had eaten for years.

On the first day of April, the *Chantier*'s sailing date was only five days away. Still Byrd was $30,000 short of the amount needed to purchase the remainder of his supplies. But it was too late to cry, "April fool!" and postpone the expedition.

"We'll take a chance," he told Bennett. "I'll be personally responsible for the difference."

In fact, he did have a financial ace-in-the-hole, having signed over the exclusive rights to newspaper and picture coverage of the expedition, and this could easily bring a sufficient financial return whether the flight succeeded or failed.

He christened the Fokker *Josephine Ford* in a tribute to Edsel Ford's daughter, and the aircraft was carefully loaded on board the *Chantier* as the moment for embarkation drew near. Another plane, a much smaller single-engined Curtiss Oriole, was also put aboard after Byrd decided it might be needed for relief flying. This plane he dubbed *Richard the Third*, in honor of his young son.

On April 5, the *Chantier* steamed out of New York Harbor and headed for Norway with Captain Brennan wondering how he was going to make out with all those landlubbers on board. Byrd feared Amundsen and his dirigible still might beat him to the Pole, but despite its age, the reconditioned *Chantier* crossed the Atlantic without a breakdown, and on Sunday, April 25, 1926, they were off Trondheim, Norway.

Again, it was full speed ahead as they proceeded up the Norwegian coast, with the midnight sun becoming brighter with each passing mile. No longer now was the day followed by night, only day followed by day. And in the absence of darkness, the inexperienced ship's crew began to find sleep difficult in the never-ending daylight. Gradually, too, the temperature was dropping as the *Chantier* sailed on beyond the Arctic Circle. The thermometer was down to zero on the afternoon of April 29, when they sighted Spitsbergen, and then steamed into King's Fjord.

A rousing Yankee cheer went up when, far in the distance, they saw a thin column of smoke rising from King's Bay, the northernmost community in the world. Spitsbergen, its history and its lore, had been basic reading during the weeks of training back at Brooklyn Navy Yard, and now they were to learn first-hand about these islands which the Vikings had discovered nearly a thousand years B.B.—BEFORE BYRD.

The early Norsemen had named the mountainous islands "Svalbard." Then came the Dutch explorers who rediscovered them in the seventeenth century and changed the name to Spitsbergen. The name stuck until the 1920s when Norway acquired sovereignty over the archipelago—and renamed it Svalbard again. The Norwegians had long known of vast coal deposits on West Spitsbergen, largest of the islands, but mining was not begun until 1904. The mines were on the west coast at King's Bay and, by 1926, more than fifty coal miners and their families were calling Spitsbergen their permanent home.

Steeped in glaciers and covered with snow much of the year, most of Spitsbergen's eastern shorelines are inaccessible except for brief periods when the Arctic relaxes its icy grip. But along the western shores the area around King's Bay is caressed by the warm North Atlantic drift, which moderates the climate and keeps the fjords open to shipping most months of the year.

April was one of these months, and the *Chantier* was making about six knots as she moved through the deep blue water of the fjord. Suddenly, on the port side, a spotted seal stuck his nose above the floating ice cakes, and then dived out of sight again in his hunt for cod and shrimp.

Standing on the bridge with field glasses, Byrd surveyed the Ice Age panorama that lay around him. Behind him to the north, a massive glacier extended along the fjord's outer limits, and on beyond rose the jagged mountains of upper Spitsbergen. To the south he saw Mount Zeppelin looming above the settlement of King's Bay. On a hill just outside the village stood the huge hangar that was to house the dirigible *Norge*. And nearby, towering 130 feet above the shoreline, was a mooring mast, the highest man-made structure north of the Arctic Circle.

As the *Chantier* approached shore, it was apparent that the docking facilities at King's Bay consisted of one small coal-loading pier and there, occupying the only available space, was a slate-colored Norwegian gunboat, the *Heimdal*. Anticipating such a contingency, Byrd had cabled Oslo weeks before, explaining that dock facilities would be needed to unload the expedition's two airplanes and requesting a berth for the *Chantier*. In reply, the Norwegian authorities had assured him that all would be in readiness, and that whenever the *Chantier* arrived at King's Bay, it would encounter no docking problem whatsoever.

Still, there was no smoke coming from the *Heimdal*'s funnel, a clear indication that the gunboat had no intention of pulling out from the pier right away. By the time the *Chantier* moved to within hailing distance, a large crowd of Norwegian sailors had appeared on the deck, all fully uniformed and wearing their familiar round blue hats and seaboots. Shouting across the floating ice, Byrd asked to speak to the gunboat's captain, and then he explained his problem with a request that *Heimdal* move out into the fjord long enough to permit unloading of the two airplanes.

But Captain Tank-Nielsen of the Norwegian Navy had some bad news. Shouting his reply with as much grace as possible, he told Byrd he could not move the *Heimdal* for at least several days because coal had to be taken on and his vessel was up for repairs. Tank-Nielsen also went on to explain that he was under strict orders to keep his ship in readiness for possible relief duty in case the *Norge* was forced down on its flight from Leningrad.

Byrd listened quietly and wondered—were they deliberately trying to block him? After all, a delay of a few days could make all the difference in a race to reach the Pole first. He gave Tank-Nielsen a curt "thank you," then instructed Captain Brennan to pull the *Chantier* farther out into the fjord and drop anchor at a point several hundred yards from shore.

Ten minutes later, Byrd and three of his top men climbed into a whaleboat and were lowered from the *Chantier*. Curious for a look at the Americans, a few coal miners and their families were waiting when they stepped ashore. The dour Norwegians made no comments, and only the barking of their dogs broke the silence as Byrd, in full Navy uniform with every button of his blue overcoat precisely fastened, led his group across the snow flats toward Amundsen's camp.

King's Bay was located on a small plain which, in most places, reached down to the water's edge, and was sealed off on the other three sides by a semicircle of snow-draped mountains, ascending in sharp contrast against the azure sky. Only two days before, a blizzard had struck the village with 50-mile-an-hour winds, piling up huge snowdrifts against the buildings and burying some up to the second story.

As he trudged through the snow, Byrd noted the narrow gauge railway extending down from the mine to the dockside, also the busy-looking commissary, the white hospital buildings barely discernible in the snow, and the dark outlines of the huge dirigible hangar in the distance. He lifted his eyes to scan the top of the mooring mast, then paused to gaze at the wooden huts where Nobile's Italian advance party was quartered, awaiting the arrival of the *Norge.*

When Byrd and his men reached the mess hall, a couple of hostile-looking cooks were standing in the doorway, grumbling to themselves in Norwegian, but the Americans pretended not to hear as they walked by. As they approached another building, the machine shop, a young Norwegian came out of the doorway to meet them, but his face wore a friendly smile. Encouraged by this development, Byrd offered his hand.

"I'm Commander Byrd," he said. "Can you tell me where I'll find Captain Amundsen?"

The sociable Norwegian paused long enough to pull a piece of cloth from his pocket, and wipe some grease from his right hand before extending it to Byrd.

"It's a pleasure to meet you, Commander Byrd," he said. "My name is Balchen."

When he met Byrd that day in the snows of Spitsbergen, Bernt Balchen was twenty-six years old, a young flight lieutenant on leave from the Norwegian Air Force to serve with Amundsen's expedition. Years before, all through his boyhood in Norway, he had been impatient with the process of growing up, anxious to reach manhood and become an explorer. He was only twelve when he first met his hero, Roald Amundsen, who came to Bernt's home in Kristiansand one evening to have dinner with his parents. Discipline was a strict affair in Norwegian families, and Bernt's mother told him he could come into the parlor before dinner and shake hands with Captain Amundsen, but he was not to speak unless spoken to and, in any event, he must leave at once.

When the little boy was led into the parlor, the benignly smiling Amundsen asked him that perennial question of the elderly to the young:

"Well, Bernt, what do you want to do when you grow up?"

While his parents gasped in surprise, Bernt blurted out: "I want to be an explorer and go on an expedition with you, and hunt seals and maybe polar bears."

Later, he became a student pilot at Norway's military aviation school, and by the time he joined Amundsen's expedition at King's Bay, Bernt was generally credited with more hours of flying over snow and ice than any other pilot, anywhere. He of course had heard about Commander Byrd, so it was with more than ordinary interest that he regarded the handsome clean-shaven American.

"Follow me," he said, "I'll take you to Captain Amundsen." Whereupon he led the way up the hill toward the headquarters building, with Byrd and the others following close behind.

When they walked inside, Amundsen was seated behind a table piled high with maps and charts, but he promptly arose from his chair. A balding, white-haired man of slender build, Amundsen had eyes with a permanent squint, brought on by years of exposure to the white glare of the polar snows. But he opened them wide as he shook hands with Byrd.

"Glad you're here safely, Commander," he said cordially. "Welcome to Spitsbergen."

Byrd, still bristling over the rebuff he had just received from the *Heimdal*'s captain, was cool but polite as he introduced his companions.

"This is Lieutenant Noville, my executive officer, and Lieutenant Oertell, who is handling our fuel supplies." Then Byrd turned to the tall chap who was leaning against the doorway. "And this is my pilot, Floyd Bennett."

At that moment, Amundsen's American partner and financial backer, Lincoln Ellsworth, came in from the kitchen and rather casually went through the motions of shaking hands. Perhaps Ellsworth also was somewhat concerned over the possibility that Byrd would become the first to fly over the North Pole.

Three months earlier, before they left New York City for Spitsbergen, both Amundsen and Ellsworth had talked with Byrd in a general exchange of information about their separate, though simultaneous, assaults on the Pole. Ellsworth had followed the discussion with rapt attention because, like Byrd, he too was looking for new worlds to conquer. At the age of forty-four, Ellsworth was the widely traveled son of a wealthy Midwestern industrialist. An ardent sportsman who also liked to do the unusual, he had explored in the Mara country of Yucatán, traveled afoot across the Andes, and stalked bighorn in the Pacific Northwest. As a youngster, he had worked with railroad construction gangs in western Canada.

In New York City, one October evening in 1924, the telephone rang in Roald Amundsen's room at the old Waldorf-Astoria Hotel. It had been a hard day for Amundsen. He was in New York trying to raise funds for another expedition. Things had not been going well, and his financial picture was bleak, so he was just a trifle weary with it all when he picked up the telephone.

"Captain Amundsen?" the voice asked.

"Yes."

"This is Lincoln Ellsworth. I haven't met you before but I'd appreciate very much the opportunity to talk with you for about an hour."

Although his caller was a complete stranger, Amundsen invited him up, and an hour later one of exploration's most famous teams had been formed—with Ellsworth offering to supply any needed funds. A few months afterward when Ellsworth produced a check for $85,000, Amundsen couldn't have been more astonished had he found the money lying in the street.

They purchased two Dornier-Wal flying boats and, one day in the summer of 1925, both planes took off from Spitsbergen on a flight discovery to the North Pole. But the venture fell short of its mark when one plane was forced down by engine trouble and the other landed nearby to provide relief. For weeks, Amundsen and Ellsworth were lost to the outside world until they were rescued by a Norwegian sealer.

It was the second time Amundsen had been involved in an

unsuccessful attempt to reach the North Pole in a plane, and it was not surprising that he began to weigh the possible advantages of a dirigible. Italy's lighter-than-air engineer, Colonel Umberto Nobile, had designed a highly successful airship for the Italian Air Force and Amundsen decided to purchase it—with more Ellsworth money.

But the Italians were exploration-minded themselves, in keeping with Mussolini's campaign to revive the "ancient glory of Rome" by whatever means possible, regardless of how far-fetched some of the means might be. It was hard to picture the Italians giving each other the Fascist salute as they cracked their heels together at the North Pole. Nevertheless, Amundsen and Mussolini agreed on a joint expedition. The dirigible was renamed the *Norge*, displaying both the Norwegian and Italian flags. Amundsen had the overall command while Colonel Nobile operated the airship with a predominantly Italian crew. It became the Amundsen-Ellsworth-Nobile Polar Expedition, and the American's name in the top billing gave the enterprise even more of an international flavor. It also meant something else—a population explosion for Spitsbergen.

In fact, by the time Amundsen and Ellsworth were exchanging greetings with Byrd in the headquarters building at King's Bay, the population of Spitsbergen had already tripled, with nearly a hundred Norwegian, American, and Italian explorers, plus more to come on the *Norge*.

Amundsen motioned Byrd over to the table where they began poring over the maps.

"Yes, that's the route," said Byrd and, indirectly hinting at the trouble he had encountered with the gunboat, added: "But, how are we to get our plane into the air?"

If Amundsen was aware of the *Chantier*'s docking problem, he made no reference to it, but he did make a gracious offer.

"There's a flat area in front of this building, running north through the center of the camp right to the edge of the fjord. You can tramp it level if you wish, and use it for your strip."

Byrd gazed at Amundsen meditatively.

"You're being very generous for a rival."

"But we are not rivals," Amundsen was emphatic in replying. "We are collaborators in a joint assault on the polar regions, an attack by two vehicles, one lighter and one heavier than air. We are partners in this venture together."

As far as Byrd was concerned, the venture would not take on his name to become the Amundsen-Ellsworth-Nobile-Byrd expedition. They had their plans, and he had his. And besides, none of the Norwegians, Amundsen nor anyone else, had offered him the slightest assistance in getting his planes ashore. That, certainly, would have to be an all-American enterprise, and he had an idea on how it could be done.

It was well past 6 P.M. when Byrd and his group returned to the beach and set out in the whaleboat toward the *Chantier*, still at anchor some three hundred yards away.

"Row like hell," he told Noville and Oertell who were manning the oars. As they came close to the *Chantier*, Byrd was so keyed up that he leaped across a short gap of water and grabbed the ship's ladder in mid-air, just like the old flying-ring days back at Annapolis. He clambered to the deck and promptly called a meeting of all his officers. Quickly, he outlined his plan.

They would immediately begin the construction of a raft by lashing four of the ship's whaleboats together with boards spread across to form a platform. The two planes, first the Curtiss Oriole and then the Fokker, would be lowered to the raft, in turn, and towed to shore. Another whaleboat, manned by the expedition's most muscular seamen, would do the towing. The beach was lined with a 10-foot wall of ice, but an advance party would take care of that by chopping an opening large enough to let the planes through.

Some of the officers took a dim view of Byrd's plan, pointing out that the Fokker weighed three tons and ferrying it on a clumsy raft through the floating ice would be disastrous if a sudden Arctic storm should arise.

One even insisted: "It can't be done! A bit of wind, a single ice floe—pouf! Goodbye plane and expedition."

Byrd listened patiently, but refused to yield. If his plan meant gambling with the safety of the planes, then so be it.

"It can be done," he said, "and we'll do it right now."

It was long after midnight and a snowstorm was raging before the raft was finally pronounced ready. The little Curtiss Oriole, with its bright, orange-colored fuselage and yellow wings, was quickly lowered from the ship and towed safely to shore, although it was snowing so hard the oarsmen could scarcely see where they were going.

On the return trip to pick up the *Josephine Ford*, it took the raft fully two hours to get through the drifting ice and reach the side of the *Chantier*. Then, slowly the crane lifted the Fokker's fuselage from the deck, gently swinging it over the side and down to the platform. Next, the iron hook came back for the 74-foot wing and, just as it was in mid-air, a gale came belting across the fjord, rocking the *Chantier* and nearly tearing the wing from the crane.

Working with frantic speed, Byrd's seamen managed to pull the wing back on deck and fasten it down with ropes. But the raft, with the fuselage aboard, was banging against the iron sides of the ship. Gradually, they dragged the raft around to the *Chantier's* stern where the ship's bulk afforded some protection. But the storm raged on for another twelve hours before it ceased, leaving a water-soaked, shivering band of seamen who, somehow, had saved the Fokker.

The big wing was lowered and attached to the fuselage, then began the long hard pull for the shore. Byrd stood forward on the raft, and it was a bit like Washington crossing the Delaware, even though Floyd Bennett privately said it was more like Eliza crossing the ice. The task was difficult enough as it was, but some of the landlubbers didn't even know how to row. Several times they misinterpreted Byrd's nautical commands, but they gingerly made their way through the ice floes without a mishap, and soon the *Josephine Ford* was on the takeoff strip, almost ready for the flight.

Commander Richard Byrd's tri-motored Fokker at Spitsbergen before the historic first flight to the North Pole, 1926. Byrd and his crew won the race to the Pole from Norwegian explorer, Roald Amundsen. (*National Geographic Photo*)

For the next few days, some of the men found the subzero cold intolerable, and were confined to the ship with frostbitten hands and feet. But the other crewmen worked day and night, tramping the snow along the runway and hauling equipment to the plane, including the skis which had been custom-made to serve as landing gear.

The Fokker was parked near the hangar, poised at the end of the strip which Amundsen had turned over to the Americans. Bernt Balchen, perhaps more than anyone else among the Norwegians, was taking a special interest in the preparations, and he had some uneasy doubts about the *Josephine Ford*'s skis. As a Norwegian ski champion, Balchen, by instinct, knew what kind of wood was best suited for the task. What bothered him about the Fokker's skis was their design—they just didn't seem to be either large enough or strong enough—and it was his private hunch that Byrd might have trouble getting off the ground.

Balchen's analysis proved to be correct. Shortly past noon on Tuesday, May 3, Byrd and Bennett gunned the Fokker down the runway for a test flight. The plane was beginning to gather speed when one of the skis wobbled and came loose, plunging the plane sideways into a snowdrift.

Balchen was in the machine shop and didn't see the mishap, but moments later, Amundsen came running through the door and motioned him outside.

"There's been an accident," he said. "The Fokker's broken a ski. See what you can do."

Balchen hurried to where Byrd, Bennett and their ground crew were glumly looking at the *Josephine Ford* which was tilted against the snowbank like a wounded bird. Bennett, now aware that the skis were too light to carry the load, was the first to speak.

"I'm a float-plane pilot myself," he said, "and I don't know the first thing about skis. We've got a set of spares on the ship, but they're exactly the same as the one that broke loose."

"Maybe we could shore up the spares with some strips of hardwood," Balchen was quick to suggest.

"But where are we going to find any hickory or ash around here?"

Balchen thought for a moment. "How about the lifeboat oars on the *Chantier?*"

Despite Captain Brennan's vigorous protests, an armful of lifeboat oars was removed from the ship and carried to Balchen's machine shop where Amundsen's own woodworkers joined the *Chantier*'s carpenter in reinforcing the Fokker's spare skis. But the following day, as he watched the *Josephine Ford* speed down the strip and take off on a perfect test flight, Balchen didn't know whether to be happy or sad. Captain Amundsen had given them a landing strip, and now the matter of the skis. Once again, he thought, the Norwegians have turned the odds against themselves in the race.

That evening, the receiving set in the King's Bay radio station was crackling with messages from Alaska. Hubert Wilkins and his pilot, Ben Eielson, wanted to know about the weather and landing conditions at Spitsbergen. For two weeks, storms and fog had kept them grounded at Point Barrow, forcing a delay in their plans to cross the Arctic in a single-engined Fokker, and now they were anxious to get away. They were told that good weather appeared to be developing over the Arctic Ocean, even though conditions over Alaska were still bad.

The report of favorable weather was also cabled to Nobile at Leningrad, and on the morning of May 7, the throbbing of motors was heard in the skies above King's Bay as the *Norge* came stealing over the hills. Etched in silver against the blue Arctic sky, it was 348 feet in length—longer than a football field.

A ground crew of Italians seized the dangling ropes, and suddenly they were yanked off their feet when a gust of wind caught the dirigible and sent it aloft again. Then, the wind subsided and the ship was walked into its hangar.

Colonel Nobile, the gold braid on his uniform sparkling in the sunlight, was the first to step from the big airship and he was warmly greeted by Amundsen and Ellsworth. As they walked toward the headquarters building, Nobile caught sight of the *Josephine Ford*, and a frown crossed his face. Several times previously, he had urged Amundsen to concentrate on the single objective of becoming the first to reach the Pole by air, and then turn back to Spitsbergen once this was achieved. So by the time they reached Amundsen's quarters, Nobile was excitedly waving his arms.

"There's no time to lose," he was saying. "We did have engine trouble on the way, but replacing the motor would take another three days and we shouldn't waste time on such details now. The *Norge* must be off at once."

Amundsen shook his head. "We will not be rushed," he said calmly. "We'll take every necessary precaution and leave only when the ship and weather are right."

Nobile spread his arms in a gesture of despair, and Ellsworth joined him in a plea that every effort be made to reach the

Pole first. Still, Amundsen would only say: "Our flight is not a race. We're trying to chart a shorter route to the New World, and the North Pole is just a point we shall cross on the way."

That was final—and the Italian crewmen began the task of replacing the ailing engine and hauling fuel supplies to the *Norge*. There were now twenty-four Italians among the explorers at King's Bay and some had never seen snow before. Between stints of work, they spent their time learning to ski and engaging in snowball battles, while tumbling gleefully about in the snow. Colonel Nobile took no part in the merrymaking but he did have some difficulty standing up on the ice and Amundsen, on several occasions, saved him from a fall.

The relations between the two, never really good, began gradually deteriorating, especially after Amundsen was told that the Norwegian members of the *Norge*'s crew were not allowed to wear their warm flying suits on the flight from Leningrad. Nobile said the suits were too heavy, would overload the airship, so the Norwegians wore ordinary street clothes on the flight and were chilled through and through—even for Norwegians!

With the arrival of the *Norge*, Byrd asked his mechanics to work with all possible speed to get the *Josephine Ford* ready for the flight. Byrd seemed in such a hurry that Amundsen was worried about the safety precautions the Americans were taking against the possibility of being forced down in the Arctic Ocean. Amundsen didn't want to see that happen for one reason—he would be obliged to set aside his own plans and go to the rescue. To increase their chances of survival in case of an emergency, Amundsen gave Byrd and Bennett two pairs of snowshoes and also instructed the *Norge*'s carpenter to construct a light sledge.

Just before noon on Sunday, May 8, little groups of seamen from the *Chantier* began coming ashore and walking up the hill to the spot where the *Josephine Ford* was poised, ready for the takeoff. They were soon joined by the Italians and Norwegians who were idle that day because Amundsen, a religious man, allowed no work on Sundays. Even though there had been no official announcement that Byrd was ready to leave, the weather was perfect for flying with the temperatures in the thirties and the sun high in the sky.

Byrd had, indeed, received the most favorable weather report by far since his arrival at Spitsbergen. A high pressure area was developing over the entire polar basin. Favorable conditions were expected to last for at least forty-eight hours, with a probable tail wind all the way from King's Bay to the Pole, which of course could mean a head wind on return.

It was shortly past noon when Byrd and Bennett, wearing their reindeer flying suits, joined the crowd around the plane. Byrd, as immaculate as ever, saluted his staff as he mounted the steps and closed the cabin door.

Bennett fired up his three engines, advancing the throttle to full power as the plane moved down the sloping runway toward the fjord. Sliding slowly across the ice for 300 feet, it finally picked up enough speed to leave the surface, but only briefly. After clearing the end of the runway, the *Josephine Ford* came abruptly down again to bounce along over a row of snow hummocks and then flutter to a halt, with one wing buried in a snowdrift.

The crowd rushed down the hill to find Byrd and Bennett already outside, digging around the plane in a search for damage, but to their relief they found none. While Bennett crouched low over the skis to give them a closer inspection, Byrd spotted Balchen in the crowd and beckoned to him.

"Wonder what's wrong this time?" Byrd asked.

Once again the ski-minded Balchen had the answer.

"During the spring breakup period," he told Byrd, "the temperature sometimes rises above freezing and the snow becomes sticky, holding down the skis. The only thing to do is to wait until just after twelve o'clock midnight, when the colder air should make the snow hard and slick enough for a takeoff."

Balchen's advice seemed like common sense. Also, a closer inspection of the plane's storage compartment revealed something else that might help. What about all the assorted items, such as trinkets, hats, coats and pictures, the ground crew had smuggled on board, hoping to reclaim them later as souvenirs of the first flight over the North Pole? The entire lot added some two hundred pounds—an overload. Byrd now ordered it removed along with a large supply of extra fuel they had hoped to take along.

Quiet settled over the camp that evening and most of Amundsen's men were asleep in their barracks while Byrd's crewmen gave the plane a final going over. Shortly past midnight on Monday, May 9, the sun was a molten ball, hanging just above the northern horizon. It was colder now, and the icy runway was in better shape as Byrd and Bennett again climbed aboard, with their fingers crossed.

Bennett gave the plane full power and it slid swiftly down the runway, this time showing every intention of taking off. Gradually, the skis left the frozen snow and Bennett nosed the aircraft sharply upward out over the fjord. As King's Bay fell away behind them, Byrd and Bennett could see their jubilant shipmates running and skidding along the ice as they waved and tossed their hats.

Climbing to around 2000 feet they leveled off, and headed for the Pole. As they flew on across the Arctic Ocean, Byrd and Bennett saw no land, no birds, no polar bears, nothing but the limitless ice pack, reaching out toward the horizon. Byrd now concentrated on navigating a straight course toward a rather obscure distant point in the Polar Sea which had never been spotted from the air, and only once by human beings. That was when Peary was there with Matt Henson and their four Eskimo companions, Ootah, Egingwah, Seegloo, and Ooqueath. Byrd now had to do it without the aid of landmarks, for there were none in that unexplored realm at the top of the world. Nor were there any stars or a moon above to point the way toward "90 Degrees North"—the Pole, 700 miles distant.

In addition to the wind drift indicator and bubble horizon sextant which he had helped design for the Navy, Byrd had brought along a third navigational instrument, a sun compass. It had been constructed specially for the polar flight by Albert Bumstead, chief cartographer of the National Geographic Society. With Old Sol his only celestial guide, Byrd obviously would find the sun compass most important. It operated on the reverse principle of the familiar sundial. As for the conventional magnetic compass, it would be useless, because the North Magnetic Pole was located on one of Canada's Arctic islands, a thousand miles south of the geographic North Pole.

Byrd soon gave the sign that all was "O.K.," and both fliers turned to survey the endless panorama of ice. From a half-mile up, the pack looked like a great "white plain" that offered a score of landing places, but when Bennett nosed down to 300 feet to get a closer view they found themselves skimming above great frozen waves of ice—pressure ridges 10 feet high and more.

With the choice—or so it seemed—of remaining airborne or courting disaster, Bennett took the plane to 2000 feet again and leveled off at 90 miles an hour. When Byrd relieved him at the controls, Bennett busied himself pouring gasoline into the tanks from the five-gallon tins in the cabin, then throwing the empty cans overboard.

One of the mysteries of exploration was still unsolved—how about land in the Arctic? Suddenly, rising out of the sea, a line of snowcapped mountains came into view. But as Byrd turned to motion to Bennett, the "mountain peaks" proved to be an Arctic mirage, merely white clouds across the sky. So what might have been a newly discovered Byrdland, simply wasn't there.

Just as Byrd completed another sun observation, fixing their position at about 90 miles from the Pole, Bennett waved toward the starboard window. Something seemed wrong with the starboard engine! Byrd spotted oil bubbling from a leak with the "wash" from the propeller whipping the fluid back against the windows and fuselage, coating them with a heavy film that froze the moment it struck. With a pencil and pad, Bennett scrawled out his analysis of the situation.

"That motor," Bennett wrote, *"is going to stop."*

Byrd wrote back: *"Is it a bad leak?"*

Bennett scribbled: *"Yes, and we may lose the motor at any time,"* and he added: *"We'd better try to make a landing. Can't go on like this. We'll burn out the motor. If we land we'll have a chance of fixing it."*

Byrd looked at the ice field below. It seemed smooth enough. But even if they did come down and make a smooth landing, it would still be risky because the heavy plane might go through the ice. With their goal now less than an hour away, Byrd decided that even a forced landing right at the Pole couldn't leave them in any worse fix, so he wrote his reply, *"We'll keep going."*

With a shrug Bennett nodded agreement, and the oil-splattered Fokker pounded on toward the Ultimate North. They did throttle down the ailing engine, just to see if the plane would hold its altitude. All went well, but it cut down their speed, so they turned it up again with the hope of making it back on two engines, if that became necessary.

Among the magic charms in Byrd's pocket was a religious medal, put there by a friend who had explained that it belonged to his fiancée; also, a tiny horseshoe forged by a famous blacksmith; and a coin Peary had carried across the ice to the Pole and back seventeen years before. And, oh yes, what about the crisis that arose last Christmas Eve when his three small children, Katherine, Bolling, and Dickie-Byrd, first heard about his plans to fly to the North Pole and confronted him with that obvious question:

"Daddy, will you see Santa Claus?"

"I am not so sure about that," he had told them, "but when I get back I'll tell you all about his place at the North Pole."

"But there is a Santa Claus, isn't there?" asked Dickie.

The hour-hand of the clock brought Byrd back to the charting board. It was almost 9 o'clock, and that long-elusive North Pole couldn't be more than a few minutes away. With his head through the upper trapdoor, he swung the compass into position and sighted the sun, picking up a slight case of frostbitten nose in the process. The plane was at 89 degrees 55.3 minutes, and Byrd was tense as he watched the seconds ticking off on the chronometer. At 9:02 A.M. he tapped Bennett on the shoulder, and shouted above the roar of the engines: "This is it, you're over the Pole!"

As many have discovered since that day, including both authors of this book, the North Pole is nothing but a geographical spot in that sea of moving pack ice. At times it's a series of pressure ridges, or again there may even be open water right at the Ultimate North—where the ocean is some 14,000 feet deep.

Byrd motioned Bennett into a right bank for two quick confirming observations of the sun. Then back the other way for two more, and finally into a great circle for a three-minute flight around the top of the world. While Bennett swung the plane into a broad bank, Byrd cranked their movie camera, capturing on film man's first aerial view of the North Pole. Then, he opened a bottom trapdoor and sent an American flag fluttering to the ice below.

Byrd later told how he gave a silent salute to Peary and his men, as well as to the many who had lost their lives in the quest for the Pole.

With the starboard motor still losing its oil, they fervently hoped there was a benign Santa Claus. After spending thirteen minutes over the Pole, they headed south—south being the only direction in which to go. This, again, was a matter of precise navigation back across that sea of ice. The vital question was— would the oil leak and dwindling supplies of fuel, force them down? As Byrd reached for the sextant, Bennett put the plane into a steep bank and the instrument slid off the charting table and crashed to the floor, smashing its glass bubble. Now the return flight would have to be navigated by dead reckoning and the sun compass.

The hours passed, and then, Byrd sang out: "Floyd! The oil's stopped leaking!"

Bennett got up to see for himself.

The drone of the motors was like a soporific, and several

times Byrd relieved the drowsy Bennett who was having trouble keeping his eyes open. Speeding along at one hundred miles an hour now with an unexpected tail wind behind them, things looked much brighter, and when the clock read 6 P.M., almost nine hours since leaving the Pole, they again sighted land.

All through the afternoon at King's Bay, Amundsen's men had been preparing the *Norge* for its flight while occasionally pausing to scan the skies for some sign of Byrd and Bennett. And the tension was heightened by the lack of radio communication with the plane.

One of the Italians among Nobile's crew had been foresighted enough to bring along some spaghetti, and that afternoon at 6 P.M., he fashioned a white towel into a chef's hat and strode triumphantly into the mess hall with a platter of steaming

Commander Richard Byrd with the *Josephine Ford*, the plane used in the historic first crossing of the North Pole, 1926. (*Wide World Photos*)

spaghetti and tomatoes while his cohorts shouted with delight. It may have been the first spaghetti ever served at Spitsbergen. The dinner was only half finished when someone shouted: "She come—a motor!"

Chairs were overturned and tables shoved aside as everybody rushed for the door, and once outside they could see a silver speck moving toward them, high above the mountain peaks to the north.

Soon the runway was swarming with so many people that Bennett was forced to circle until the crowd got out of the way. Balchen looked at his watch and the hour was 6:07 P.M. when the plane's skis touched down at the end of the strip, then came to a stop at the foot of the ramp.

Amundsen was the first to greet them as they stepped from the plane, and there were tears in those squinty Norwegian eyes as he put his arms around both Byrd and Bennett. Then he turned to his men and called on them to give "nine good Viking cheers," for the Americans.

The following morning, Bennett examined the oil tank on the starboard engine and discovered why the leak had started, and then so mysteriously stopped. About halfway up the tank, a rivet had jarred out, but when the oil level had dropped below the rivet hole, the leak had ended.

It was a gala scene that night on the *Chantier*, with Amundsen, Ellsworth, and Nobile as special dinner guests, and the strains of "The Star-Spangled Banner" were heard coming from the *Heimdal*. Toward the end of the dinner, Amundsen called Byrd to one side and asked him:

"Well, what next?"

To which Byrd replied: "The South Pole."

"A big job," said Amundsen, "but it can be done. You have the right idea. The old order is changing. Aircraft is the new way, and the one way to beat the Antarctic."

Early the next morning, Amundsen, Ellsworth, Nobile, and thirteen crewmen filed on board the *Norge* to begin their flight across the Polar Basin to Alaska. The weather was still good northward from Spitsbergen, but violent sleetstorms were reported all along the Alaskan coast near Point Barrow. Weight problems also arose and Amundsen, with regrets, found it necessary to leave three of his men behind, including young Balchen who was much disappointed as he watched the *Norge* disappear into the northern sky.

Floyd Bennett interrupted Bernt's reverie: "Byrd would like to see you. Come over to the *Chantier*."

Byrd went right to the point, saying: "I'm planning another expedition and we can use your experience with skis and cold weather flying. How about a year's leave of absence from the Norwegian Air Force? We'd like you to sail back with us on the *Chantier*."

Balchen wanted to accept the invitation which he believed had been offered at Bennett's suggestion.

"Can I give you my answer in a couple of days, sir?" Bernt replied. "When I have word that Amundsen has reached Alaska."

Three days later on May 14, the radio reported that the *Norge* had safely landed in Alaska, after crossing the Pole and running into severe ice storms along the way. It had come down at Teller, an Eskimo village between Nome and Point Barrow, where Hubert Wilkins and Ben Eielson were still awaiting good weather before attempting their own flight over the Arctic. That afternoon, Balchen told Byrd that he would join his team. It was the origin of the Byrd-Balchen association that resulted in Bernt flying Byrd's plane over the South Pole, and many more honors for both, including a permanent commission in the U. S. Air Force for the young Viking who had given the American naval officer so much help at Spitsbergen.

Now came a young man—seemingly out of nowhere, for whom Destiny had arranged a special role.

CHAPTER IX

Lindbergh Flies Alone

Ghostlike, the moon shadow of the mail plane was moving northeastward across the Illinois prairie on that September night in 1926. High above the advancing shadow, the biplane's silver wings had turned sea-green in the light of the moon, as though some sky-dwelling astrologer were mixing colors to foretell things to come. Inside the cockpit and flying alone as usual, Captain Charles Augustus Lindbergh glanced at the instrument board, just to make sure his St. Louis-to-Chicago mail run was on course. It was. So he settled back and relaxed, and his thoughts stretched far into the distance.

What if this plane carried nothing but gasoline . . . no mail . . . just gasoline—how far would it go? Beyond Chicago, of course—even beyond Canada. If only this plane were a single-wing Bellanca with a Wright Whirlwind engine, then the horizons would go by like railway ties beneath an onrushing train. A mail plane like that could fly from St. Louis to New York without stopping . . . wait a minute, it could even fly all the way to Paris, something bigger and heavier planes somehow can't seem to do. That's it! His thoughts were tumbling one over the other now . . . "I'll attempt that too . . . I'll organize a flight to Paris!"

Charles A. Lindbergh was not the first man to fly the Atlantic. By the time he did so in 1927, many other fliers before him had completed the hazardous crossing, either by island-hopping, refueling at sea, or by winging it non-stop on a prayer and a pair of stuffed cats as Alcock and Brown had done in 1919.

Still, Lindbergh's flight had something special. The most notable aspect of his achievement was, of course, that it was the first time anyone had ever flown non-stop across the Atlantic *all by himself*. While others had made the crossing, or tried it, in planes loaded with mechanics, navigators, and co-pilots, Lindbergh's lone companion in the cabin space ahead was an extra tankful of gasoline. Here was a man who played solitaire with the unpredictable forces of nature, and won. And, as almost everyone now knows, his flight captured the imagination of a world in which the available supply of Grand Adventures was rapidly running out.

At any rate, it all began on that moonlit night over Illinois when he took stock of his own resources and decided that, as meager as they were, he was going to fly to Paris in his own plane, no matter what the odds. And the odds? Only last year, didn't a friend of his disappear without a trace in a flight over Lake Michigan, and how many times would Lake Michigan fit into the Atlantic Ocean?

Besides, there was the money—who would provide the money for a flight to Paris? His personal savings would yield only about $2000. A Bellanca monoplane with a Whirlwind engine would cost perhaps $10,000, and of course there would be other expenses before he finally landed in France. But there was the $25,000 prize which Raymond Orteig, the New York hotel owner, had offered the first man to fly non-stop between New York and France, in either direction—a prize that had gone unclaimed since 1919. That would cover the cost and then some, but you would have to get there first to win.

Other aviators were building their transatlantic planes and laying their strategy, still they all had ample financial backing. Commander Richard E. Byrd, the North Pole hero, had the Wanamaker millions behind him. The American Legion was asking its members to contribute $100,000 to finance another flight planned by Commander Noel Davis and Lieutenant Stanton Wooster in a biplane to be christened, *The American Legion*. And the Columbia Aircraft Corporation was rushing preparations to send its own famed Bellanca monoplane to Paris and win the Orteig prize. On the other side of the Atlantic, several French aviators were busily going about their transatlantic projects, and they too seemed to have plenty of financial support. To Lindbergh, all this made one thing unavoidably clear. Even though he would fly to Paris alone, the influence and financial help of others would be needed to get him off the ground.

Returning to St. Louis in his mail plane, he moved swiftly to carry out what had suddenly become a mandate to himself. And his position was not entirely without advantage. Admittedly he was short of cash, but he had a lot of experience banked away for a young aviator whose twenty-fifth birthday was still some months off. He had learned to fly at Lincoln, Nebraska, in 1922, when he also took his first parachute jump and trained himself in the insecure profession of wing-walking. That same year, he joined a flying circus and barnstormed through Kansas, Nebraska, and Montana, with the handbills spelling it out in bold, black letters: COME SEE DAREDEVIL LINDBERGH. And the cowboys, farmers and merchants flocked from miles around to stare with awestruck disbelief, while he strolled about the wings, and then "hit the silk" with a leap off into space.

In April 1923, while Kelly and Macready were getting ready to fly from coast-to-coast, Lindbergh laid out $500 of his precariously earned money and bought his first airplane, one of those "flying crates" known as government surplus "Jennies." The Army Air Service beckoned in 1924 and, taking it in easy stages, he flew his old "Jenny" from the Midwest down to Texas to enroll as a cadet flier at Brooks Field. When Lindbergh arrived, the commanding officer took just one look at "Jenny" with her haywire patches, and ordered the plane off the field.

Learning to fly for the Army proved no problem for a wing-walking barnstormer, and he was a second lieutenant in the Air Service Reserve when he decided to quit the Army,

eventually to head for St. Louis to become an airmail pilot.
Then, as soon as he had settled into his new job, he enlisted in
the 110th Observation Squadron of the Missouri National Guard
and the outfit made him a captain and flight commander.

Little wonder then that around aviation-conscious St. Louis,
"Slim" Lindbergh became known as one of the best fliers in
those parts. Tall, sandy-haired, blue-eyed, and handsome, he
came by friends easily and his modest manner even won over
some who might have preferred to dislike him. As a flight instructor at Lambert Field, he had come to know a number of
the city's influential citizens, some of whom either had money
to finance a transatlantic flight, or knew where to get it. So he
began making the rounds.

This was, in a way, the beginning of an uncharted flight
that rivaled the actual New York-to-Paris journey itself. This
flight was over neither land nor water, but Lindbergh had to
summon all of his navigational skill as he moved through a maze
of wealthy homes, banks, aircraft plants, and newspaper offices
in search of an airplane.

The insurance executive, Earl Thompson, was understandably
cautious. After all, wasn't flying the Atlantic a pretty risky
business? "Sounds like an interesting idea," he smiled encourag-
ingly, "but don't you think you should use a tri-motored Fokker, like Commander Byrd's?"

Seated in the living room of Thompson's home, and maybe a
bit ill at ease because it wasn't a hangar, Lindbergh gave his
answers: "A three-engined Fokker is big and heavy, and might
cost as much as $30,000. Even then, if one engine failed, with
all that weight there's no assurance the other two would get
you back to land safely. A single-engined plane trimmed of
every ounce of excess weight, would probably be the safest of
all."

The editor of the St. Louis *Post-Dispatch* was emphatic in
turning him down. "This newspaper wouldn't think of taking
part in such a hazardous flight . . . one pilot flying the Atlantic
in a single-engined plane. We have our reputation to consider."

Several days later, after Flying Club president Harry Knight had set up the appointment, Lindbergh walked into the State National Bank to see Harold Bixby, a banking executive who also served as president of the local Chamber of Commerce. They shook hands and Bixby began to talk, not with words, but with lyrics.

"Slim, you've sold us on that proposition of yours, and we're with you. From now on you'd better leave the financial end to us, and we'll arrange whatever organization we need. Put in your $2000, keep the cost figures down, and concentrate on getting a plane ready for the flight."

It was wintertime, but the young airmail pilot must have had a warm feeling as he reached the sidewalk outside. And for some strange reason the tallest building in St. Louis was beginning to resemble the Eiffel Tower.

The quest for a plane finally came to an end in San Diego where, in February 1927, shortly after Lindbergh's twenty-fifth birthday, an order was placed with Ryan Airlines—an almost unheard-of firm with a factory in a dilapidated building near the waterfront. After getting a go-ahead from his St. Louis backers, Lindbergh personally closed the deal for the construction of a monoplane, equipped with a 200-hp Wright Whirl-wind engine, along with the standard instruments. Delivery would be within sixty days—and the price was set at exactly $10,580.

But time was growing short, and for Lindbergh the pace of construction must have been agonizingly slow. Three American transatlantic expeditions were speeding their plans to completion, while the French war ace, Charles Nungesser, had decided to fly from Paris to New York as soon as possible rather than wait until summer.

Then, within the space of eleven ill-starred days in April, there was a series of crackups, one of them tragic. Both the Columbia Aircraft's Bellanca and Byrd's tri-motored Fokker, the *America*, were damaged in test flights, sending Byrd's pilot, Floyd Bennett, to a hospital with injuries from which he never really recovered.

Commander Davis and Lieutenant Wooster lost their lives when their plane *The American Legion* crashed at Hampton, Virginia, shortly after taking off on a final test run. Twelve days later on May 8, as the sun rose above Paris, Captain Nungesser and his co-pilot, François Coli, gunned their biplane, the *White Bird,* down the runway at Le Bourget Field and took off into the western sky—New York-bound. Ships at sea reported sighting the plane several times, but it never reached New York. Somewhere over the Atlantic the *White Bird* vanished, leaving not even a stray piece of fuselage as a clue to what had happened.

Spurred by the knowledge that Lindbergh was preparing to fly from San Diego to New York, Byrd and Columbia Aircraft's veteran pilot, Clarence Chamberlain, hurriedly went about repairing their damaged planes. Byrd's *America* was in a hangar at the far end of Roosevelt Field, and Chamberlain's *Columbia* was based at Curtiss Field, right next door to Roosevelt. By mid-May, Curtiss had become the teeming center of preparations in the race for the Orteig prize with newsmen and their "seeing eyes," the cameramen, swarming around the field. Publicity men, pilots, and mechanics moved in pinwheel formations about the hangars, while uniformed guards rushed here and there, trying to keep aviation buffs away from the planes.

It was into this supercharged arena of excitement that, on the afternoon of May 12, a silver-winged monoplane came circling out of the sky and rolled to a stop on Curtiss Field. Lindbergh leaned from the cockpit, waving a greeting and giving out with a rather shy smile that was soon to become another American emblem. The forward fuselage bore the neatly lettered words, *Spirit of St. Louis.* Harold Bixby had provided the name, and for this exercise in nomenclature he was destined to become just about the most envied Chamber of Commerce president of all time.

For months there had been a definite, and often discouraging, "gap" between Lindbergh's efforts and those of his rivals but it was certainly non-existent now. The airmail pilot had finally

Lindbergh in the *Spirit of St. Louis* en route from California to New York, when he hoped to be the first to fly to Paris non-stop. (*Brown Brothers*)

landed his plane on Long Island, and he was standing at the starting line, toe-to-toe with Chamberlain and Byrd. Still, it was a waiting game, because far out over the Atlantic the routes to Paris were shrouded in fog and rocked by storms.

For seven days, those North Atlantic demons held back the planes, until early on the morning of Friday, May 20, the Weather Bureau issued a shaky prediction—conditions might be clearing out over the ocean. However, at that very moment the rain was pelting New York, turning the Long Island airfields into mud flats, and nobody was convinced—nobody, that is, except Lindbergh. No matter how flimsy the weather report might be, he knew it was time to go. Even more important, he was the only one of the three contenders who was actually ready to take off. The *Columbia* was restrained by a court injunction because of a quarrel between Levine, the owner, and the crew. While Byrd, leaving nothing to chance, had decided to delay things a bit more and run the *America* through another series of tests.

Captain Charles Lindbergh, twenty-five-year-old former airmail pilot after arrival at Curtiss Field, New York, in the *Spirit of St. Louis*. This was his last stop before his historic solo flight. (*Wide World Photos*)

As dawn broke over Long Island, the rain began to slacken but a heavy mist still clouded the reaches out into the Atlantic. The neon beacon lights were flashing red, imparting a feverish look to the faces of an excited crowd that had quickly gathered on Curtiss Field after the word got out that Lindbergh was ready. A truck rolled up and towed the *Spirit of St. Louis* from its hangar, then across the rainy stretches to Roosevelt Field for the takeoff on a longer, but even muddier, runway.

It was 7:30 A.M. when Lindbergh took a final look around. Straight ahead, nearly a mile away, he could see a tractor someone had parked at the end of the runway. Above the tractor, a mesh of telephone wires stretched across his path, and beyond that was a low tree-studded hill, the outer limits of a golf course.

Suddenly he sensed a change of wind. Instead of a helpful head wind, something he had counted on, now it was a five-mile-an-hour tail wind that would certainly heighten the danger of taking off with a heavily loaded plane. The *Spirit of St. Louis* was standing patiently beside him in the mud, its tires bulging under a cargo of 425 gallons of gasoline—2550 pounds—more than it had ever carried on its test flights.

But there was no time now to worry. At 7:40 A.M., he donned a one-piece flying suit and eased himself into the wicker chair in the cockpit. One of the more privileged reporters on the field, Frank Tichenor, editor of the *Aero Digest*, stepped up to the plane.

"I hear you're taking only five sandwiches. Is that true?"

"That's all," Lindbergh replied, "outside of seven days' emergency Army fare. If I get to Paris, I won't need any more. And if I don't get there, I won't need any more either."

The engine roared to life, and he alternately idled and raced it for a final check across the instrument panel. His mechanic walked to the cockpit and Lindbergh gave him a long look then threw out the big question.

"How's she running? Everything all right?"

There was a hint of apprehension in the mechanic's eyes, and he hesitated a moment before answering. "She's running about thirty revolutions low, but doing as well as you can expect in this muggy weather."

For a moment, Lindbergh added up the latest tidings, none of them good. Wind, weather, power and load—all were discouraging. Then he buckled his safety belt, closed the door to his cramped cabin, and nodded to the men to take away the wheel blocks. At 7:52 A.M., the *Spirit of St. Louis* began to roll, moving more like an overweighted mud turtle than an airplane.

Slowly, ever so slowly, it lumbered forward, the tail-skid plowing a deep furrow in the mud for at least 2000 feet. Lindbergh was obviously taking his time, trying to keep the tail down and the nose up until he had gained enough speed to leave the runway. The plane wallowed on and on through the mud and then—a shout from the crowd as it left the ground, but the cheers turned to groans when it flopped right back again.

A few hundred feet more and up it went again, only to bound a few yards and come down once more, though all the while the engine was pulling for all it was worth and the *Spirit of St. Louis* was slowly gathering flying speed. Now the plane had passed the point of no return, a white cloth waving from a stick planted along the runway. From here on out it would be impossible to stop and come back for another try. Lindbergh must get the plane off the ground and over the tractor and telephone wires, or pile up at the end of the runway, perhaps in an inferno of blazing gasoline. While the crowd watched in agonized silence, an automobile raced along abreast of the plane. It carried Nassau County Police Chief Abraham Skidmore who had a fire extinguisher in his lap.

For the third time, the *Spirit of St. Louis* bounds off the ground, and dead ahead stands the tractor, now only a thousand feet away. Taut and straining, the plane continues to climb, from 5 feet to 20, and Lindbergh peers from the side window to see the tractor flash by underneath with barely 15 feet to spare! Still gaining speed, the plane climbs to 40 feet—and he's over the telephone wires!

Below him now he sees the white upturned faces on the green golf links, and ahead is that final hurdle—the tree-lined hill. He banks the plane a little to the right, sweeping the hilltop with the periscope he had brought along to peer around the gasoline tank that blocked the forward view. Faster and faster the plane climbs, over the hill, over the treetops, while through the overcast he can see a soft red glow, the day's first reassurance that the sun is still there, trying to break through. And Paris is still there, too, gleaming and dreaming by the Seine—3610 miles away.

Through the mist Lindbergh can see only three miles ahead, even though the ground is clearly visible below as the well-groomed landscape of Long Island's horse country glides by at a hundred miles an hour. He sets a compass course northward, heading toward Long Island Sound and the first segment of a carefully determined Great Circle route across the ocean. Soon a line of water appears on his left, the shoreline of the Sound, and suddenly he's aware that he's not alone. A plane loaded with newspapermen and photographers is circling off to his right, with cameras protruding from the cabin windows.

The engine is literally purring smoothly and easily, like the kitten he had reluctantly decided to leave behind just before the takeoff. After all, he had reasoned, why endanger the life of a kitten? A harbor full of boats looms ahead, and it's Port Jefferson with the open water of the Sound stretching beyond toward the Connecticut shore. He turns in the cockpit to see the newspaper plane call it quits, dipping a wing in a farewell salute as it heads back to Roosevelt.

A few minutes pass and the coast of Long Island is lost in the haze behind him, the water calm with not even a boat to break the glassy stillness. It's only 35 miles to Connecticut, but never in all his accumulated flying time has he ever flown across that much water before. Look, no hands! If Louis Blériot, who is still alive and in Paris, could only see him now!

The mouth of the Connecticut River is approaching, and rising beyond are the trees and hills of New England. He folds a map of New York State and puts it away, then takes out one of Connecticut. Just as he opens it across his knees, the plane begins to joggle, only slightly, but enough to make him throw an anxious glance at the wings, loaded down with those many extra pounds of gasoline. Turbulent air—something to reckon with wherever land meets water, and it's a great feeling to know the plane will grow lighter and lighter as the mileage consumes the gas.

The clock reads 8:50 A.M. and the haze is gradually clearing. Connecticut drops away to the west and already he's over Rhode Island. The first hundred miles are behind him, and the plane is about a hundred pounds lighter. Populous Rhode Island, a lot of people on a little square of land with a labyrinth of railroad tracks extending in all directions across the terrain. The city of Providence lies to his left, sprawling its suburbs across the Massachusetts line, and less than half an hour away lies the open sweep of the North Atlantic. The Atlantic! Even now, the first vague glimpses of a coastline can be seen far in the distance.

All along the flight path, people are gathered in the streets, standing on the roofs and in the trees, hoping to catch a glimpse of the plane. If he didn't know better, he'd guess they were viewing an eclipse of the sun. Over Halifax, Massachusetts, he dips down low to give the plane-watchers a good look, flying barely a hundred feet above the ground and almost brushing the treetops. Just like the old barnstorming days! Then he regains altitude and pulls out the most treasured map of all—his Mercator's projection of the Great Circle route across the North Atlantic, with the thirty-seven heading changes he had carefully worked out to take him to Paris in the shortest possible time.

Out over the rolling water, he aims his course toward the coast of Nova Scotia, 250 miles away. Banking the plane into a wide arc he glides gracefully downward to fly above the ocean at a height of less than six feet. Soon a few fishing boats dot the sea around him and he prudently rises again to a hundred feet where he's suddenly rewarded with the first blazing flash of sunlight from a sky of vivid blue.

The panel clock now reads 11:15 A.M., and he's steadily growing annoyed by two brown clumps of mud, thrown up on the bottom of the wings during the takeoff. They're stuck there, and he can't reach out and knock them off, they're too far away. After all his careful calculations to keep down the weight of the plane, even to the point of tearing the blank pages out of his notebook, why should he have to carry two stupid clods of mud to Paris? Why should he . . . his head nods forward. Then he jerks himself backward, almost violently. He's half asleep. Quickly he reaches a hand outside the cabin, not to knock off the mud, but to deflect a stream of fresh air against this face.

The grassy coastline of Nova Scotia passes under the wings, and soon it's one o'clock, time for lunch. But he's not hungry and a drink of water from one of his two canteens is sufficient. No need now, and hopefully never, to use that new Armburst cup which condenses the moisture of human breath into drinking water. That's strictly for an emergency. As he reaches up to replace the canteen, he makes a frantic grab for the Mercator's chart which nearly blows through the open window. Be careful now—there's no such item as a spare chart aboard this plane.

Haze begins to blur the bright sunlight, while little flocks of white clouds scurry here and there, joining in a conspiracy to spoil the weather. Far ahead to the north, a massive black wall reaches from the horizon up to the top of the sky itself. Green-banked lakes and ponds are passing underneath, rocking and bumping the plane as it moves through the turbulence above the waterlines. And the wind—it's beginning to be downright unfriendly, increasing in velocity as he approaches the big, black storm clouds ahead. The gusts are coming on stronger now,

flapping and bouncing him around in the cockpit like a mari-
onette. He tightens his safety belt and looks at the wings. In
the gale they are straining to hold their own, but how long
can they take this kind of punishment—and, of course, there's
no parachute aboard this plane.

The rainsqualls come, giving the *Spirit of St. Louis* its first
bath since the muddy takeoff, and he weaves in and out of
the clouds, trying to find the patches of blue. Time and again,
he abandons course rather than head straight into the meteorological monster ahead.

For an hour he plays hide-and-seek with the clouds until
the rains begin to recede, chasing the edge of the storm as it
moves away. The last of Nova Scotia is below and beyond
him lies more water—200 miles of it—then, the coast of Newfoundland. Out over the ocean again and great blocks of ice
are everywhere, throwing out a blinding glare in the bright
sunlight. Time is passing and the ice field stretches on and on
as far as he can see . . . but wait a minute . . . there's a streak
of ocean blue up there ahead. And beyond that, the plum-
colored mountains of Newfoundland are reaching into the sky.

The clock reads 7:15 P.M., and the rugged landscape of Newfoundland is silently marching by when, almost abruptly, the
city of St. John's comes beneath the plane. A deep harbor,
shaped like a bathtub, with the mountains coming right down
to the water's edge, leaving only a narrow gap in one corner
as a doorway out into the Atlantic. The flat-topped homes and
buildings are clustered together, a jumbled collection of boxes
on a steep incline extending up from the waterline.

Lindbergh pushes the stick forward and dives to within a
hundred feet of the streets and buildings, and the brightly
colored fishing boats in the harbor. Startled faces turn upward
on the wharves, staring at him as he lets them know that, yes,
he has reached his final landfall on the North American continent so tell the folks back home. Then the *Spirit of St. Louis*
flies straight and true between the perpendicular walls of the
ocean gateway and out into the wild, gray Atlantic. Two thou-

sand miles away lies Ireland—that little bit of heaven that fell from out of the sky one day.

Now he must get down to the rigid business of hard-and-fast navigation. That little visit to St. John's took him 90 miles south of the Great Circle course, but it was worth it—getting a sure "fix" on the continent as he flew away. The ocean is hardly discernible in the gathering dusk, but it looks black . . . black, with little ripples of gray twisting across the surface. A giant white ghost glides by under the wings . . . an iceberg, then several more, rising gauntly through scattered patches of fog that dapple the waves.

It's 7:52 P.M., and the Thirteenth Hour begins. Why does there have to be a *thirteenth* hour on a transatlantic flight? They say it's definitely unlucky for the bride to be run over by a truck on the left side of the road on Friday the 13th, but what's that got to do with flying the Atlantic? The icebergs are cropping up everywhere, so watch out for those on the left side of the plane. But other problems are coming on. Straight ahead, coming up fast is a barricade of fog, blocking everything from view. He'll have to get above that, so he puts the plane into a steady climb and when he levels off, some new companions, the stars, are twinkling above.

Another hour passes and the fog beneath him has changed to steadily rising clouds, forcing him higher and higher until the altimeter reads 10,000 feet. What was that forecast about weather clearing out over the Atlantic? The clouds are still ascending and now there's no avoiding it—he'll have to meet some of them head-on, and that means blind flying. He plunges into the first tower of cumulus at 85 miles an hour, and it's a maelstrom, turning the cockpit into a clothes-wringer.

Suddenly a new demon appears at his window—freezing rain —and that's ice on the wings! He throws the beam of his flashlight through the window and, as far as he can see along the wing, ice is collecting and staying there. Ice quickly weighs a plane down. He's got to get out of this, fast. Already the altimeter is dropping as the plane feels the heavy load. He banks cautiously to the right, then turns around completely, heading back toward Newfoundland in search of a canyon through the clouds. He throws the flashlight beam along the wings again. The ice is getting thicker!

The altimeter reads 10,300 feet but the clouds are still there—towering walls of gray, loaded with freezing moisture. Can he find a way out, or would it be better if . . . for the first time he seriously considers heading back to New York. But what would that accomplish? By now, the icing conditions probably extend all the way back to Newfoundland. It could be just as bad to the west, as it is to the east.

He turns southward and down and around he goes, spiraling and weaving through the misty labyrinths, trying to find his way out of a crazy house in the sky. Still, the shepherding stars shine through, guiding him along the corridors and gradually the plane resumes its eastward course.

The clock reads 10:20 P.M., and the sky is clearing. In the flashlight's beam, the ice is still on the wing but it's slowly melting away. The gaps between the clouds are growing wider, and the moon is moving up the sky. His eyes keep closing . . . only a little sleep last night and none at all tonight. He kicks his legs up and down, shakes his head vigorously, swings his arms, cups his hands outside the window to channel fresh air against his face—anything to remain conscious. Before long, the sun will rise, and then maybe staying awake will be easier.

Four hours pass and Roosevelt Field is 1800 miles behind him—the halfway mark. Morning twilight is seeping into the sky, but a billowy blanket of clouds covers the ocean below, and huge cumulus formations loom around him. He heads the plane into one white colossus, then out again . . . into another, and out again. Down he dives through a sunlit opening in the gray mass, and the altimeter unwinds to 2000 feet before he emerges between the clouds and the sea.

A gale is sweeping the ocean, with the waves rolling and breaking into swirling showers of mist. He noses the plane down again until he's barely 50 feet above the churning sea.

On he flies, with the waves crashing and lunging at the wheels, until a vast carpet of fog rolls out and he's flying once again by instrument. He eases back the stick and starts to climb . . . 300 . . . 500 . . . 1000 feet, but the fog still clings to the plane.

In Scandinavian mythology, Niflheim was the world of fog and mist on the northern limits of cold and darkness. Now it seems that Niflheim has moved out into the Atlantic. The fog is everywhere, and will it never go away? The plane drones on through the mist with the instrument panel his only guide—and with Morpheus, the unrelenting God of Sleep, nagging him like a fishwife.

Across the wide expanse of the forty-eight states, millions of people are gazing hopefully at newspaper bulletin boards or leaning over their radios, anxiously awaiting the news that all goes well. But the *Spirit of St. Louis* carries no radio and the reports of progress, or disaster, can only come from eye-witnesses on the land or from ships at sea. In Detroit, his mother, Mrs. Evangeline Lindbergh, turns from her radio and through the front windows of her home she sees a large crowd gathered on the sidewalk. Across the nation many newspapers are carrying, as usual, the humorous comments of Will Rogers, and this is what he says: "No attempt at jokes today, folks. A tall, slim, bashful, smiling American boy is somewhere over the middle of the Atlantic Ocean, where no lone human being has ever ventured before."

Brilliant sunshine strikes the plane, and the mists fall away. Even the sea is calmer now, and the clouds ahead are full of wide channels, inviting him to sail through. No longer can his instruments call him a slave.

A cloud floats across his course. The plane knifes through it into the blazing sunshine beyond—and he can't believe what he sees. A coastline! And it's running parallel to his plane to the north. But there's no land out here! He blinks his eyes, shakes his head, and takes another look. Hills, covered with a purple haze. Cliffs, and small islands dotting the shoreline. Has his compass gone berserk? Is he off course . . . is it Greenland . . . Labrador? Or is it the Lost Atlantis? Mirages, that's all they can possibly be . . . mirages, manufactured by the fog. And it's getting hot in the cockpit, the shade of the wing looks cool and inviting . . . motor droning . . . cool and inviting . . . eyelids . . . drooping . . . eyes sleeping . . .

He jerks back his head with alarm. He must do something to stay awake, chase away this paralyzing monotony. He glides the plane down to the water and levels off barely ten feet above the waves. Two seagulls swerve lazily into view, circling and flapping their wings as his mechanical bird flies past. Seagulls! Does that mean land is near, or do those creatures merely follow the ships around to pick up the table-scrappings?

He eases the stick back and the *Spirit of St. Louis* begins to climb, up to where the view is more far-reaching. But there's nothing on the ocean, no ships, no hint of land . . . but wait . . . what are those black dots to the southeast? He squints his eyes for another look and this time the dots gradually resolve into definite shapes . . . boats . . . fishing boats! Europe, or some part of Europe, has to be near. He sets his course toward the boats and noses down to within 50 feet, just in time to see a man's face emerge from a porthole and peer up toward the intruding plane. Closing the throttle to cut down the noise, Lindbergh leans forward from his window and shouts above the idling motor:

"Which way is Ireland?"

But the face in the porthole remains expressionless, and continues to stare as the plane flies away.

A sense of frustration begins to pester his thoughts. Where were those boats when he saw them—somewhere north of Scotland, or south of Ireland? His course is still eastward—but eastward to *where?*

To the north, heavy storm clouds are gathering and shrouds of rain already sweep the horizon ahead. He aims straight for the squalls, making no effort to skirt them and soon the rain is rolling off the wings. But helpful patches of blue appear through the clouds, and he keeps on looking for the elusive land.

What's that to the northeast? Another mirage? He angles the plane off course, heading for a thin line of purple that could be a coastline, real or imaginary, about ten miles away. As he approaches it becomes clearer, sharper, and gradually the rugged features of a seacoast come into view. It is land! It has to be Ireland, because it's much too early to be flying over England or France.

Quickly he turns the chart across his knees, looking back and forth from the cabin window, trying to find a point of reference to match the shoreline beneath. In less than a minute he has the answer—he's over Valentia and Dingle Bay on the southwest coast of Ireland, almost the exact point he wanted to hit. In spite of all the detours, blind flying, and backtracking through the clouds, dead reckoning has brought him across the Atlantic and right through the eye of a navigational needle. Paris lies only 600 miles away now, with the sun still high in a clearing sky. And far below, people are running from their homes, waving to him.

The waters of St. George's Channel, the southwest tip of England, the tempestuous waters of the English Channel, then the coast of France itself, and the Port of Cherbourg—all glide by as the afternoon sky blends into twilight. He finally eats one of those five sandwiches, draws out a map of France, and soon the River Seine winds into view from the north, a glistening highroad to Paris. The *Spirit of St. Louis* flies on across the French farmlands, and its motor is a musical instrument with wings.

That night, shortly after 10 o'clock, the floodlights were switched on at Le Bourget Field where an emotionally charged crowd of about 100,000 had gathered either to attend Lindbergh's wake, or to witness his arrival. The tension was slowly rising to the boiling stage, for the word from Cherbourg was that the American had positively passed over the French coastline and soon would be over Paris.

At 10:20 P.M., the huge crowd heard a faint drone in the night sky, and a roaring cheer went up when a silver-winged plane appeared overhead. Then the shouts and cries of amazement reached a crescendo as the *Spirit of St. Louis* came down for a perfect landing, right in front of the Administration Building.

LINDBERGH DOES IT! TO PARIS IN 33½ HOURS;
FLIES 1,000 MILES THROUGH SNOW AND SLEET;
CHEERING FRENCH CARRY HIM OFF THE FIELD

The New York *Times* told the story in three banner headlines across page one. But the cheering French who carried him off the field also nearly wrecked his plane, and Lindbergh himself called his reception at Le Bourget the most dangerous part of the entire flight. Before leaving for home on board the U.S. cruiser *Memphis*, which President Coolidge had ordered to stand by at Cherbourg, he received tumultuous welcomes in Brussels and London. And his arrival in England had all the elements of a James Bond suspense story, as reported in that most conservative British magazine, *The Aeroplane:*

"On Sunday afternoon, May 29th, Lindbergh and the *Spirit of St. Louis* landed at Croydon Aerodrome—but only just. He very nearly landed on some hundreds of congenital idiots who, even before he appeared, had crowded onto the field in defiance of warnings that aeroplanes must have room to land. Miraculously, he missed them all, and managed to get down on clear ground. If he had hit a few, what would that have mattered, unless the plane was damaged."

The rest of the story is in the history books. The entire world hastened to honor the young pilot who had conquered time, distance and the North Atlantic, alone in a single-engined plane. In due course he received the $25,000 Orteig prize and the War Department made him a colonel in the U. S. Army Air Force Reserve. Louis Blériot, in a moment of nostalgia gave him a fragment of the plane that had carried him across the Channel back in 1909.

How did Lindbergh do it? Over the years aviation experts have argued the question, calling it brilliant navigational technique, superior flying with a first-class plane, or attributing his success to careful, detailed planning and favorable flying conditions most of the way, or to just plain luck. The answer lies in a combination of all of these, with luck being the least significant of all. However, one minor detail of the flight has never been satisfactorily explained:

Why was a tractor left standing on Roosevelt Field at the end of the runway, the point of takeoff for a transatlantic flight?

With our other airmen who have made long-distance firsts, whenever possible we have told something about what happened after the flight. In the case of Charles A. Lindbergh the story is, or should be, known to all. First he convinced America that the age of air travel had come. He tried to warn his countrymen of the threat of war. When that war overwhelmed the world, he helped the Air Force solve some of its urgent problems—and avoided publicity while doing so. Since then he has continued as an adviser to the aviation world in general, and to Pan American World Airways in particular—always working modestly and selflessly behind the scenes, a story that may never be told. But it all began in September 1926 when a young pilot was on his run from St. Louis to Chicago with the night mail.

What next? Explorers had long sought for a missing continent. Was there one in the Arctic Ocean? Although the Australian with the beard didn't find it, he did win a knighthood.

CHAPTER X

The Wilkins-Eielson
Trans-Arctic Flight

In April 1928, Barrow, Alaska, the northernmost community under the Stars and Stripes, was an Arctic trading post surrounded by a sparsely populated Eskimo village—with nothing between it and the North Pole but water and ice. Dominated by a church spire that rose like a white needle from the barren, frozen coast, it was a cheerless scene—Eskimo huts, quonsets, whaling boats, and discarded oil drums scattered helter-skelter along the beach. The entire population numbered only a few hundred, mostly Eskimos whose main occupation was still the pursuit of seals, walrus, polar bear, and whales. There were a few outsiders who were on duty at the Point Barrow Hospital, the schoolhouse, a mission, and the Cape Smyth Whaling and Trading Post on the far side of the lagoon, half a mile distant. As for the sea ice, it seemed to fill the Arctic Ocean all the way to the Pole, some 1290 miles on farther north across a still little known region at the top of the world.

The first white man to come this close to the Pole had been the British explorer, Captain Frederick W. Beechey, who sailed into these waters in 1826 and named this northernmost point of land after Sir John Barrow, one of England's most enthusiastic supporters of Arctic research. Among the whalers who braved the rigors of this forbidding coast was one, Charley Brower, who pitched his camp there and established a trading post in

1880. With him came his Eskimo wife, and his cook, Fred Hopson who brought along Mrs. Hopson. Within a few years a passel of little Browers and Hopsons were added to Alaska's farthest north population.

Over the years, Charley Brower and the natives swapped and traded on the best of terms, but as time went on and civilization crept in the Eskimos picked up some shrewd business ideas. After learning English in the white man's school, they wrote letters requesting catalogues from the big fur companies in the United States. Then they put the squeeze on Brower by demanding the same fur prices that were being quoted on the New York markets. All of which Charley Brower took in stride by simply charging the Eskimos higher prices for the goods they took in trade. And it was a tribute to his diplomacy that everybody stayed happy on both sides of the counter.

Then, the Eskimos and the white trader were astonished when Captain George Hubert Wilkins and his pilot, Lieutenant Ben Eielson, came down out of the clouds one day in an orange-colored airplane. Although the natives had never seen a bird like this before, as they gathered around to inspect the strange "winged duck," they asked only one question:

"How can it fly? It has no feathers."

Wilkins and Eielson looked at each other and, frankly, they wondered too. For three years they had been trying to fly an airplane over the unexplored Arctic Ocean—perhaps even to Spitsbergen, on the other side of the globe. But their every attempt had ended in heart-breaking failure. Their hopes had reached such a low ebb that any kind of a suggestion was welcome, even if it called for pasting feathers on the fuselage in order to make that flight.

Wilkins, already a veteran explorer, had known frustrations before. In 1919, as we have seen, his Blackburn "Kangaroo" biplane developed engine trouble over the Mediterranean and made a crash landing on Crete, ending his dream of winning the London-to-Australia Air Derby. Later that same year, he tried to obtain a dirigible for a flight across the Arctic Ocean, but no one would take him seriously, even though his credentials included the solid experience of three grueling years in the Arctic with famed Canadian explorer, Vilhjalmur Stefansson.

Born in 1888 on a South Australian sheep station, Wilkins was a tall, rather unusually keen young man of twenty-five and didn't have his famous beard when he joined a Stefansson Arctic expedition in 1913. Later, he had hurried south from the Arctic to join the Australian Flying Corps when he belatedly learned there was a war on with Germany. From then on he was busy along the Western Front, taking part in every major Australian engagement of World War I and distinguishing himself as a combat photographer. At times, he put down his camera to help bring in the wounded, and on at least one occasion he even assumed the role of a combat officer to rally the troops under fire.

When the war came to an end, Wilkins seemed to have a choice of a wide range of professions, for he was a man of many talents. During his student years in Australia at Adelaide University, he had mastered mechanical engineering while, at the same time, learning to sing and play the organ, flute, violin, and cello. But the call to the wild unexplored areas of the earth was too much to resist, and in 1921 he joined Sir Ernest Shackleton's final expedition to the Antarctic.

By the time he was thirty-seven years old, Wilkins had spent nearly half his life traveling to the far reaches of the globe, and still owned but one suit of conventional clothes to wear during his infrequent visits to civilization. He had walked more than 5000 miles across the icy terrain of the Arctic and Antarctic, but he had not—repeat not—enjoyed one minute of it, so he said, and readily admitted his reasons why.

"I disliked walking," Wilkins complained, "and derived little enjoyment in wandering along the ice-strewn beaches in the long winter darkness, or in following the dogs, or running ahead of them to break trail." His eyes had ached from strain of snow-blindness. But he had learned to handle an airplane while flying with friends in 1910, and dreamed of exploring by air, with all that ice far below.

To put it plainly, Wilkins was an explorer who much preferred to have the ice and snow beneath his wings instead of
under his feet. By 1925 when he arrived in Detroit, he was
determined to have it that way. Wearing his one and only suit,
he toured the city in a public appeal for funds to finance a
flight that would determine once and for all whether a land mass,
an undiscovered continent or islands, existed up near the North
Pole.

There were, indeed, sound historical reasons for his ambition
to remove the Arctic from the province of mystery and
speculation into the realm of scientific fact. Tens of thousands
of square miles of the Arctic Ocean remained unseen by human
eyes, and no one could positively say that land did not exist in
the polar seas. After he reached the North Pole by dog sled in
1909, Peary had conjectured that the pattern of bird migrations
and the flow of ocean currents indicated that undiscovered land
could exist. Later, long after Peary, Byrd had flown from
Spitsbergen to the Pole and back. Also Amundsen and Nobile
had crossed the high Arctic from Europe to Alaska in the
dirigible *Norge*. But these flights had covered only a fraction
of the unknown surface of the vast Arctic Ocean, and the
map-makers were still taking great pains to protect their professional reputations by sketching in question marks to desig-
nate the unexplored areas.

In seeking an answer to this fascinating riddle, Wilkins proposed to take off from Barrow and fly on a northeast course
across the polar sea to Spitsbergen, a distance of 2200 miles.
His line of flight would by-pass the North Pole completely,
taking him instead across the vast unexplored ocean north of the
islands of the Canadian Archipelago and Greenland. Aside from
the possibility of discovering unknown land, Wilkins also wanted
to determine whether the Arctic, be it ice or *terra firma*, was
suitable for the establishment of a polar weather station, a
project he had dreamed of for years.

He succeeded in enlisting the support of Detroit's most
prominent citizens, and the collection of funds went forward
with all the drum-beating and ballyhoo of an old-fashioned

Chamber of Commerce campaign. But modest Captain Wilkins himself took a dim view of all that. The Detroit *News* lent its support to the drive, and more than 80,000 individuals subscribed their dollars, quarters, and pennies. Many of the donors were school children who were not permitted to contribute more than five cents each. The donation of any amount, large or small, gave the donors the right to have their names inscribed on a monument to be erected if the flight were successful. All of which didn't keep some unexploration-minded individuals from roundly criticizing Wilkins for, as they put it, "extracting money from defenseless infants for his personal use."

However, the campaign did produce the needed funds, and Wilkins purchased two Fokker airplanes which were shipped to Alaska in preparation for the flight. On the day of his departure, he was called to the steps of Detroit's City Hall where the mayor bade him a public farewell, and a brass band escorted him to the railway station through streets lined with thousands of cheering, also some jeering, people.

Even before he boarded the train that would take him to Seattle, Wilkins already had chosen the man who would pilot his plane across the Arctic. His old comrade-in-exploration, Vilhjalmur Stefansson, had introduced him to Lieutenant Carl Ben Eielson, a twenty-eight-year-old Army aviator who had flown so many hours over Alaska that the Yukon Indians called him "Brother-to-the-Eagle."

Ben Eielson, at that time, may have been the most popular man in Alaska. Lean, gray-eyed and about 5-foot-10 in height, he was a Norwegian-American who had come to the Territory from his home state of North Dakota in 1922. He had learned to fly during the closing months of World War I, and held the rank of second lieutenant when he left the Army Air Service and took a job as a guard at the House Office Building in Washington. But he became more of a lobbyist than a guard as, day by day, he buttonholed the congressmen, urging them to do more to open up Alaska to aviation. When his efforts failed, he gave up his job and went to Alaska where he temporarily grounded himself as a teacher of English and mathematics in the high school at Fairbanks.

Within only a few months, he persuaded two partners, one a banker, to join him in forming a commercial flying company which he named the Fairbanks Aviation Corporation. The firm bought an Army surplus "Jenny," and for the next two years Eielson carried passengers to all parts of the Territory and even engaged in some stunt-flying on the side. When the first airmail service was established between Fairbanks and McGrath, Eielson was given the contract. He also became a "Good Samaritan of the Air," carrying doctors to isolated patients, and flying through storms into remote areas to pick up expectant mothers, trappers, and sick miners, and speed them to hospitals. By 1924 Eielson was so greatly admired throughout the Territory that no one was surprised when a tribe of Indians at McGrath asked the government to make him their tribal chief.

Stefansson couldn't have recommended a better man, and Wilkins was quick to realize his good fortune in getting the Alaskan sky hero even though, curiously enough, Eielson expressed no interest in exploration. He was merely all for the idea of flying an airplane over the boundless snows and ice of the Arctic.

Then, in spite of all their careful preparations, everything started going wrong. First, their efforts to fly to Spitsbergen in 1926 ended in a dismal failure when both of their planes were wrecked. Again a year later they tried, but engine trouble forced them down on the frozen pack ice more than a hundred miles north of Point Barrow. All they did was prove that a plane could land on the ice, something many pseudo-Arctic experts had said couldn't be done. Even so, the achievement was small consolation, for they abandoned their Stinson skiplane to walk and crawl all the way back to Alaska, battling freezing cold and howling blizzards for thirteen days. The ordeal was so intense that Eielson's right hand became badly frostbitten, and the little finger had to be amputated when they finally reached Barrow.

Wilkins returned to the United States and late in 1927 he was in San Francisco, nursing his wounded fortunes while trying to raise enough money to equip another expedition—the third one, which he hoped would be the charmed one. One afternoon as he sat in his room at the St. Francis Hotel, looking out the window at nothing in particular, a small, sleek-looking monoplane suddenly and providentially crossed his line of vision. At first he watched the plane almost absent-mindedly as it came in low and banked away to the east, apparently heading for a landing field. Then he rushed to the telephone to begin calling every air facility in the San Francisco area until he finally located the plane at Oakland Airport. Like a man who had fallen in love at first sight, he immediately drove to the field and gave the plane a careful inspection.

On the fuselage and tail were the markings, "Vega-Lockheed Aircraft Corporation, Los Angeles." Weighing 2000 pounds, it had a bullet-shaped body with no visible struts and wires to offer wind resistance. Up front was a 225-hp Wright Whirlwind engine, the same type that had carried Lindbergh across the Atlantic the year before. The wing, which spanned 41 feet, contained extra gasoline tanks, and the entire construction was of wood, eliminating any chance of metallic interference with a compass. The fuselage had ample room for navigation instruments, emergency rations, and sledging equipment. Wilkins was told the plane's maximum speed was 136 miles per hour.

Still moving like a man possessed, he drove to Los Angeles and closed a deal with the Lockheed people who promised to have a similar plane equipped with ski landing gear off the assembly lines within a few months. For money he had an ace-in-the-hole. His two Fokkers, wrecked on the 1926 expedition, had since been rebuilt, and he succeeded in selling one of them to Charles Kingsford-Smith, a young Australian aviator who was planning a long-distance flight across the Pacific from California to Australia. So by the spring of 1928, Wilkins and Eielson had their spanking new Lockheed-Vega sitting in the snows

Wilkins and Lieutenant Ben Eielson take off from Fairbanks, Alaska, for Point Barrow, the first stop en route to Spitsbergen on the historic trans-Arctic flight, 1928. This was when Sir Hubert sent back his famous message "No foxes seen." (*United Press International Photo*)

at Point Barrow, ready for another do-or-die attempt to fly across that frozen empty ocean to Spitsbergen.

As soon as word got around that Ben Eielson was back, Wilkins was swamped by whites and natives who offered to work, day or night, in preparing a runway for the takeoff. Ancient Eskimo women carefully tailored the reindeer suits the fliers were to wear, while young Eskimo girls stretched the tissues with their teeth and strong young arms until the clothing fitted perfectly. The Eskimo men were busy, too, sharpening spears and fashioning ice-picks that could be used to retrieve dead seals from the water in case the fliers were forced again to land on the ice.

"If your flying machine fails," one old Eskimo told Wilkins, "you must walk to a land visited by one of our ancestors who walked over to the ice to Ast, where he found a new land and people, and was tattooed on the back to prove it. That was his story, but our fathers didn't know whether to believe him. Perhaps you'll prove that he was right."

The Land of Ast! Could it have been Spitsbergen, or one of the islands of the Canadian Archipelago? And if so, was the mysterious tattooer an ancient Indian medicine man, or a shipwrecked sailor who had wandered far to the North? Understandably, these questions fired Wilkins' imagination as two dog teams slowly pulled the Vega across the snow to Elson Lagoon, the spot chosen for the takeoff. For two days, a work force of thirty-three Eskimos dug and shoveled an open lane through the drifts, until finally on the morning of Sunday, April 15, a runway 14 feet wide and 5000 feet in length stretched along the Arctic shore. Stoves were lit to pre-heat the Vega's engines, and Eielson brought over a large can of warm oil wrapped in a double sleeping bag. The tanks were filled with 370 gallons of gasoline, and when fully loaded the Vega weighed 3400 pounds. Favorable weather was forecast for the first part of the journey out across that geographical "blind spot" northeast of Alaska. Still, no one could predict what awaited them over the mist-shrouded waters of Spitsbergen.

The hour was approaching 10 A.M. with only one important chore remaining before the getaway. Wilkins had brought along a small radio set, and he left the receiving apparatus with Leon Vincent, a government schoolteacher at Barrow, while the hand-operated transmitter was placed on board the plane. The Vega had been assigned a wave length of 33.1 meters with the call letters, KDZ, and throughout the flight Wilkins hoped to keep in touch with Vincent. Also, if new land was discovered a code message would be relayed to Dr. Isaiah Bowman, president of the American Geographical Society—scientific sponsor of the flight. If the new land should be mountainous, Wilkins would convey the information with the code message, "black foxes seen." And if Wilkins found it possible to estimate the extent of such land, the hundreds of square miles would be designated by the "number of foxes seen."

Wilkins stood in front of the plane with his hands on the propeller.

"Switch off?" he shouted to Eielson, who was in the cockpit.

"Switch off," Eielson answered.

"Gas on?"

"Gas on."

Wilkins swung the propeller sharply through several turns to suck gas into the cylinders, and then shouted to Eielson again.

"All clear?"

"All clear," Eielson called in reply.

The engine coughed once, and then the propeller became a whirling, purring disc in the morning sunlight. Wilkins ran to the side of the plane and jumped into the cabin with a final shout:

"Let's go!"

The Eskimos, holding down the tail, loosened their grip and the Vega began moving down the icy runway, swaying slightly to the left and right as it gathered momentum. The wing was clear of the snowbanks on either side, but as the speed increased to 30 . . . 40 . . . and 50 miles an hour, the tail began swinging dangerously wide, narrowly missing the runway's hard-packed sides. With the rudder, Eielson skillfully kept the plane under control and the Vega left the runway at a speed of 70 miles an hour, trailing a cloud of propeller-blown snow.

As they headed out over the uncharted sea, an easterly wind was a little against the plane, but Wilkins was confident it would soon change, perhaps becoming a steady tail wind that would help them along. For the first 50 miles the horizons were clear to the north and east. As for the sea below, it was mostly drifting ice floes, and Wilkins quickly dismissed the painful thought of history repeating itself with another forced landing. Eielson gradually eased the plane upward to 3000 feet as the first hundred miles of ocean fell away behind them, and Wilkins began straining his eyes in all directions, looking for land.

Two hundred miles passed, then 300 and 400, with still no sign of either islands or a lost continent. There was nothing to arrest the eye—nothing except the pack ice, interspersed with leads of open water. From time to time Wilkins put aside his navigation instruments and radio transmitter to take motion pictures, although he wondered how he ever could give a lecture on Arctic exploration with such monotonous film.

Clear visibility and a gradually changing wind favored them for 700 miles until late in the afternoon the skies began to darken. Soon they were flying through a low-hanging layer of clouds and Eielson nosed the plane downward, hoping to keep the sea in view. Still, 120 miles passed with no change in the visibility and Wilkins reluctantly made a note in the logbook—if land lay beneath that cloud cover, it remained hidden from view.

Before long, the Vega emerged from the clouds and for the next 700 miles the view below them was excellent, still there was nothing that remotely resembled land. Even so, they had already added more than 1400 miles to the known map of the world. Another hour passed, and far to the south they could see the mountains of Grant Land rising through a towering mass of ice clouds. It was a reassuring sight for Wilkins because it meant, so far at least, his navigation had kept them on course to Spitsbergen. Grant Land, the northern part of huge Ellesmere Island in the Canadian Archipelago, was a checkpoint on the flight and their goal was now only 800 miles away.

As the plane swung away from Grant Land and continued eastward over the sea north of Greenland, the signs of a heavy storm appeared ahead. Clouds were rising to heights far above the maximum ceiling of their plane. Eielson, determined not to give up ahead of time, kept the Vega in a steady climb until they reached 8000 feet—as high as their plane could go. Yet, the clouds were still above them, blocking the way to Spitsbergen.

By now they had been in the air more than thirteen hours, long enough to become tired and cramped, and not a little worried about the gas consumption which had been greater than expected. Although the tanks had enough fuel for another four hours, Eielson was facing the necessity of weaving in and out of the clouds in a never-ending search for better visibility, and more than four hours might pass before they could even hope to see land. Now and then the plane emerged briefly into patches of sunlight, enabling Wilkins to take quick readings with his sextant as he steered Eielson toward the western side of Spitsbergen. But the difficult cross-longitude navigation, and the high curling masses of clouds, had turned the flight into an exercise in guesswork.

Shortly past midnight something went wrong with the wind-driven generator and the wireless transmitter ceased to function. Meanwhile back at Point Barrow, Leon Vincent was huddled over the radio when he received a final message from the Vega . . . "KDZ, KDZ, KDZ Wilkins Arctic Expedition . . . Greenland . . . storm . . . our tanks . . ." and then the transmitter's buzz gradually faded into silence.

Another hour passed, and Wilkins felt sure they were over the peaks of northern Spitsbergen. The cloud bank had grown even thicker and no longer was the sun favoring them with an occasional breakthrough. With the gasoline supply rapidly dwindling and visibility showing no sign of improving, Wilkins passed a note up to Eielson, advising him to try to get beneath the cloud layer, even at the risk of crashing into a mountain peak.

Eielson promptly sent the Vega into a dive through the swirling white mist and, within seconds, a break in the clouds revealed the rugged sides of a mountain far to the east. The plane dived lower and suddenly, Wilkins saw the surface of the sea heaving in row after row of gigantic waves. Eielson quickly came out of the dive, and it wasn't a moment too soon.

As the plane zoomed up from the sea, the wind-whipped waves drenched the cabin windows, leaving the windshield coated with icy spray. Realizing that Eielson was now flying completely blind, Wilkins peered through the side windows and caught a fleeting glimpse of a smooth stretch of ice along the coast parallel to the sea. He shouted to Eielson, directing him to circle and bring the plane back again so they could try for a landing before the icy stretch was lost to view in a driving snowstorm raging along the coast.

Even though he was still unable to see clearly through his windshield, Eielson banked the plane out to sea, then steered it back toward the shore. It was almost blind flying but Wilkins performed as a human radar, waving his hands right and left to give the directions. The wind was against them now as Eielson crabbed low over the water and gently brought the Vega down on the ice-smooth beach.

Outside, the fierce blizzard obscured their view beyond a few feet on either side of the plane. Numb and exhausted, Eielson said nothing as he reached over to cut off the engine, mindful that every ounce of gasoline must be conserved like a miser's horde. Wilkins jumped from the cabin with an empty can in his hands, and struggled forward to drain the tanks before the oil had a chance to freeze.

"Open the tap," he called to Eielson, who was still in something of a trance and failed to hear. Wilkins repeated his request, this time with a shout, then Eielson slowly opened the valve and the precious oil began flowing out into the can. The wind was howling with gale force when Eielson finally leaped from the cabin to join Wilkins in stamping the snow around the skis so it would freeze, thereby preventing the plane from overturning in the storm. Then they crawled back into the cabin to ponder the question—where were they? Without a doubt they were in the Spitsbergen Archipelago, but again—where? They had hoped to reach the mining village of King's Bay, Byrd's takeoff point on his flight to the North Pole. Here, however, there was no sign of life anywhere around them and even if there were, it would be hidden from view in the blinding snow.

Wilkins made a few notes. They had been in the air 20 hours and 20 minutes since the takeoff on Sunday morning, and their flight of exploration was completed. Except for that stretch of about 120 miles where the clouds had prevented a proper view, they could positively say that no land mass existed between Alaska and Spitsbergen—in fact, there was nothing but ocean and ice. Analyzing his last sighting with the sextant, Wilkins decided they must have landed on a small island, perhaps less than a hundred miles from either King's Bay or Green Harbor, another community in the Spitsbergen Archipelago. Just before they came down, Eielson was almost certain the gasoline gauge showed 20 gallons remaining, which should be enough to take them the rest of the way—if only they could get the plane up out of the snow.

For the moment, however, they had to face the hard fact that they were snowbound, with drifts piling high around them as the blizzard continued to rage. Debating a course of action was pointless, because there was only one—with absolutely no alternatives. So for five days and nights they stayed in the cabin of their little plane while the storm swirled around them. They had their sleeping bags, and a few nuts and raisins for food. Then, as the storm subsided after the fifth day, they put on their snowshoes and dug the plane out of the drifts.

The sky had cleared and far in the distance they could see tiny black specks that resembled the houses of a village. Wilkins well knew that a mirage always appeared to be anything the viewer desired, whether it be palm trees in the desert or homes in the Arctic. So they turned their eyes away from the horizon with its mocking outlines.

By some twist of fortune, a stretch of ice in front of the plane had been left clear of snow and they lost little time in fire-potting the engine in preparation for a takeoff. But when Ben Eielson opened the throttle the skis remained stationary, refusing to budge until Wilkins jumped down and gave the plane a push. In trying to get back on board, he missed his step and Eielson took off without him, then circled and came back when he looked down to see Wilkins standing there in the snow. They tried again, and for the second time Wilkins lost his footing while the plane sped across the ice and into the air without him. Again Eielson circled and came back.

By now the engine had been running for a least an hour, using up half their precious supply of gasoline and they were right back where they were before. Faced with a critical decision, Wilkins came up with a plan of action. If he failed to get aboard on the third try, Eielson was to drop him a tent and some supplies, then return for him by boat or dog sled. This time, however, they tried something different. A long piece of tough driftwood was brought up from the beach, and Wilkins kept one foot inside the cabin while he used his hands to furiously push the driftwood against the hard-packed snow—poling the plane along as though it were a Venetian canal boat. The ingenious trick worked and the Vega slid across the icy surface until, at long last, it was in the air—with both men aboard.

Eielson took the plane to 3000 feet and just as they circled a headland, he turned and shouted to Wilkins: "What's that over in the bay to the left?"

In the clear sunlight Wilkins saw two wireless masts rising from a group of houses, but the community bore no resemblance to King's Bay. Quickly he penned a note to the cockpit: *It's not King's Bay, so it must be Green Harbor. Go over and land where you think best.*

The plane crossed about five miles of open water and within minutes Eielson spotted a likely place, then came down for a perfect landing in front of a wireless station where two Norwegian flags were flying in the breeze. They also saw four men on skis moving swiftly down a slope toward the plane. When greetings were exchanged, Wilkins and Eielson learned they had, indeed, arrived at Green Harbor, and for five days they had been reported lost. In fact, they had been marooned on a strip of land known as Dead Man's Island.

Their historic flight was over and soon Wilkins would be returning to England where he would be knighted by King George for his achievements as an explorer—henceforth to be known as Sir Hubert Wilkins. Still, before saying farewell to Green Harbor there was one important detail remaining, and he went inside the wireless station to give it his personal attention. By radiogram he sent a message to Dr. Isaiah Bowman of the American Geographical Society, putting it in just three words: NO FOXES SEEN.

Nevertheless, Wilkins and Eielson had made one of the most

important long-range flights in the history of aviation, and they had solved for all time one of the mysteries of the Arctic.

After making numerous other exploratory flights with Wilkins, Carl Ben Eielson returned to Alaska in 1929 to fly chartered planes in the Arctic region. In November, he was requested to go to the aid of an American vessel, the *Nanook*, which was icebound in Siberian waters with a million dollars worth of furs aboard. The Swenson Fur Company of Seattle offered Eielson $50,000 to bring back the fur cargo and the ship's fifteen passengers. Eielson succeeded in making a first

Carl Ben Eielson and Sir Hubert Wilkins with New York's Mayor James J. Walker (center) at a 1929 City Hall reception honoring them for their flight explorations of both Arctic and Antarctic. In Antarctica they had observed land never seen before by civilized man, and in the Arctic they proved it was possible to land on and take off from the ice of the Arctic Ocean. (*Wide World Photos*)

Sir G. Hubert Wilkins talking with Lowell Thomas, Sr., at a Ford
Motor Company dinner given in his honor in New York, 1940.
Wilkins later became an adviser to the U. S. Army on polar matters.
(*Culver Pictures, Inc.*)

trip to the stranded vessel, but on the second flight he disappeared forever.

Sir Hubert Wilkins went on to make countless other flights over the Arctic and Antarctic, engaging in rescue work, exploration, and scientific research. As we will see in a later chapter, he and Eielson were the first to fly an airplane over the Antarctic, and later Wilkins served as an adviser to Lincoln Ellsworth in the south polar region. Sir Hubert married the beautiful actress and artist, Suzanne Bennett, who, like himself, was an Australian. He became an adviser to the U. S. Army on polar matters and continued his fabulous life of adventure and exploration until 1958, when death overtook him at the age of seventy.

Apparently 1928 was to be Australia's year. Now came another historic trail-blazing flight, one of the most perilous, in a plane named the Southern Cross.

These indeed were "the days when knighthood was in flower."

CHAPTER XI

The Saga of the Southern Cross

Aviation was in a dismal slump on the West Coast of the United States in August 1927, with every airport and landing field from Seattle to San Diego in mourning over the loss of twelve lives. Within the space of nine tragic days, a dozen fliers, one of them a woman, had plunged to their deaths in accidents that were related, either directly or indirectly, to the big race of its day—the Dole Air Derby from Oakland to Honolulu. Three fliers were killed as they were getting their planes ready for the contest, five others lost their lives at sea after the race began, and even while the sorrowful news was coming in, four more aviators died in heroic attempts to rescue those who were missing. When the starter fired his pistol at Oakland Airport on August 16, eight contesting airplanes had soared above the Golden Gate and headed out across the Pacific toward Honolulu —2400 miles away. But only two planes made it to the finish line, while the others either crashed at sea, or turned around and came back with mechanical troubles.

The winning team was Arthur Goebel, a movie stunt flier, and his navigator, Navy Lieutenant William Davis, and when they landed their single-engined *Woolaroc* at Honolulu's Wheeler Field, a roaring crowd of 30,000 was on hand to greet them. Waiting for them, too, was James Dole, the Hawaiian pineapple king, who was ready with the check for $25,000 he had offered as the first prize. Bands played, hula girls swayed in their native costumes, while Goebel and Davis found themselves up to their ears in leis. But, as the hours wore on and the days passed with no word from the missing fliers, gloom came over the field and the celebration turned into a wake. The race had boomeranged into a depressing setback for Pacific aviation, and the long-awaited commercial air service between California and Hawaii seemed farther away than ever.

During that same disastrous month of August, a liner arrived in San Francisco from Sydney, and among the passengers were two young Australian fliers who had two things very much in common. Both had the same given name, Charles, and they were obsessed with the same fixed purpose—to pilot an airplane from California on across the Pacific Ocean to Australia, blazing an air trail that no one had ever dared fly before. Charles Kingsford-Smith and Charles T. P. Ulm had no intention of calling it quits after flying the 2400 miles from Oakland to Honolulu. For them, Hawaii would merely be a refueling stop. From there they would continue on across the Pacific another 3000 miles to the Fiji Islands, then take off for Brisbane on the Australian coast still another 1700 miles away. For several years a great trans-Pacific flight such as this had been their dream, but when they began making the rounds in California to ask for financial support, they were told it was a nightmare.

Before they left Australia, a group of businessmen in Sydney, and even the Australian government, had promised to raise the needed funds, but most of the money was not yet available. They had already set their sights on the plane of their choice, a three-engined Fokker, owned by none other than Captain George Hubert Wilkins who had flown it on one of his Arctic expeditions. Most of all, Smith and Ulm needed immediate funds to close the deal with Wilkins who was equally anxious to get his hands on some ready cash to buy the Lockheed-Vega which, as we have seen, soon was to carry him across the Arctic Ocean to Spitsbergen.

The Australians quickly found a financial angel in Mr. Sidney

Myer, a wealthy Melbourne businessman who was living in San Francisco. He advanced them $15,000 to buy the plane, even though he was aghast over the thought of a flight from California to Australia and felt certain that Smith and Ulm were out to break their collective necks. Myer was so apprehensive that, several days later, he called on the fliers at their hotel to make a personal plea.

"Look, boys," he told them, "you have that money and it's yours. But I'm not associated in any way with what you intend to do. Seriously and earnestly, I want you to put that money in your pockets, and don't risk your lives on this flight."

Smith and Ulm were moved by their friend's concern for their safety, and expressed their gratitude for his generosity, but they also told him they could not be swerved from their plans. It was a downcast Mr. Myer who left the hotel, even though he knew the flight was a cherished ambition that couldn't be blithely tossed aside.

Almost as soon as Myer closed the room door, Smith got in touch with Wilkins and purchased the plane. Actually, it was a composite airplane, constructed from parts of the two Fokkers Wilkins had flown and crashed while on his 1926 expedition up North. The wing of one plane was attached to the fuselage of the other. The three Wright Whirlwind engines were not included in the deal, and the Australians would have to look elsewhere for their motors. In giving the Fokker a name, Smith decided on the *Southern Cross,* a most appropriate choice since Australia had adopted that constellation as its insignia. When news of the transaction got around, one West Coast newspaper columnist reported it as follows:

> In the glow of the Midnight Sun, with a mass of wreckage as the father, with necessity as the mother, and with Captain Wilkins as the midwife, The Southern Cross was born.

Smith and Ulm had their plane, but it had no means of locomotion, and they were determined to settle for nothing less than three new Wright Whirlwind engines. Then to their dismay, they learned that the Wright Corporation was already eighty to ninety engines behind in current orders, mainly because the

U. S. Navy was clamoring for immediate deliveries. By now, Kingsford-Smith had met quite a few influential people on the West Coast and he began pulling every possible string. An oil company executive, Locke T. Harper, agreed to introduce them to Rear Admiral Christian J. Peoples at Navy Headquarters in San Francisco, and a few days later he ushered them into the admiral's office.

"These boys," Harper began, without batting an eyelash, "are going to fly the Pacific to Australia."

They say the admiral's face turned so red his visitors thought he was on the verge of apoplexy.

"I . . . I . . ." he began, groping for words, then he pounded the desk with his fist, rattling the windows behind him, and exploded:

"I'm not interested in this thing in any way! You're crazy. Flying to Australia! I don't want to be brought into this thing at all. Look what happened to the Dole fliers!"

Pausing for breath, Peoples gave his blood pressure a chance to recede, then went on:

"Look," he said earnestly, "don't you realize the Navy is already spending hundreds of thousands of dollars searching for the fliers lost in the Dole race? Think, boys, don't do it. Anyhow, I don't want to become mixed up in any negotiations that might start this crazy thing of yours going."

Reaching across his desk, the admiral pushed a button to summon his aide, Lieutenant Ben Wyatt, who had been a member of the Dole Race Committee.

As Wyatt walked into the room, he told him: "These fellows are talking about flying the Pacific to Australia. To Australia—get that. Give them some advice. They're crazy."

Wyatt took one brief glance at Smith and Ulm, then spoke in calm and measured tones: "I don't even want to know anything about such a scheme. Anyway, I don't know what type of equipment you intend to use, or anything about it."

If the phrasing of Wyatt's statement offered a ray of hope, Smith was quick to seize it. "We," he cautiously informed the two officers, "are going to use a tri-motored Fokker."

The words were magic. Peoples and Wyatt looked at each other, then turned and regarded the fliers with a keen new interest.

"Now, that's different," they said, almost in unison.

It was quite a change of attitude and before they left the admiral's office, Smith and Ulm were promised that the Navy would release its priority on three Wright engines for installation on the Fokker at the earliest possible moment.

It was a heartening development, but things were going to get much worse before they got better. Word came from Australia that the state elections had placed a new government administration in power, and the officials were flatly refusing to advance or guarantee the fliers any further finances. They had already strained their shaky credit to purchase many items of equipment, including the engines, and each day when they returned to their hotel they were finding their mailbox crammed with letters demanding immediate payment of their bills.

Their good friend, Locke Harper, temporarily came to the rescue by lending them $7500, but it became necessary to mortgage the Fokker in order to guarantee the loan. Then, shortly after New Year's Day, 1928, the situation became really desperate when the new Australian government formally asked them to sell their plane and abandon the flight for once and for all. Coming as it did from their own government it was more of an order than a request, and Smith and Ulm were forced to comply. But they clung to one faint hope—if only they could sell the plane to a private individual, perhaps the new owner could be prevailed upon to sponsor the flight himself.

Three months later, in the middle of March, that's precisely what happened. Smith and Ulm were introduced to Captain G. Allan Hancock, a California oil and railway magnate who was intensely interested in aviation. They told him their entire story, and within a matter of days Hancock decided to see the flight through by providing the fliers with all the money they needed. He bought the plane and told them to concentrate on getting ready for the takeoff while leaving the financial worries

to him. Considering what they had been through, it was hard
to believe—and it proved once again that the toughest part of
every great flight is simply getting off the ground.

Moving swiftly to wrap up every pre-flight detail, Smith acquired all the necessary equipment, and by the first of May he
had lined up a crew of four by choosing two Americans as his
navigator and radioman. The newly hired navigator, an expert
in his field, was Harry W. Lyon, Jr., a forty-one-year-old lieutenant commander in the U. S. Naval Reserve who had sailed
with merchant marine and Navy vessels for thirteen years. The
son of a rear admiral, Lyon had attended Annapolis and, for a
time, served as a "soldier of fortune" in the Mexican and Central
American rebel wars. As radioman, Smith chose thirty-six-year-
old James W. Warner who had retired from the Navy only a
month before. A native of Michigan, Warner had spent sixteen
years at sea, and when he put away his uniform he held the
rating of Chief Radioman USN.

As chief pilot of his own flight, Charles Edward Kingsford-
Smith was well qualified for the task of selecting personnel,
perhaps even more so than his relief pilot, Charley Ulm. At the
age of thirty, "Smithy," as he was called by his closest friends,
had already taken his place among Australia's leading airmen.
Born in Brisbane in 1897, he was the son of William Charles
Smith, a bank manager. When he was only six, Smithy's family
moved to Canada, and it was there that his last name was
hyphenated into Kingsford-Smith. There were several other
Smiths on the street where they lived and, for the postman's
sake, his mother thought it best to avoid confusion by attaching
her maiden name, Kingsford, to the family surname, Smith.

A few years later, the Kingsford-Smiths returned to Australia
to make their permanent home in Sydney, and when England
went to war with the Kaiser, young Smithy distinguished himself in the Royal Flying Corps by shooting down eight enemy
planes. After the Armistice, he drifted to California where he
engaged in a brief career of "odd-job" flying. He barnstormed
with a flying circus, thrilling the local yokels by walking the

wings and hanging by his heels from the landing gear. Then he turned to movie stunt-flying and finally, some Japanese-American farmers in Southern California gave him the job of scaring wild ducks away from their rice fields. During those days he sent photographs back home to Australia, showing him standing by his plane with duck feathers draped all over his flying togs, as well as the wings and fuselage. Whenever he had a moment to spare, he sometimes stood on the seashore, gazing out over the blue Pacific and asking himself how long it would take to fly home.

On returning to Australia, Smithy met Lieutenant Charles Ulm, but several years passed before they realized they had the same ambition to fly the 7332 miles of ocean between California and Australia. When he teamed up with his friend for the Pacific flight, Ulm didn't even have official status as a pilot, but he had an unshakable self-confidence that went well with his wiry physique and fighter's jaw. Smithy was dapper, short in figure, and spoke with a rapid terseness, but he listened attentively to everything anyone had to say. And he found Ulm a man with plenty of sound flying advice.

A native of Melbourne and about the same age as Kingsford-Smith, Ulm had been wounded three times in the Gallipoli campaign, but it happened on the ground, not in the air. After the war he applied for flight training in England, but was rejected, whereupon he began spending his spare time at airfields, urging a pilot friend to give him lessons. His friend obliged, but when he went up for his first solo, Ulm crash-landed the Royal Air Force plane, setting off quite a fireworks display of official repercussions.

The test flights were completed and curtains of gray fog hung over the Golden Gate on the morning of May 31, 1928, when the *Southern Cross*, painted in bright blue, was taxied out to the dirt runway at Oakland Airport. Kingsford-Smith and Ulm were wearing flying togs, but Lyon and Warner showed up in civilian clothes, with Lyon even sporting a bow tie as he climbed into the roomy radio-navigation cabin behind the pilot's cockpit. At 8:54 A.M., a tense silence fell over a farewell crowd of about a thousand people as Kingsford-Smith gave the signal to remove the wheel chocks. Then, just as the plane was about to roll, Lyon stuck his head out of the cabin window and seized a lighted cigarette from a reporter's hand.

"This may be my last drag," Lyon grinned at the startled newsman as he drew the smoke into his lungs, then returned the cigarette to its owner.

The 220-hp engines roared into action and the big plane lumbered across the field, its tires bulging under a heavy load of gasoline and the wheels struggling to overcome the law of gravity. Twice the tires left the ground only to settle back again, and every man and woman on the field began "helping" Kingsford-Smith with their "body-english" as he desperately tried to get into the air. With the end of the runway just ahead, the plane left the dirt for a third time and gingerly began to climb, while the crowd twisted and strained, trying to lift it above the housetops. The group calisthenics came to an end, and the spectators heaved an audible sigh of relief as the *Southern Cross* finally cleared the last barrier of a row of homes and soared out of sight above the misty Pacific.

After rising to 1500 feet, Smith took a parting glance at the California coast, and the great white skyscrapers of San Francisco rising through the wreath of fog around the Bay area. Soon the dim gray outlines of the offshore Farallon Islands were beneath the wings, the last bits of solid land they would see between the Embarcadero and the sands of Waikiki. In the navigation cabin, Warner picked up the radio beacon that was beaming outward from the coast behind them, and on out over the ocean they would eventually zero in on another reassuring beacon, flung toward them from Honolulu. The weather forecast had been excellent, although it carried a reservation of possible clouds along the way, and sure enough, in less than two hours after the takeoff, they had to climb to 2000 feet to get above the first billowy white wall. By late afternoon the ceiling lowered as the clouds beneath them literally exploded and disintegrated in a mushroom of vapor that enveloped the plane.

Soon the blue Pacific was tinged with gold and the fiery ball of the sun doused itself in the sea, and then was gone. As the stars came out, Kingsford-Smith took the plane to nearly 4000 feet, and Lyon cast overboard the first of the calcium flares that would help indicate the all-important rate of drift. As they struck the water one by one, each flare burst into a blaze of blinding white, and the fliers watched as the burning calcium drifted slightly to the south—a clear indication the plane was holding its course.

Shortly past midnight, while Ulm was at the controls, the tiny lights of a steamer were seen twinkling far below, the first sign of life on the sea since the takeoff. Ulm nosed the plane downward, and Smith manned a searchlight to signal the ship with a 6000-foot beam. The shaft of electric light shot through the black void, catching the vessel squarely amidships, and back came the answering signal of a blinking white flash.

Two hours passed and another ship passed beneath the wings, and then until well into the early hours of morning they struggled against those Twin Furies of all transocean fliers— boredom and monotony. The moon went down with the dawn, and with daylight the Fool's Land of cloud mirages appeared on the horizon of the steel-blue sea. Just before 11 A.M., Navigator Lyon, aware of the haunting visions of land, scribbled a note and sent it forward, insisting that the Hawaiian Islands had to be just over the horizon or else the plane had wandered badly off course.

It was a prophetic note, for only moments later they saw the snow-capped heights of Mauna Kea, the extinct Hawaiian volcano rising from the sea to the southwest. Within minutes, the *Southern Cross* was soaring around the bold promontory of Diamond Head, and then over Honolulu itself where thousands of people were standing in the streets, gaily waving amid the ringing of bells and shrieking of whistles. When the plane came down and rolled to a stop at Wheeler Field, the fliers were lassoed with leis in a tumultuous welcome led by Hawaii's

The *Southern Cross* lands at Honolulu, Hawaii, first stop on a 7000-mile trip from Oakland, California, to Brisbane, Australia, 1928. Kingsford-Smith's monoplane was the first to make this long aerial journey. (*Wide World Photos*)

Governor, Wallace R. Farrington. Among those who came forward to greet them were Art Goebel, the winner of the Dole Race, and Captain Lowell Smith, the man who had led the Army round-the-world fliers four years before.

Nearly one-third of the journey was behind them, and now they faced a flight of 3144 miles across the trackless ocean to Suva in the Fiji Islands. In a sense, during this flight they would be upgraded from mere aviators to the status of aerial explorers for no plane had ever spanned that area before. In order to take off with a load of 1300 gallons of gasoline, an exceptionally long runway was needed, and Kingsford-Smith decided to utilize the beach at Barking Sands on the Island of Kauai, some one hundred miles from Honolulu.

The *Southern Cross* was flown to the beach, and early on the morning of June 3 while the surf was rolling in from the sea, the big blue monoplane pounded along the sandy runway to begin the second, and most hazardous lap of the voyage. The plane skimmed low above the ocean, then climbed to 500 feet as the fliers saw the last of the Hawaiian Islands fade away to the northeast. Almost immediately, a cloud bank arose to challenge their passage, and for at least an hour they raced in and out of the misty corridors in an effort to keep the sea in view.

As suddenly as they had appeared, the clouds vanished at 7 A.M., and the sun rode high in the sky as the plane sped on southward, its motors droning with perfection. The long, blue water trail stretched away into the distance, with neither ship nor coral to break its glassy smoothness. It was a moment that invited relaxation in the cockpit, and Charley Ulm was just about to unlimber his cramped legs when he caught sight of a trickle of liquid that dropped from the wing gasoline tank to splatter on the cockpit floor near Smithy, who was at the controls.

A gas leak!

Ulm grabbed Smithy's arm and pointed to the innocent-looking fluid as it trickled its way along the steel lining of the lower wing, creating that always terrifying hazard of a fire in flight. Smithy promptly gave Ulm the controls, then reached up for a sample of the liquid and tasted it. With a grin on his face, he turned back to Ulm.

"Glory be!" Smithy reported. "It's not gas. It's only water, probably formed by the air condensing around that cold gas pipe."

So it was recorded as a crisis that failed to happen, and for the first time since leaving Barking Sands they opened the food hamper to polish off several sandwiches and a couple of oranges. They chose the right moment to fortify themselves with food for, as night fell, dark clouds began merging into colossal thunderheads all around them, and every hand would be needed in the battle against a storm they couldn't avoid. The matter of gasoline conservation was so important that Kingsford-Smith decided to plow right through the rain, rather than consume extra fuel trying to climb above the clouds. The plane was bucking heavy winds at 3000 feet when the floodgates seemed to open, and a deluge crashed down upon them.

Driving with a tremendous force, the tropic rain seeped through the fuselage, leaving the cockpit ankle-deep in water.

The storm's fury gave Smithy some second thoughts and he decided to get above the clouds, even if it meant draining away some of that precious gasoline. Sending the *Southern Cross* into a steady climb, he reached 5000 feet, but the storm was still there. Shaking his head in discouragement, Smithy nosed the plane up again, and at 8000 feet they broke into the clear. And there, hanging in the dark blue sky, was their constellation the *Southern Cross,* beckoning to its soaking wet namesake with the three roaring engines.

The night passed, and when dawn came the southeast trade winds began giving them a bumpy ride. They had been in the air 32 hours, and the heavy atmosphere suggested that the tropical heat of the Fiji Islands was not far away. With Ulm at the controls, they were flying 750 feet above the white-crested waves when far out on the starboard bow a small brown dome seemed to rise from the sea. No believer in mirages, Ulm recognized it as land and swung sharply in that direction. Jarred from his sleep by the sudden turn, Kingsford-Smith joined the others to see the green islands of Fiji appear on the southern horizon. The clock read 2:20 P.M. when they looked down on the cane fields, the rubber plantations, and the red, yellow, and purple landscape of the Fijis. Then they were over the waterfront and red-roofed bungalows of Suva where the entire population of some 10,000 was out in the streets to honor the *Southern Cross.* Smithy took over the controls and prepared to come in for a landing at Albert Park Sports Oval, a cricket field barely 400 yards long. The surrounding area had been cleared of trees and telegraph wires for their arrival, still there remained the vital question of whether the plane would have enough room to land.

Coming in at 65 miles an hour, Smithy brought the wheels down midway in the field, leaving only 200 yards in which to check the forward motion or else crash into a thickly forested grove that bordered the playing oval. The plane rolled on toward the trees, then just as a crash seemed inevitable, he ground-looped sharply to the left, and the *Southern Cross* had landed safely at Fiji. They had completed history's longest non-stop flight over water—a distance of 3144 miles in 34 hours and 30 minutes.

Anxious as they were to complete the rest of the journey to Australia, the fliers found it necessary to remain in the Fijis for a few days. Another field, or a beach, was needed because the Sports Oval was not nearly long enough for their takeoff. Also, the matter of refueling would have to be attended to before the *Southern Cross* could head for its final target—Brisbane on the Australian coast.

The presence of the fliers and their "big blue bird" caused immense excitement among the Fiji Islanders, virtually none of whom had ever seen a flying machine before. They ascribed supernatural qualities to the white aviators, and donned their native bronze-green costumes and gaudy headdress to stage colorful "meke" dances and ceremonies in their honor. From one of the natives the fliers heard a strange story about their airplane coming to a stop, and suspending itself in the night sky.

Turaga was the spokesman for a small group of natives who had been on a lookout for the plane as it approached the islands the night before. "Yes," Turaga told them in his native tongue, "and I will tell you how he actually did it, we saw him so plainly. He found he must be ahead of time, and he had to wait till daylight before he came to Suva. So he decided to have a rest and he went up to the moon and hooked his plane to the moon. We saw him hook it on with the big hooks, and the plane rested there. It stayed there for an hour. Boss, we saw him stay there, true!"

The fliers were puzzled by the weird story, but finally the answer became apparent. Before their arrival, the newspapers had carried a story about a lunar eclipse. The natives had seen the dark shadow across the eclipsed moon and were convinced it was the *Southern Cross*—moored to a pinnacle in the mountains of the moon and swinging lazily over the lunar valleys.

For their takeoff they selected Naselai Beach, 20 miles east of Suva, and on the afternoon of June 8 they began the final

1780-mile flight to Australia—the shortest leg of their historic journey. After circling Suva where the streets and parks were thronged with thousands of waving and cheering islanders, the *Southern Cross* winged its way over the open sea, heading now for the Land Down Under. Layers of feathery clouds floated across the horizon though the weather was ideal, and Kingsford-Smith gave the instrument panel a final check before settling back to relax at the controls.

Victory seemed so near that it was something of a shock when Harry Lyon passed a message forward, informing the cockpit that the earth inductor compass had gone out of action. It was far and away their most valuable navigation instrument, but in their haste to refuel the tanks at Naselai Beach they had forgotten to oil the compass. There was no retrieving the error now, and for the rest of the flight they would have to depend upon their highly inaccurate steering compasses.

The tropical sunset painted the western sky at 6 P.M. Then with darkness came a chill, and they put on their fur-lined overalls. The hours passed, the night grew colder and blacker, with nothing to be seen except the blue-tipped flames that spouted from the engines. Trying to get above the overcast, they climbed to 4300 feet and then, without warning, the plane ran into another heavy rainstorm. With it came cyclonic gusts of wind that rocked the wings and fuselage so violently that Smithy could hardly keep the plane on an even keel. Climbing to 7000 feet there was still no relief from the cascades of water that pounded the windshield with such force that it seemed on the verge of breaking. Streaks of red and blue lightning ripped through the night, illuminating the giant thunderheads that towered around them. Inside the cabin, Lyon threw up his hands in surrender, for navigation was futile under such conditions. Worse yet, he had no idea where they were. If only, he thought, they *could* hook the plane on the moon and ride out the storm!

All through the night the deluge continued, but with the dawn it ended and the sun ascended in the sky behind them, lighting the way toward the coast of Australia. And it was 9:50

A.M. when a line of violet hills and brown cliffs unrolled along the western horizon to give them their first sight of home. Swinging over the coast, Lyon announced that their landfall was about 110 miles south of Brisbane, so Kingsford-Smith turned the plane northward, determined to end the flight according to plan. Approaching the suburbs of Brisbane, he picked up the winding trail of Breakfast Creek that led them to Eagle Farm Aerodrome on the outskirts of the city where some 15,000 people were waiting as the *Southern Cross* came in for a perfect landing. It was an almost dream-like ending to one of the most remarkable flights in history. As the crowds surged forward, a lone police inspector tried to restrain them, shouting:

"Get back! Get back! This is no ordinary plane."

A motorcade carried the fliers triumphantly into Brisbane where the streets were lined with 40,000 more wildly cheering Australians. And when they arrived at City Hall, they were handed a cablegram from San Francisco. It was from their friend and benefactor Captain Allan Hancock, and the message read:

I AM DELIVERING TO THE CALIFORNIA BANK AT LOS ANGELES FOR TRANSMISSION TO THE COMMERCIAL BANKING COMPANY OF SYDNEY, A BILL OF SALE TRANSFERRING TO KINGSFORD-SMITH AND ULM THE SOUTHERN CROSS, TOGETHER WITH RELEASE AND DISCHARGE OF ALL YOUR INDEBTEDNESS TO ME. I BEG YOU TO ACCEPT THIS GIFT AS A TOKEN OF OUR MUTUAL FRIENDSHIP, AND ALSO TO COMMEMORATE THE MAGNIFICENT ACHIEVEMENT OF YOURSELVES AND YOUR BRAVE AMERICAN COMPANIONS IN BRINGING OUR TWO GREAT COUNTRIES CLOSER TOGETHER. YOUR FRIENDS HERE JOIN ME IN SAYING— ADVANCE AUSTRALIA!

As Kingsford-Smith finished reading this message he said to himself: "Thank God for the wonderful people there are in this world!"

Within the next seven years, both Kingsford-Smith and Ulm lost their lives, still trying to further the cause of long-distance flying. On December 3, 1934, Ulm and two companions took off from San Francisco in a small, twin-engined plane, bound for

The crew of the *Southern Cross:* (from left to right) Harry W. Lyon, navigator; Charles Kingsford-Smith, captain; Charles Ulm, relief pilot, and James Warner, radioman. Lyon and Warner were Americans; Kingsford-Smith and Ulm Australians. (*Wide World Photos*)

Honolulu in another attempt to fly to Australia. Somehow they missed the Hawaiian Islands and became hopelessly lost as their fuel supply dwindled to nothing. Ulm sent out a final message: "We are now landing in the sea. Please come pick us out." Despite a massive air and sea search, they were never found.

Early in November of the following year, 1935, Kingsford-Smith left England on a flight to Australia, but somewhere off the coast of Malaya his plane vanished, and Australia's most famous aviator was never seen again. It was a tragic loss, for Kingsford-Smith never lived to see the realization of his dream —the trans-Pacific airlines he had so valiantly pioneered.

Which brings us to the second installment of our story of "The Admiral of the Poles."

CHAPTER XII

Byrd, Balchen, June, and McKinley Fly over the South Pole

The daily life of an Adelie penguin down near the South Pole is not always routine. As he waddles along the ice with that Charlie Chaplin shuffle, in his white shirt and black tuxedo-like feathers, he—or she—sometimes encounters unusual experiences in the course of the day.

If, for instance, the penguin has a mind to go a-courtin', he may find himself in some embarrassing circumstance that keeps life from becoming unbearably dull. Scientists and zoologists generally agree that the male and female penguins look exactly alike, with nothing to enable even the experts to tell them apart. This does bring on some romantic complications, because, unfortunately, the penguins have the same trouble, and the males often have the jarring experience of trying to pitch woo with birds who, alas, turn out to be males themselves.

This can be disconcerting enough, but still more frustrating must be the rueful knowledge that, although he is a bird, he cannot fly. He has a beak, yes, and he has sleek, shiny feathers and flipper-like wings that propel him through the water, but somewhere along the line of evolutionary development he failed to learn to fly. So as he waddles earthbound over the ice it must be with pangs of jealousy that he watches the snow petrels and the skua gulls spread their wings and soar away into the Antarctic sky.

But on Thanksgiving Day, November 28, 1929, Mr. Penguin's black opaque eye might have turned livid green with envy, for on that afternoon, the latest creature to join him in the ice and snow—man (*Homo Sapiens Antarcticus*, if you like)—spread his wings and took off toward the South Pole. And it was perhaps an ornithological coincidence that this man's name was, Byrd.

More than a year before, in the summer of 1928, Commander Richard Evelyn Byrd had established his Antarctic expedition headquarters in a well-known New York igloo called the Hotel Biltmore. The luxurious Biltmore, with its 23 floors and 950 rooms, had been dedicated on New Year's Eve, 1913, but as they raised a toast to that new venture, the owners little dreamed that fifteen years later their Manhattan caravanserai would become the base for exploration's greatest assault against the almost unknown Antarctic continent.

In organizing his Arctic flight in 1926, Byrd's intentions had been limited to one goal—to become the first to fly across the North Pole. If new land should be discovered on the way, all well and good—but the idea was to fly to the Pole and back, and do it first. For the Antarctic, it would be different.

For one thing, money had been a problem on the North Pole venture. But by 1928 two spectacular aerial achievements had given Byrd's prestige a big boost in the fund-raising department. He had of course reached the North Pole, and a year later in 1927, thanks again to the young Norseman Bernt Balchen, Byrd added another laurel by flying non-stop from New York to France. Taking off from Roosevelt Field five weeks after Lindbergh, Byrd's tri-motored monoplane, the *America*, arrived over France in fog, rain, and darkness and came down for a forced landing near the little village of Ver-Sur-Mer. Byrd was acclaimed second only to Lindbergh when he arrived at Paris, and on returning to the United States he received his second hero's welcome in two years. Then he set out to raise a million dollars for Antarctic exploration. Now he was at the Biltmore, organizing an expedition so vast and so elaborate that it would make his Arctic adventure look like a weekend outing in the snow. Also it would include, so he hoped, a first flight to the South Pole and back.

Time had virtually stood still on Antarctica, the only uninhabited continent of the world. Its 5,500,000 square miles remained in the grip of the Ice Age. It was a vast realm of ice, a lofty two-mile-high plateau swept by cyclonic winds, a continent of unseen, nameless mountains. Of living things, there were the sea birds, the skua gulls, the petrels and the penguins, along with the killer whales, the blue whales, the sea leopards and the seals, all of whom took their food from the sea because there was none to be found on the icebound continent. Even then, it was largely a matter of consuming each other.

Still, it had not always been that way. Fossils, petrified trees, plants, and animals, had been found beneath the ice, so it was known that flora and living organisms had once thrived there in the remote prehistoric past. The plant remains, rocks, and beds of coal were similar in age and description to those found on other Southern Hemisphere continents, all of which gave rise to the theory that Antarctica was once joined to South America, South Africa, India and Australia, forming a gigantic land mass before it all broke up into separate continents to drift into their present positions. But that had been 200 million years ago.

In mounting an assault against this inhospitable region, Byrd dreamed of making it the most long-drawn-out, the biggest, the most expensive, the most efficient, and the most scientific expedition ever to head for the Far South. Thousands of tons of equipment and supplies would be transported on two ships. There would be three airplanes, one of which would fly him to the South Pole. Prefabricated insulation panels for buildings, a snowmobile, steel for three radio towers, eighty Eskimo dogs and a fleet of sledges, skis, fur clothing, kerosene stoves, a complete machine shop, a gymnasium, pins, matches, toothbrushes, tons of food, a kitchen, sewing machines, gasoline engines to generate electricity, a physician complete with medical supplies for a clinic, enough books to fill a small library—

all of this and more would enable him to establish a self-sufficient village to be known as Little America—population 42. Also, for the first time, this seventh continent would have a post office.

Even as late as the middle 1920s, to most Americans the Antarctic was as remote as the moon, perhaps more so because, after all, they could see the moon. The southern continent remained the world's number one geographic mystery, guarded by icebergs as large as islands. For centuries, navigators had sailed south in search of this other world, always to be driven back by the howling winds and the ice barrier. It will never be known how many ships went down, and how many men died during those early days in Antarctic seas. The screaming gales, the crushing weight of ice against wooden hulls, the commands to abandon ship—and then, perhaps, came the worst ordeals of all.

Finally in 1773, that indomitable British explorer, Captain James Cook, the first voyager in recorded history ever to cross the Antarctic Circle, arrived in these waters with his ship, the *Resolution,* in search of the elusive continent. Indeed, he came within 150 miles of its coast, but just as it had in the voyages before him—the ice won. Even so, Cook had set a new record by sailing farther south than anyone else.

The first well-organized American expedition to the Antarctic was not until the years 1838 to 1842 when the U. S. Navy sent four ships south under the command of Lieutenant Charles Wilkes. He sighted land while sailing along the Antarctic coast south of the Indian Ocean, even though he failed to get a landing party ashore. His ships couldn't cope with the ice and his shivering crews had little enthusiasm for a region that offered them naught but hardship.

During that same period a British expedition led by Sir James Clark Ross, sailed into the southern seas and did make a discovery. Ross, known as the Adonis of the British Navy, approached Antarctica from a point south of New Zealand through what today is known as the Ross Sea. One morning he found his passage blocked by a wall of ice that rose nearly 200 feet above the sea and stretched east and west beyond the limits of vision.

Although he didn't know it at the time, Ross had discovered a layer of ice nearly a thousand feet thick and as big as France— its outer wall, facing the sea, was 500 miles long and its immense, flat-topped surface extended 400 miles farther south to the continent, where it was fed by ice pushing down from lofty glacial mountains. Naturally enough, the discoverer called it an "ice barrier," simply because it blocked both his ship and his view. All explorers who were to follow him would call it— the Ross Ice Shelf.

By the year 1900, the curtain of mystery was slowly rising and the vast outline of the shadowy continent was gradually coming into focus. A few years later, viewed from high over the Pacific in one of those new-fangled flying machines invented by the Wright Brothers, the mountains of the Antarctic Peninsula zigzagged across the sky to the east, reaching toward South America through an archipelago of islands extending toward Cape Horn. These mountains, in fact, were an extension of the Andes. On farther south stretched an unknown land of more mountains, and then the great south polar plateau.

The tempo of Antarctic exploration was stepped up in the years between 1900 and 1910—a period when nineteen expeditions set forth from six different countries. Among them was the British National Expedition, headed by Commander Robert Falcon Scott who was destined to become one of the Antarctic's immortals. Scott brought along a veteran cameraman and a captive balloon, and soon after his arrival the first aerial photos of the Antarctic were made from a height of 800 feet over Ross Island. In shooting these pictures, Scott's photographer set the stage for the great age of aerial exploration by camera which began in earnest with Byrd's Antarctic expedition and has continued on down to our own day of close-up pictures of the moon.

In January 1911, Scott led a second expedition to Antarctica, and this time his goal was to reach the South Pole. But competition came unexpectedly from Norway, with the veteran explorer Roald Amundsen, conqueror of the Northwest Passage, dramatically changing plans to head for the South Pole. Originally, Amundsen had been headed for the North Pole until he heard that Peary had beaten him to it. From then on, the race to the South would be to the swift, and as everyone knows, the Scott-Amundsen story is one of the most dramatic, most tragic, pages of history. Amundsen left the Bay of Whales at the eastern end of the Ice Shelf and headed south on October 19, 1911. With him were four Norwegian companions, all expert dog-drivers with four sledges, each pulled by thirteen huskies. Supply depots were set up along the route, and after duelling with blizzards and crevasses on the Ice Shelf, they scaled the heights of Axel Heiberg Glacier and made the dash across the polar plateau. The 800-mile journey was completed on December 14 when Amundsen raised the Norwegian flag at the Ultimate South. Then, less than two months later, they returned safely to their base after one of the most successful polar journeys on record.

Meanwhile, Scott had established his base at the opposite far western end of the Ice Shelf on Ross Island on the shores of McMurdo Sound, where volcanic Mount Erebus was belching its smoke and flames into the sky. His party started for the Pole on November 1, some two weeks after Amundsen's departure, but Scott had no way of knowing whether he was ahead or behind in the race. Unwisely, he had chosen snow ponies as sledge animals and they soon gave out, forcing him and his four English companions to haul their loads by hand for hundreds of miles over glaciers, mountains and that trackless Antarctic plateau. To make matters even worse, their route was 60 miles longer than the one Amundsen had chosen.

The story has been told again and again of how they finally reached the Pole on January 18, only to find a tent which still flew the Norwegian flag—for Amundsen had beaten Scott. It was a blow for the British, but for them the ultimate in exploration tragedy was yet to come.

They now faced a return journey of more than 850 miles, and

again they would have to pull their sledges across the ice cap. Scott already had his doubts. *"Now for the run home and a desperate struggle,"* he wrote in his diary, *"I wonder if we can make it."* They didn't. Within the next two and a half months all five men perished, some from exhaustion and others from cold and starvation, even though three of their frozen bodies were found only 11 miles from a cache of food and fuel. Scott's diary was found in his clothing with the last entry dated March 29, 1912. It included that now-famous "letter to the public," one of the most moving and heart-rending messages ever written:

> I do not regret this journey, which has shown that Englishmen can endure hardships, help one another, and meet death with as great a fortitude as ever in the past. We took risks; we knew we took them; things have come out against us, and therefore we have no cause for complaint, but bow to the will of Providence, determined still to do our best to the last . . . Had we lived, I should have had a tale to tell of the hardihood, endurance, and courage of my companions, which would have stirred the hearts of every Englishman. These rough notes and our dead bodies must tell the tale . . .
>
> R. Scott

Dr. Edward A. Wilson was found with a bag containing thirty-five pounds of geological specimens he had collected on the way down Beardmore Glacier and hauled all the way to the spot where he collapsed and died. The gallant Scott and his heroic companions gave their lives trying to advance man's knowledge of one of earth's last great frontiers, and after them were to come such other explorers as Sir Douglas Mawson, Sir Ernest Shackleton, Sir Hubert Wilkins, and many more. But it was left to Commander Byrd to throw the full weight of modern technology into that land of forgotten time.

New York Harbor was a festive scene on August 25, 1928, when an old-fashioned, three-master, bark-rigged whaling ship, the vanguard of Byrd's "Antarctic Armada," sailed out of the Hudson into the Atlantic. As they passed through the harbor, hundreds of ships, tugs, fireboats, and launches turned on their

Bernt Balchen, the Norwegian who flew Byrd over the South Pole. A former associate of Roald Amundsen, Balchen had been Byrd's chief pilot on his earlier transatlantic flight. (*Culver Pictures, Inc.*)

whistles full-blast, with the giant, oceangoing liner, *Leviathan,* adding its deep rolling bass.

Byrd had searched throughout the world for a ship that could weather the rough seas of the polar regions and the one he finally purchased had been built in New Zealand a half-century before. Amundsen had taken it to sea under the name *Viking,* and now the stout old bark, her main masts set to the wind, bore the name *City of New York,* across her bows.

Two years before at Spitsbergen, when Byrd discussed his South Pole idea with Amundsen, some of the old Norwegian's advice had been in the form of a warning. "Look to your men," Amundsen cautioned him. "Men are the doubtful quantities in the Antarctic. The most thorough kind of preparation, the shrewdest plan, can be destroyed by an incompetent or worthless man."

Trying to heed the advice, Byrd surrounded himself with some of the nation's top experts in aviation, aerial photography, meteorology, geography, and geology. His pilot of North Pole days, Floyd Bennett, had died while trying to aid the survivors of the transatlantic plane, *Bremen*. And now, heading the list of Byrd's pilots was Bernt Balchen, the Viking who had saved the day for him on the flight across the Atlantic. Reaching the South Pole by air, or by any means for that matter, had long been one of Balchen's dreams.

Byrd also chose three other fliers, for the expedition had three planes—virtually an Antarctic squadron. They included six-foot-four Dean Smith, a veteran airmail pilot; Captain Alton Parker, formerly of the U. S. Marines; and Harold June, a Navy pilot, expert radio operator and skilled mechanic. Byrd appointed the noted geologist and geographer, Dr. Laurence M. Gould, as his second in command; as third, Captain Ashley McKinley, a veteran aerial photographer who had served as a kite-balloonist in World War I; and, fourth, William "Cyclone" Haines, the meteorologist who had been with him in the Arctic.

After stopping at Dunedin, New Zealand, for supplies and coal, the *City of New York* sailed on south through the ice fields and finally arrived off the Ross Ice Shelf on Christmas Day. For three days they cruised eastward along the barrier to the Bay of Whales, the ice-locked arm of the Ross Sea where Amundsen had made his base seventeen years before. The far eastern end of the barrier held the ship's harbor closest to the South Pole, and after a look around, Byrd decided to establish his headquarters high up on the Ice Shelf. He chose an area as near the edge as possible where it was wide and flat enough for a good landing strip. Along the bay's shores, drifting snow had formed an inclined platform that sloped upward to the top of the 110-foot barrier, providing a ready-made access route for hauling supplies from the ship.

Byrd sent his second in command, Larry Gould, ashore to take charge of the construction of Little America and, like Rome, it wasn't to be built in a day. For weeks, the dog teams pulled building materials and supplies over an eight-mile route, while the ever-lengthening shadows of the sledges warned that the Antarctic winter was not too far away. Soon the kerosene-heated, prefabricated buildings were going up—a mess hall, bunkhouses, the administration building, and seventy-foot radio towers that would keep Little America in constant touch with the world in general, and with the New York *Times* in particular.

Because of fire hazard, special precautions were taken to construct the buildings well apart from each other, with a labyrinth of connecting tunnels, six feet deep, assuring an all-weather route between the main buildings and the mess hall. Before long, electric lights, running water and artificial ventilation were installed in the buildings.

It wasn't the first time the Byrd family had put a town or a city on the map. Commander Byrd's ancestor, Colonel William Byrd, had founded the city of Richmond, Virginia, in 1733. But, unlike Richmond, as soon as Little America was built it disappeared from sight after the first snowfall, leaving only the smokestacks and three radio towers sticking up out of the drifts.

On January 14, the first of the three planes was put ashore—a Fairchild monoplane with a 425-hp Wasp engine capable of speeding 140 miles an hour. Designed primarily for high altitude photography, this plane had wide windows along the sides and a glass floor under the cockpit. It was named the *Stars and Stripes* and the following day Byrd sent the aircraft aloft on the expedition's first exploratory flight. Still, it was not the first time an airplane had been flown over the Antarctic. Sir Hubert Wilkins and his pilot, Ben Eielson, had gained that distinction in December only a few weeks before. Taking off from Deception Island in the Lockheed-Vega that had carried them across the Arctic, Wilkins and Eielson flew south on a mapping expedition along the eastern coast of the Antarctic Peninsula, thus winning the distinction of being the first ever to fly over *both* the north and the south polar regions.

Before the Antarctic winter set in, Byrd made several exploratory flights over unknown territory east of the Alexandra

Mountains which had been discovered and named by Commander Scott. With Balchen as his pilot on one of these trips, Byrd sighted a chain of uncharted mountain peaks extending north and south for about 30 miles, and named them the Rockefeller Mountains in honor of John D., Jr. Three weeks later, Byrd flew farther east and found new territory that he called Marie Byrd Land, claiming it for the United States.

The supply vessel, *Eleanor Bolling*—named for Byrd's mother —soon arrived from New Zealand, bringing additional dogs, more gasoline and the other two airplanes which, in Balchen's words, would "enable them to assault the Antarctic in mass formation." One of the aircraft, a tri-motored Ford monoplane which Byrd had named the *Floyd Bennett*, was being primed for the flight to the South Pole. All-metal in construction and mounted on skis, it had a pair of 225-hp Wright Whirlwind engines on the wings and a special 525-hp Wright Cyclone in the nose. The third monoplane, called the *Virginia*, was a single-engined Fokker with a 425-hp engine.

On Saturday evenings, there was always a two-way broadcast with the United States, when the men gathered around to talk directly with their families and friends many thousands of miles away. One evening a radio message came through from a Ziegfeld Follies girl in New York who apparently thought one of the men was being neglected.

"Hello, big boy," she said, "I been noticing you never get no messages from nobody, so here's one from me. If you and I was down there together, baby, we'd melt a hole right through the ice!"

When the winter storms were at their worst, the gymnasium became the most popular spot on the Ice Shelf. Both Bernt Balchen and Sverre Strom had been amateur boxing champions back in Norway, and they donned the gloves to entertain the men with rousing exhibitions, or spent the afternoon instructing them in self-defense. Byrd came to the gym regularly, either to watch the boxing or to keep himself trim with weight-lifting devices. One afternoon Byrd was feeling especially chipper and he challenged Strom to a round of Indian wrestling, a form of foot-to-foot combat. The match was a brief one. Strom, a six-footer with muscles like the village blacksmith, sent Byrd flying head over heels into a corner where he landed against a stove and gashed his forehead. Embarrassed by his own show of strength, Strom promptly rushed over to offer his apologies.

Midwinter, July 21, was celebrated by presenting the *Antarctic Follies of 1929.* To the tune of catcalls and wolf-whistles, a muscular line of "chorus girls," some of them bearded, danced out onto the stage—clad in costumes resembling ballet skirts and blond wigs that looked suspiciously like pieces of frayed rope. From the "orchestra pit" came the jolly strains of an accordion played by Sverre Strom—a man of many talents indeed.

During the long winter months, valuable observations were made in physics, meteorology, and glaciology. There were busy preparations also for the South Pole flight and the 400-mile journey of Dr. Gould's geological party which would spend nearly three months in the field.

Due south from the base and some 400 miles across the Ice Shelf stood the 14,000-foot Queen Maud Range, and beyond that, it was another 393 miles across the polar plateau to the Pole. To get over the Queen Maud mountains and above the plateau, Byrd's plane would have to navigate its way through one of the glacial passes where the altitude was lower than the tops of those icy mountains. But first, two supply bases would be established at the foot of the mountains and stocked with food and gasoline, ready for an emergency should one arise. The *Floyd Bennett* would be flown on one of these missions, the other would go by dog sledge.

A supporting party of four men and several dog teams left on October 15 and returned several weeks later after planting supplies along the trail southward. Soon afterward, Dr. Larry Gould's geological survey party of six men and ten sledges set out over the same trail. They cached even more supplies along the way and pushed on toward the Queen Maud Range to establish a base for the geological party's work in the mountains.

Byrd's tri-motored Ford plane, the *Floyd Bennett* that made the South Pole flight. (*Wide World Photos*)

The *Floyd Bennett* was hauled out of its snow and ice hangar and given a complete going over—the engines were checked and tuned, new gas lines installed, and the ski pedestals were fitted and aligned, with some of the work being done in temperatures of 50-below. Then on November 19, two weeks after Gould's overland party had left, the big tri-motored plane was pronounced ready and it took off on the base-laying flight to the mountains.

On board for this flight were Commander Byrd, radioman Harold June, photographer Ashley McKinley, and airmail pilot Dean Smith who appeared to be moving into first place as Byrd's choice to fly the plane to the Pole. They were about 200 miles out when, far below, they spotted Larry Gould and his dog teams trudging along the trail. After dropping mail and supplies, the *Floyd Bennett* continued on to land at the foot of the Queen Maud Range where a supply cache was set up, then the return journey began. About a hundred miles from Little America the motors began to miss, and June informed

Byrd that they were running out of gas. He had hardly spoken before all three engines stopped cold, but Dean Smith managed to bring them down to a safe though bumpy landing on some extremely rough terrain.

When the engines quit, the radio transmitter also went out of commission, and back at Little America apprehension began to mount over the missing plane. Balchen warmed up the Fairchild monoplane, took off, and finally spotted the *Floyd Bennett* and its crew in the snow, very close to the edge of a yawning crevasse. He found them unharmed, but the Ford's tanks were indeed empty. Just in case, Balchen had brought along an extra one hundred gallons of gas, and when the plane was refueled he offered to assist them in getting the engines started again. But the stranded fliers waved him aside, saying they could manage by themselves.

So Balchen flew the Fairchild back to Little America, still the remainder of the day passed with no sign of the *Floyd Bennett*. So he took off again with radioman Carl Petersen and they found the grounded plane in the same spot, its engine still refusing to fire up. When heaters were applied to the cold motors, it solved the problem. Then less than two hours later the *Floyd Bennett* took off with the Fairchild as an escort, and soon they were back at their air strip on the Ross Ice Shelf.

Obviously concerned about the *Floyd Bennett*'s performance, Byrd called Balchen aside the next day and asked him if he knew why the gasoline consumption had been higher than expected. Balchen said he didn't, but promised to go over the entire fuel system and completely recheck the engines before the plane left for the Pole.

"All right," Byrd agreed, "but get started right away, just to make sure."

The conversation apparently over, Balchen turned to walk back to the bunkhouse—but Byrd stopped him.

"Oh, by the way," the commander added, "I'll want you to pilot the plane. You will fly with me to the South Pole."

Now began the period of final preparation with Byrd facing

a dilemma that had to be resolved before the takeoff. One objective of the Pole flight would be a photographic record of some thousands of square miles of unknown Antarctica between Little America and the Pole. This would be McKinley's job. Still, there was the question of how much weight the plane could carry. In order to get through one of the passes and above the polar plateau, the *Floyd Bennett* would have to climb to at least 10,500 feet. When fully loaded and with all personnel on board, the plane would weigh about 14,500 pounds—its cargo including enough food and supplies for at least forty-five days in the event of a forced landing. Captain McKinley and his big mapping camera, taken together with his food and equipment, weighed a total of 600 pounds. The weight-and-load factor was so critical that it boiled down to this:

Without McKinley and the camera, it would be possible to fly all the way to the Pole and back, non-stop. With McKinley and the camera, at least one landing to refuel would be necessary and a non-stop flight was out of the question. The reasoning was simple enough—without McKinley, the plane could carry more gasoline.

However, Byrd would not be satisfied unless he had both the Pole and pictures, even if it meant stopping to refuel on the way back. On the other hand, there were the hazards of landing on the polar ice, with the white glare sometimes making it impossible to judge distances, and the freezing cold making it difficult to start the engines again. And there were the sudden squalls which could come out of nowhere to dash a plane against a glacier. On balance, however, Byrd decided that McKinley and his camera had to go along—they'd take that added risk.

For two reasons, it was necessary to have clear weather on the day of the flight. From the exploration point of view, little could be done if the visibility were poor. Unfavorable weather would also introduce the factor or danger in climbing above the mountains, with the prospect of colliding with one of those uncharted peaks.

On the morning of Thanksgiving Day, November 28, the geological party reached a point about a hundred miles from the Queen Maud Range and Gould flashed a radio report that the weather was excellent for flying over the polar plateau. Still, there was an overcast at Little America. "Cyclone" Haines evaluated the information, sent a weather balloon aloft to make his own observations, then stuck a wet finger into the wind. Turning to Byrd, Haines said:

"Could be more nearly perfect, but you'd better go now. Another chance may not come."

Shortly after noon, the ground crew formed a bucket line and began passing five-gallon tins of gasoline to the plane, along with food and equipment, all of which was carefully weighed and counted. Even so, Byrd decided at the last minute to take along two extra sacks of food, each weighing 150 pounds.

By 3 o'clock, Byrd was all decked out for the flight, wearing a big fur cap, parka, and a caribou flying suit, and he posed for a farewell picture. In his hands was a small American flag attached to a stone taken from Floyd Bennett's grave in Arlington National Cemetery, and this would be dropped over the South Pole. Movie cameras were grinding as he waved to the crowd and climbed aboard to join his three companions. Balchen was seated at the controls and Byrd gave him the nod. Then, at 3:29 P.M. the *Floyd Bennett* sped across the snow and took off for the South Pole.

The flight began in a hazy overcast, a milk-white sky blending with the snow-covered surface to create a visibility condition known as a "whiteout." There was no horizon, no shadows, and the plane seemed to be flying inside a giant ping-pong ball. Byrd took his seat at the navigator's table in the rear of the cabin and unfolded the same old charts Roald Amundsen had used when he followed the same route with dog sleds years before. Radioman Harold June was at his transmitter on the port side of the cabin, already maintaining constant radio contact with Little America. Ashley McKinley, unlimbering his camera, began shooting pictures from both port and starboard windows only moments after the takeoff.

An hour passed and, suddenly, the "whiteout" was gone and sunshine flooded the cabin. June sent back optimistic messages while to the west the mountains were coming into view, their icy peaks sparkling in the sunlight and their glaciers spilling down onto the Ice Shelf. The plane was 325 miles out of Little America when Larry Gould and his men were spotted in the snow, waving a greeting as Balchen flew low to drop a parachute-bag with cigarettes, chocolate, and mail. By radio, Byrd received the ground party's exact latitude and longitude, checking it against his own figures as the plane sped on southward with the Queen Maud mountains now just ahead.

Their course would eventually bring them to Axel Heiberg Glacier, the highway of ice Amundsen had climbed to reach the polar plateau. It was one of only two passes in the Queen Maud Range, the other being Liv's Glacier, located farther west and named for the daughter of Norwegian explorer Fridtjof Nansen. As the plane approached the mountains, Balchen gave the engines full throttle and went into a steady climb to 5000 feet.

Soon now a critical decision would have to be made—which pass should they take through the mountains? Success or failure could hinge on their choice, and they had to decide in a hurry.

Amundsen had reported that the highest point in Axel Heiberg Glacier was 10,500 feet, but they had no way of knowing whether the pass was wide enough to allow the plane maneuvering room should it fail to gain the needed altitude. Also, on each side of the gradually ascending sheet of ice there were sharply rising peaks, reaching much higher than the maximum ceiling of their heavily loaded plane. To the west was the other choice, Liv's Glacier, which they knew little about—except that it appeared wider, and some 1000 feet lower than Axel Heiberg. Liv's seemed to be the best course—but would they find unknown mountains blocking the way once they flew through the pass? Or, should they follow Amundsen's more familiar route up the Axel Heiberg? With time running out, Byrd and Balchen made their decision. They chose the unknown glacier, and swung the plane sharply to the right toward Liv's.

The wild and jagged mountains, eerie in their patterns of light and shadow, were much closer now as Balchen battled for more altitude. As they approached Liv's, the lowest point on the glacier was still above the nose of the plane, and more altitude would be needed to get over the hump. Harold June left his radio for a moment to help lighten the plane, opening the last of the fuel cans and pouring the gasoline in the tanks, then dropping the empty tins through the trapdoor. Each can weighed only two pounds, but for the next few minutes every ounce would count.

When the plane reached a point just above Liv's lower reaches, they could see what lay before them—Mount Nansen on the left, the walls of Fisher Mountain on the right, and straight ahead the glacier ascended gradually to level off some 30 miles up the pass. That would be the edge of the polar plateau— the level top of the Antarctic Ice Cap. Even as he increased the rate of climb, Balchen could see that the pass went up at a gradient he was sure they couldn't make. Even worse, down currents were hampering his efforts to gain more altitude, while beneath them the glacier floor was a maze of ice terraces and crevasses where no plane could land without a crash. When the altimeter warned the maximum ceiling was near, Balchen turned to yell over the roar of the motors:

"It's drop two hundred pounds, or go back!"

June jumped to the gasoline dump valve, but both Byrd and Balchen waved him off. Some of that extra food Byrd had put aboard would have to go. McKinley left his camera, grabbed a brown bag weighing 150 pounds and sent it spinning through the trapdoor. Like a buoyant balloon, the plane seemed to leap upward but it wasn't enough—so Balchen shouted again:

"More! Another bag!"

McKinley shoved a second 150-pound bag of food through the trapdoor, and the *Floyd Bennett* rose sharply another hundred feet, enough to clear the barrier while still maintaining its climb. Suddenly, the pilot grinned—that familiar, and rather special, Balchen grin. They had made the pass. In front of them now lay the open plateau, with the South Pole less than 400 miles away.

They were crossing a region no man had ever seen before— a land where the snow met the horizon in a thin line of blue and white, with nothing to break the monotonous expanse except the lonely peak of some mountain whose base was buried deep in the gigantic dome of ice. From a thousand feet above, the plateau for the most part appeared to be smooth enough to permit a landing, except where sastrugi—those hard, wind-honed ridges of ice—jutted up through the drifts.

About an hour out over the plateau, trouble developed in the starboard engine which began to backfire, and Balchen nosed the plane down while June rushed to the gasoline dump valves. Flying at a height of 11,000 feet, two engines could never keep the plane airborne but Balchen quickly discovered the trouble. In his efforts to conserve fuel, he had been "leaning the mixture" a bit too thin, that is, reducing the amount of gasoline that mixes with air as it passes through the carburetor. After he adjusted the mixture slightly, the sputtering engine began to sing its tune again as on and on they sped toward their goal.

Soon, a chain of mountains was marching across the eastern horizon, many of them standing in bold relief above the rim of the 10,000-foot tableland. They seemed to stretch in an endless procession toward the southeast, peaks of ice silhouetted against the blue—a panorama of the Ice Age.

Their course to the Pole lay along the 171st meridian, and Byrd began to notice a peculiar trend in his calculations. Even though the plane was maintaining a fairly steady altitude, the level of the plateau seemed to be falling away, slanting down-hill as they drew near the Pole. A variable wind was blowing from the east and to compensate for this, Byrd got Balchen's attention, waving him on a new course about 12 degrees to the left. The wind drift indicator was fitted into the trapdoor and Byrd also was using his old friend of the North Pole flight—the Bumstead sun compass.

At intervals, June went forward to take over the controls, giving Balchen a chance to walk back through the cabin and relax. With the climax of the flight rapidly drawing near, all nerves and senses were attuned to the goal that was almost at hand, even though a strong head wind had developed, holding their speed to 90 miles an hour. Shortly past 12 o'clock midnight it was a new day, November 29, when Byrd hauled out the sextant to take a reading on the sun and it showed their position to be within an hour's flying time from "90 Degrees South," the location of the South Pole.

As the hour hand moved near 1 A.M., the eastern mountains began dropping from view, one by one, leaving the horizon a circular line of blue around the plateau. With the Pole now actually in sight, Byrd was tense as he watched the chronometers, the compasses, and the drift indicators. As he prepared to resume the pilot's duties, Balchen saw dark clouds gathering in the east and a polar storm was on its way. Getting back to the Queen Maud Range in bright sunlight would be difficult enough, but high winds and poor visibility would create even more serious problems in getting through the pass.

Balchen returned to the pilot's seat and at 1:10 A.M., the countdown began. Byrd swung his sextant into position again. The position was 89 Degrees, 56 Minutes South. The Pole was barely six miles away, and the *Floyd Bennett* was on course, moving at a mile and a half a minute. Now it was a matter of watching the clock. When the hands pointed to 1:14 A.M., Byrd sent a message forward to June:

MY CALCULATIONS INDICATE WE HAVE REACHED THE VICINITY OF THE SOUTH POLE. FLYING HIGH FOR A SURVEY. SOON TURN NORTH.

June relayed this over the radio to Little America, but the signal didn't stop there. The base was in direct contact with the New York *Times* radio station in New York City, and

Byrd's message traveled on through the air waves, thousands of miles north to Times Square where it was transmitted by loudspeaker to the thousands who jammed the streets for blocks around.

The temperature was 15-below zero and the visibility was only fair as the plane circled above the Pole. The only sounds were drone of the engines and the hum of McKinley's camera. Below them there were no mountains, no life, no water—nothing but the ice of the Antarctic. Byrd opened the trapdoor and the little American flag, weighted with the stone from Floyd Bennett's grave, fluttered down toward the white plateau. Then they turned and headed for Little America, far to the north on the edge of the continent.

Now the clouds were growing darker along the eastern horizon, challenging the plane to a race with the mountain passes as the finish line. Byrd set the return course along the 168th meridian toward Axel Heiberg Glacier—a route east of the one they had taken on the way to the plateau. This course would give them a look at more unexplored country, and also bring them to the supply depot at the foot of the Queen Maud Range where gasoline could be taken on board.

In spite of threatening clouds, there was a friendly, helpful side to the weather. The head wind which previously had cut their speed, was now a tail wind—blowing with even more force than before. Balchen climbed several hundred feet higher where he found the wind even stronger, boosting them at 125 miles per hour. Outrunning the storm, they flew down the Axel Heiberg Glacier and landed at the foot of the Queen Maud mountains at 5 A.M.

Here they took on 200 gallons of fuel from their cache, leaving all the food for the geological party. In the air again, they flew on across the Ice Shelf and four hours later the radio spires of Little America came into view. When the *Floyd Bennett* came down to a triumphant landing, it was like Spitsbergen all over again, with Byrd and his companions being carried to the mess hall for a rousing celebration.

Byrd, Balchen, June, and McKinley had made Antarctic his-

Richard E. Byrd, one of the legendary explorers of our time. The rank of rear admiral was awarded him by an act of Congress and President Roosevelt called him "Admiral of the Poles." (*Brown Brothers*)

tory, and for the third time in four years Dick Byrd was a national hero. President Herbert Hoover wired his congratulations, and the world heaped lavish praise on the young Virginian and his companions who had pushed back the aerial frontiers of the world. Byrd now claimed both Poles—and a few years later Balchen won a special place in polar history when he became the first to pilot a plane over both poles.

Even before he returned to the United States, Commander Byrd was promoted to rear admiral by a special act of Congress—and he became known as "The Admiral of the Poles." As for Bernt Balchen, the exceedingly able and versatile young man from Norway, honors were given to him rather grudgingly —or so many of his fellow airmen felt. During World War II he performed other feats equally important and perhaps more dangerous. Eventually, after years had gone by, Congress did give him a colonel's eagles in the U. S. Air Force. But for the fame he deserves, he may have to wait till the Muse of History gets around to it, a hundred years from now.

Still no one had succeeded in flying non-stop across the wide expanse of the mid-Pacific Ocean, all the way from Asia to America. The airman who did it, a barnstorming wing-walker whose pals called him "Upside-Down Pang."

CHAPTER XIII

"Pang" Flies the Pacific

It happened on an autumn afternoon during the barnstorming era of the "Roaring Twenties" with the New York *Times* telling the story:

"Major Clyde (Upside-Down) Pangborn, one of the few aviators to perfect the art of flying a plane upside down, caused a sensation at Teterboro Airport this afternoon when the engine of his G. D. Standard plane went dead while he was flying head downwards at a height of 3000 feet. Thousands at the Airshow feared that the stunt flier would be killed as his machine commenced to drop, but Pangborn shoved the nose of the plane down in order to give the aircraft increased speed, and then after a drop of about 1000 feet he righted his ship and glided to the ground, making a perfect three-point landing."

The fine art of press agentry probably had a hand in shaping this thrilling story of Clyde Pangborn's miraculous escape, but nevertheless, such episodes were for years a part of Pang's everyday life. The date of this particular brush with death was September 5, 1927, and for several years he had been barnstorming through the United States with the well-known Gates Flying Circus—an organization of stunt fliers, wing-walkers, and parachute-jumpers. These daredevils kept the local citizens awestruck with their aerial acrobatics. As chief pilot and part-owner of the company, Pangborn was in charge of a fleet of five planes that flew from one town to another, taking passengers on short hops as soon as the afternoon's aerial acrobatics were over. The customers paid fees ranging from $5 to $25, and Pangborn himself introduced thousands to the thrills of aviation.

Most of them were enjoying their first flight, even though Pang once said in telling about his experiences: "They were flying in planes that wouldn't even be allowed to leave the ground today. They held their breath through loops, rolls, spins, and other stunts—a procedure with passengers that today would result in a jail sentence for the pilot. We stunted for a number of reasons," he explained. "It was good psychology, although we didn't call it by that name then. It not only drew crowds, the stunting did more than that. Any ship that could stand it had to be good. The man who flew it had to be good, too. When the history of aviation is written, if there is any place in it for me, I would prefer to be known as the pilot who barnstormed continuously for eleven years in every state of the Union and who carried 150,000 passengers safely during those days."

But Pangborn was destined for an even more important place in the history of aviation. Within four years after he thrilled the crowds at Teterboro, he was to fly around the world, and even more important, he was to make a 4558-mile non-stop flight across the Pacific from Japan to the United States—a feat which had no precedent in aviation annals. The career which led to this crowning achievement began when Clyde Pangborn, at the age of four, learned a little about high altitudes by dangling from the windows of buildings in Seattle.

A native of the State of Washington, Pangborn was twenty-two years old in 1915 when he received a degree in civil engineering from the University of Idaho. He served a brief hitch as a deputy sheriff in Shoshone County, Idaho—in fact, he looked like a Western sheriff out of Zane Grey or Owen Wister. When the country went to war, he enlisted as a flying cadet in the U. S. Army Signal Corps and was commissioned a second lieutenant upon completion of military flight training. Throughout World War I, he served as an instructor at Ellington Field near Houston, Texas, and when he received his discharge papers in 1919, he began his commercial flying career as an aerial acrobat and barnstormer.

Pangborn was in Syracuse, New York, in 1929, trying to set a flight endurance record when he met Hugh Herndon, Jr., a twenty-five-year-old sportsman who had spent two years on the campus of Princeton University before leaving to work in the oil fields of Oklahoma and Texas. His job in the petroleum country was easily obtained because his grandfather, John J. Carter, was head of the Carter Oil Company—one of the major producers for Standard Oil. Later, Herndon went to Paris to spend a summer and while there he took flying lessons, winning a pilot's license. After he returned to the United States and met Pangborn in Syracuse, the two joined forces on a barnstorming tour that carried them through thirty-two states. In the year 1930 alone they gave some 85,000 passengers their first plane rides. Then, one evening while they were resting up from a hard day at the airfield, they decided to fly around the world, hoping to set a new record.

During the last week of June 1931, Wiley Post and Harold Gatty left New York in their plane, the *Winnie Mae*, and completed a sensational flight around the world. Following a course just a few degrees below the Arctic Circle, they made it in 8 days, 15 hours and 51 minutes. Less than a month later, on July 28, Pangborn and Herndon took off from New York in their red Bellanca monoplane and headed eastward across the Atlantic, determined to beat the Post-Gatty record.

Only two weeks before departing, Herndon had married Mary Ellen Farley of Loudonville, New York, daughter of William W. Farley, State Chairman of the Democratic Party. In planning their round-the-world flight, the Pangborn-Herndon team purchased their plane and arranged the other financial details through a group of backers, including Herndon's wealthy socialite mother, Mrs. Russell Boardman. Their cabin plane,

Clyde Pangborn (left) and his co-pilot Hugh Herndon, Jr., with their plane at Floyd Bennett Field in Brooklyn, New York, shortly before the first non-stop trans-Pacific trip. Pangborn was an early barnstorming stunt flier. (*Wide World Photos*) the *Miss Veedol*, was not as fast as the one used by Post and Gatty, but it could carry more gasoline and fewer stops would be necessary for refueling. The 425-hp Pratt & Whitney engine gave their Bellanca a top speed of 150 miles per hour, and the extra-large wing provided more lift than many standard models of the same type.

Halfway across the Atlantic, Pangborn and Herndon ran into some extremely bad weather and lost their bearings, even though they managed to land at Moylesgrove, Wales, after a trans-ocean flight of 32 hours. Stopping briefly at London's Croydon Aerodrome, they continued on to Berlin where they arrived about 22 hours behind the Post-Gatty schedule. Confident they could make up this lost time, they flew on to Moscow and then over the Urals to Siberia. After battling through the worst kind of weather, they finally reached Khabarovsk where their plane suffered a damaged wing while landing at the town's muddy airport. By now they were 27½ hours behind the Post-Gatty timetable. Forced to pause long enough to repair the wing and delayed even further by torrential storms over Siberia, they decided it would be impossible to beat the record set by Post and Gatty. So they gave up trying. Then, only a few days later, several telegrams arrived from American friends in Tokyo, urging them to try for a $25,000 prize offered by a Japanese newspaper for the first non-stop flight from Japan across the North Pacific to the United States. All of which was the beginning of the dramatic story of how they succeeded, through failure.

Pangborn and Herndon decided to seize this opportunity to retrieve something from the shambles of their world flight. First, they wired the American Embassy in Tokyo, seeking help in obtaining permission to fly over Japanese territory, but in their haste to get away they didn't wait for a reply. Japan, at that time, just happened to be at war in Manchuria and the Tokyo military authorities had laid down a strict set of regulations against flying over certain fortified areas. Whereupon, innocently enough, Pangborn and Herndon took off from Khabarovsk without a permit, and flew straight into the biggest international incident of the year.

On their monoplane they carried a 16-mm motion picture camera, and as they flew over the northern Japanese island of Hokkaido they photographed areas which, so the Japanese claimed, were fortified with concealed defenses. Every warship in the vicinity picked up their trail, and when they arrived at Tokyo's Tachikawa Airport on August 6, they were promptly arrested by the Japanese and charged with espionage.

Herndon explained that photography was merely their hobby, and they had only taken a few souvenir pictures of some ships and fishing boats along the coastline—nothing of a military nature. But the police were unconvinced. Furthermore, they accused the fliers of violating fifty-five separate Japanese military regulations. Their plane was seized, and both fliers were placed under house arrest and restricted to their quarters in the Imperial Hotel. A trial followed in Tokyo's District Court and, about a week later, the judge rendered his decision. Both were found guilty, and told to either pay fines of $1050 each, or spend 205 days in jail at hard labor. Their films were confiscated, but they were allowed to retain ownership of their plane.

Pangborn and Herndon were stunned by the verdict, for they had no funds with which to pay the fines. The American newspapers of course covered the trial's proceedings, and Mrs. Boardman and the other financial backers quickly cabled money for the fines along with some extra funds needed to get the plane in shape for a trans-Pacific flight.

Then, after the fines were paid, new complications arose the moment Pangborn and Herndon announced their intention to fly to the United States in a bid for that $25,000 prize. Already, several unsuccessful attempts had been made to win the award, and Tokyo authorities had ruled that no further Pacific flights would be made until they certified each plane as being "in condition" for the trip. For several weeks they argued and negotiated to no avail, until finally the U. S. State Department interceded and the Japanese, at long last, gave their permission. However, there were strings attached. They would be allowed only one attempt and if it failed—they would have to return home by steamer.

During the last week of September, they worked frantically to get their plane ready for the flight, and do it before the Japanese again changed their minds. They enlisted the help of American friends in rigging the wheels with steel pins and cables so the entire landing gear could be dropped into the sea as soon as they were out over the Pacific, thereby lightening the plane's weight by 300 pounds and decreasing wind resistance by about 17 percent. This bold plan meant they would have to make a belly-landing when they arrived in the United States. Still, Pang was convinced that the loss of weight and drag would provide the extra range—through an increase in fuel and airspeed —needed to cross the vast Pacific non-stop. It was also highly necessary that the rigging work be carried out in secret. The Japanese would never permit the plane to leave if they learned the landing wheels would be dropped into the ocean after the takeoff.

After several days of strenuous work, the rigging was completed and metal strips were bolted into the plane's underside to reinforce the fuselage against the prospective belly landing. The runway at Tokyo's airport was not long enough for their heavily loaded plane and the nearest suitable takeoff point was at Sabishiro Beach, some 300 miles north of the capital. So, on September 29, Pangborn and Herndon flew the plane to that more preferable jumping-off point. Still wary of the fliers' intentions, the Japanese forced them to fly well out to sea away from the coastline—an edict which added another hundred miles to their trip.

They were ready to take off on October 2, but just as they were getting into the plane, they discovered their maps were mysteriously missing—lost, strayed, or stolen. For weeks they had received threatening letters from the Black Dragon Society, an organization of super-patriotic Japanese, and the first impulse was to place the blame there. But, regardless of explanations, it all meant a delay of at least 24 hours until a new set of maps could be secured.

The plane was loaded with 915 gallons of gasoline and 45 gallons of oil, with special tanks in the cabin holding most of the fuel. This brought the aircraft's total weight to 9000 pounds which Pangborn estimated to be a new record for wing-loading. Still the plane carried no radio, no liferafts, no oxygen for use at high altitudes, no parachutes, and no cushions to sit on. It was just as though two barnstorming pilots were taking off on a weekend excursion across the Pacific.

With everything in readiness on Saturday, October 3, Herndon's twenty-seventh birthday, and with favorable weather reported out over the western Pacific, they climbed into the cabin and prepared to take off. The day was clear and cloudless as Pangborn assumed the controls for the first leg of the flight northward to Hokkaido and the Kurile Islands. Then at 2:01 P.M., Pacific Standard Time, the plane began to roll along the sandy beach.

Even though they had carefully calculated the weight and load factors, Pangborn and Herndon were not sure the Bellanca would rise from the beach. As the engine roared full throttle, Henrdon kept his hand on the dump valve, ready for any emergency, while Pangborn's two hands were on the stick, fighting to get the ship off the rough ground. The air speed mounted slowly—50, 60, 70 miles per hour—but still they were not flying. Even when the airspeed indicator showed 90, the wheels bounded off the sand only to settle back again. Then at a hundred miles an hour, they finally cleared the beach and were on their way.

A little more than two hours later they passed over Nemuro, a town on a neck of land that protrudes out into the Pacific from the island of Hokkaido. Here, Herndon checked the compass and it was squarely on 72 degrees, the reading they figured would eventually bring them over the coast of Canada. As they flew on to the northeast, a swirling fog covered most of the Kuriles—a chain of thirty-two small volcanic islands that derive their name from the Russian word, *kurit*, meaning "to smoke." Pangborn took the plane to more than 8000 feet to get above the highest of these volcanic peaks, although aside from the fog the weather was good.

When they reached a point about 300 miles out of Sabishiro Beach, Pang carefully checked the instrument panel and listened to the motor to make certain everything was in good working order. Then he pulled that secret cable rigging and the wheels fell away into a long dive toward the ocean. They had now passed their Rubicon. If engine trouble should force them to return to Japan, they undoubtedly would be jailed for coming back to belly-land without the landing gear. And, if they should be forced down at sea, there was no liferaft on board. That was the somber side of the picture. On the bright side, the departure of the heavy wheels had already increased their speed by 15 miles an hour. Even so, they still had a long, long way to go.

Night was falling when they reached a point about 500 miles up the coast of the Kuriles, and Herndon took over the controls as the plane turned out toward the open Pacific. In the distance the eastern sky was a mass of lofty clouds, while already the icy Arctic air was beginning to penetrate the cabin. Hoping to find a helpful tail wind, Herndon climbed the Bellanca to about 10,000 feet, only to find the crest of the clouds still above him. All the while the cabin temperature was dropping steadily as the outside air grew colder and colder. It was numbing their stockinged-feet for both Herndon and Pangborn were flying without their shoes—a quaint custom they had picked up in Japan.

Weaving through the open spaces in the clouds, they time and again tried to reach higher altitudes, but the heavy gasoline load kept dragging them back. Pangborn, weary from loss of sleep, took a short nap and then moved into the cockpit again. Just as he seated himself an icy glaze began forming along the wings, and within minutes the plane was coated with a dangerous load of ice. Giving the engine full throttle, they struggled on up to 17,000 feet where the clouds were spread out below them like cotton fields in the moonlight. Then, as they approached the vicinity of Attu at the western end of the Aleutian chain, the clouds rose around them again—and they could go no higher.

From the very moment he jettisoned the wheels into the ocean, Pangborn had been conscious of a new problem that could spell disaster whenever they came down to land. When the wheels fell off, two landing gear rods were left dangling and flying in the wind, and both might pierce the fuselage with fatal results when the plane plopped to the ground. Telling Herndon to take over the controls, Pang pulled himself out of the cockpit and, like the wing-walker of old, he began crawling out on the icy wing. While the plane droned on through the clouds, 17,000 feet above the Pacific, he firmly gripped a strut with one hand, using the other to unscrew the dangling rods and send them hurtling to the sea. This almost incredible feat took twenty minutes. Then carefully he made his way back to the cockpit, grinning like a barnstormer who considered it all part of the day's work.

For the next few hours they kept the engine on full power, hoping to ride out of the clouds. Shortly after they passed Dutch Harbor in the Aleutians, the ceiling did lower and they were flying above the cloud layer once more. It was already Sunday morning, and just before noon an Aleutian amateur radio operator at False Pass on Unimak Island heard an airplane passing overhead, but he couldn't see it because of the overcast. This was the first indication that the fliers had reached the halfway mark in their trans-Pacific flight. Now only the Gulf of Alaska remained between them and the coast of Canada.

A warmer strata of air had melted the ice on the wings, but as they flew on over the Gulf, they lost their bearings and Pangborn had the uneasy feeling they were heading southward to the mid-Pacific—perhaps even toward Hawaii. The flight through the clouds had placed a heavy drain on the fuel supply, and their uncertainty grew into apprehension as the hours passed with no sight of land. Then, just as the sun was setting behind them, they spotted the Queen Charlotte Islands off the coast of British Columbia. Turning their course south, they soon came over a flashing beacon on Vancouver Island and this meant Puget Sound and Seattle lay just ahead.

They were flying above the clouds at 16,000 feet—without oxygen—and keeping a wary eye on the gasoline gauge when the lights of a city glared through the undercast. Was it Seattle? There was no way of knowing for sure until, straight ahead, they saw the clouds wreathed around the lofty summit of Mount Rainier. With Seattle beneath them it was early Monday morning, and the time had arrived for an important decision.

Pangborn still had hopes of landing, installing new wheels on the record-setting Bellanca, and then taking off again with a heavy load of gasoline. For he was under the impression they were still eligible to win a second $25,000 prize which Colonel W. E. Easterwood was offering for the first one-stop flight from Japan to Dallas, Texas. But they needed a long runway for the new takeoff, which in those days Seattle didn't have. Three times they circled near Mount Rainier while discussing a course of action, then Pangborn decided to fly 200 miles farther east to Spokane's airport where he knew the runway would be long enough.

Nearly two hours later when the plane arrived over Spokane, they found that city fogbound—a landing there was impossible. Pang wanted clear weather for a "belly landing" that would keep them out of the hospital, so they turned around again and headed west—this time with the city of Wenatchee, Washington, as their goal. Wenatchee happened to be Pang's home town, and among the crowd waiting at the airport were his mother, Opal, and brother, Percy. Pangborn knew almost every foot of the ground there and was confident he could bring the plane in safely. Furthermore, he had originally planned to end the flight at the old home town.

By now it was well past dawn and the fog had lifted over central Washington as they came above Wenatchee. But when the plane came in from the east instead of the west, the big crowd on the airfield was confused, believing it couldn't be Pangborn—he was supposed to be flying in from the Pacific. Then the crowd caught a glimpse of the plane's red color and knew it must be the round-the-world Bellanca. Cheers went up, only to become mingled with groans when they saw the landing wheels were missing. What had happened?

Pang was all set now and confident—as a flier of many years of experience who could do almost anything with a plane. Down he came in a long glide, and when the armored belly struck the dirt runway it skidded along in a cloud of dust that, for moments, hid the crowd from view. The Bellanca bumped along for 30 yards or more, and then went up on its nose, smashing the propeller. As the crowd surged forward, two grimy figures

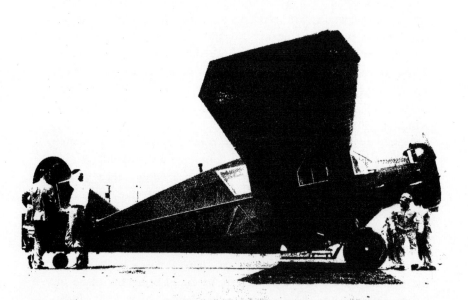

The Bellanca plane, *Miss Veedol*, flown by Pangborn and Herndon, Jr., on their unprecedented 4558-mile non-stop flight from Japan to the United States, 1931. The plane's extra-large wing span provided surplus lift, and its high fuel load capacity made the non-stop trip possible. (*Brown Brothers*)

climbed out of the cabin. Herndon had a handkerchief in hand, dabbing at a cut over his eyebrow, and Pangborn was limping slightly as though he had hurt his leg. Even so, their faces were wreathed in smiles as they stood in the center of the cheering throng. Pangborn's mother, her nerves on edge from two nights of waiting, wept as she embraced her son and exclaimed:

"Why you don't even look tired!"

They had flown 4558 miles across the Pacific in 41 hours and 13 minutes, and now Pangborn was having the homecoming of his life. But it was an out-of-towner who provided them with their greatest thrill. A Japanese representative of the Tokyo newspaper, *Asahi,* came running forward, waving a check for $25,000. "So very glad to see you," he shouted as he handed over the check, and as it turned out, that would be their only monetary reward. In Dallas, when he heard the news, Colonel Easterwood was lavish in his praise, although he said Pangborn and Herndon had not qualified for that Texas prize.

Hugh Herndon, Jr., later became a regional director for Trans World Airlines, and died of a heart attack in Cairo in 1952. As for his round-the-world pilot, poker-faced Clyde Pangborn, during World War II he made 170 trans-ocean flights as a ferry pilot for the RAF—flying bombers and transports to the United Kingdom from Canada and the United States. Then, after the war, as a test pilot he flew many new and radically designed aircraft, including Vince Buranelli's *Flying Wing.* Pang also died of a heart attack, in 1958, after one of the most impressive and colorful careers in the annals of aviation.

While fliers of many nations were winning wide acclaim with history making flights, where were the Russians? The answer is obvious—they were sticking to their aerial knitting, doing their flying within their own spacious homeland that sprawls over two great continents. Now they were to startle the world with a sensational flight from Moscow across the North Pole to the United States.

CHAPTER XIV

From Moscow to the U.S.A. via the North Pole

It wasn't until the 1930s that Valery, Georgi, Sasha, and their air-minded comrades flew out of Russia to explore the skies over other lands. On May 21, 1937, a four-engined Russian ski-plane circled out of a clear Arctic sky and came down on an ice floe only 12 miles from the North Pole. Even though eleven years before, in 1926, Richard E. Byrd and Floyd Bennett had become the first to fly to the North Pole and back, and a year later in 1927, George Hubert Wilkins and Ben Eielson confounded the skeptics by proving it possible to land on the ice of the Arctic Ocean and take off again, it was a Russian aviator, Mikhail Vodopyanov, who finally became the first man to land a plane close to the North Pole.

Vodopyanov did not come down at the Pole simply to prove it could be done. With him aboard his big *ANT-4* airplane were four other Russians who were disembarking to begin one of the most unusual and exciting Arctic expeditions in the annals of polar exploration. Their leader was Ivor Papanin, a Soviet scientist who, like Fridtjof Nansen of Norway, had long advocated putting a manned research station on an ice floe and then letting it drift across the Arctic Ocean while the scientists making the journey tried to unlock the secrets of the North. Recruited to join Papanin on the drifting ice floe were two scientists, Peter Shirshov and Eugene Fyodorov, and a radioman, Ernest Krenkel, who, as a wireless operator in the Arctic seven years before, had established the first pole-to-pole contact with Little America in the Antarctic.

Two weeks after Papanin and his group arrived, three more Russian planes touched down on that ice floe, bringing a pink silk tent with double-decker beds, a flooring made of eiderdown and tarpaulin, clothing of reindeer skin, caps of wolverine, and underwear of merino cashmere. The supplies also included two specially designed gas heaters for cooking forty-six different kinds of food products which had been brought along in water-tight cans. Rifles, sledges, canoes, a half-ton of scientific apparatus, and a windmill-powered radio were placed on the ice floe. Cannonballs had been dropped from the sky to make sure the ice was strong enough to hold the scientists and all their gear.

Their supply mission accomplished, the four planes flew back to Moscow, leaving the four men on the ice with their mascot, "Happy," one of the few Arctic dogs that was never called upon to pull a sledge. Then, a week after this polar odyssey began, a radio message came through from Moscow, reminding Papanin that the Kremlin was counting on him for some extremely important information:

"You are to supply weather reports and wireless contacts for Comrade Chkalov's flight to America over the North Pole!"

For weeks the world—or the part of it that was air-minded—had been kept guessing and waiting for an impending Soviet announcement. There was the same atmosphere of expectancy that occurred later in connection with the first Russian space launchings. The capitals of the world, particularly Washington, were buzzing with rumors and counterrumors of Soviet plans to attempt a sensational 6000-mile non-stop flight from Moscow across the North Pole to California. In a terse announcement, State Department officials disclosed that an unidentified Russian aviator had been granted official permission to fly over the United States, although they refused to elaborate and all further inquiries were referred to the Soviet Embassy. At the same time, government officials in Ottawa promised that any Russian fliers who flew down the Canadian west coast would receive full cooperation from Canada's radio stations. Even in the face of these disclosures, Soviet officials remained darkly silent about their plans.

Meanwhile, inside the Kremlin walls in Moscow, the commissars and weather experts were studying the maps, preparing for a flight that would give Russia a place among the world's great aviation powers—if it were successful. Determined not to be left behind in the race to dominate the skies, Soviet experts for years had studied the polar route as the shortest and most logical way to reach North America. Despite their careful planning, the first serious attempt to fly non-stop from Moscow over the Pole to the U.S.A. had ended in an embarrassing failure in 1935. Sigismund Levanevsky, in those days referred to as the "Lindbergh of Russia," left the Soviet capital with two companions, Victor Lenchenko and Georgi Baidukov. All went well with their *ANT-25* monoplane until they arrived over the Barents Sea north of the European mainland. Oil suddenly spurted from an engine, and Levanevsky decided to turn around and go back to the nearest landing field, even though Baidukov tried to persuade him to continue the flight when it became apparent the leak had stopped.

No one was more chagrined over this failure than Premier Joseph Stalin himself, and for two years he held a tight rein on any further attempts to fly over the Pole to the United States until success could be reasonably assured. Most of the blame for Levanevsky's fiasco was attributed to a lack of knowledge about Arctic flying conditions, and one of the main reasons for setting Papanin and his fellow scientists adrift on the ice floe was to remedy this. To reduce the chances of miscalculation even further, Stalin personally suggested a non-stop training flight of nearly 6000 miles into Eastern Siberia as a test for another attempt to reach California. As it turned out, the Siberian flight was a great success, and the three men who carried it out won the highly coveted designations, "Heroes of the Soviet Union."

In the pre-World War II period, aviators the world over argued about the real or imagined flying traits of the various nationalities. Some said the Japanese were not natural fliers, while the Chinese were; that the methodical Germans excelled at precision aviation, and the Spanish sometimes let their Latin temperament interfere with their judgment. As for the Russians? They were said to be careless about keeping their gas tanks full. Regardless of their other characteristics, the Soviet "flying *troika*," the three men who distinguished themselves on that first non-stop flight across Siberia, had two things in common—none could speak English and they had never been to the United States before.

Their leader was Valery Chkalov, a thirty-three-year-old test pilot whose father was a fireman on a river boat that plied the Volga. Chkalov had joined the Red Army at the age of fifteen, fighting in the Revolution as a foot-soldier before entering a pilot's school and becoming one of the USSR's first military fliers. As a youth, he had broken his leg in an accident, and throughout his career he often experienced extreme discomfort in the cramped quarters of a cockpit while flying over long distances. His co-pilot was thirty-year-old Georgi Baidukov, the same flier who had accompanied Levanevsky on that unsuccessful attempt to reach the United States. The son of a Siberian railwayman, Baidukov had run away from home at the age of eight, and later was expelled from a children's home because of what was officially termed his "rebellious nature." The third, and oldest, member of the crew was forty-year-old Alexander (Sasha) Beliakov who, like Chkalov, had served in the Red Army during the Revolution, soon afterward became an expert in aerial navigation and well-known as a professor at the Military Air Academy. Beliakov had inherited his teaching ability from his father who was an instructor on a collective farm near Moscow.

By early 1937, the same trio was seeking Stalin's permission to tackle that yet-unfulfilled mission of soaring across the North Pole to America. But they faced stiff competition from Sigismund Levanevsky who, despite his previous failure, was trying to get another expedition off the ground with himself as the leader. In his favor, he had the support of Stalin who still regarded him as Russia's leading Arctic flier.

Matters came to a dramatic climax at 4 o'clock on the afternoon of May 25 when Stalin summoned Levanevsky, Chkalov, and Baidukov to his office in the Kremlin. As the fliers entered the presence of the man who had more power than a czar, Stalin was seated behind a long conference table with Kliment Voroshilov, Commissar of Defense, and Vyacheslav Molotov, who, at that time, was Chairman of the Council of People's Commissars. Stalin arose and came forward to greet his visitors and then rejoined the commissars as the fliers seated themselves on the other side of the table. On the flat surface between them stood a shining new model of the *ANT-25*—the plane which made the long flight across Siberia.

"So," Stalin began, his eyes smiling, "the earth is not good enough for you? You want to fly again?"

Chkalov took it upon himself to make the reply. "Yes, Comrade Stalin, the time has come. We're here to ask the government's permission for a flight over the North Pole."

For several moments there was silence, but encouragement was written all over the commissars' faces.

"And just where do you intend to go?" asked Stalin. "Which of you will make the report on your plans?"

At this point Voroshilov spoke up, winking at Baidukov as he began: "Comrade Stalin, there's really more than one group represented and Baidukov here is in a ticklish spot. Levanevsky and Chkalov have different ideas about this flight, but both of them want Baidukov as co-pilot."

"Aha!" said Stalin, with a searching look at the fliers. "Factions, eh? Well, let's hear from you first, Comrade Chkalov."

In as few words as possible, Chkalov outlined his plan to cross the Arctic by way of the Pole to California and stoutly maintained that the single-engined *ANT-25* should be the plane. He summed up with a formal request for permission to make the flight with Baidukov as his co-pilot and Beliakov as navigator. "The *ANT-25* has been tuned up," Chkalov concluded, "and our *troika* is ready to fly."

Levanevsky then arose to state his case and, placing another model on the table to illustrate his plan, he argued in favor of a four-engined plane instead of the single-motored aircraft which Chkalov believed could do the job. Stalin and the commissars listened in silence, and finally Baidukov took the floor to throw his full support behind Chkalov's conception of how the flight should be carried out. Baidukov came up with what may have been the decisive argument. He pointed out that the single-engined *ANT-25* was entirely capable of setting a new world's record for long distance non-stop flying—an achievement which undoubtedly would be acclaimed with great enthusiasm in a country hungry for aviation honors.

The fliers had their say, the three-hour meeting came to an end, and before the day was out Stalin signed an order officially sanctioning the flight with Chkalov, Baidukov, and Beliakov as the crew. In making his decision, he was possibly influenced by an awareness of Levanevsky's previous failure on the same mission, or perhaps he was fascinated with the prospect of winning a long-distance record for Russia. In any event, Stalin insisted that if unfavorable flying conditions should develop along the route, the fliers must land somewhere in Canada instead of trying to reach the United States. Chkalov, Baidukov, and Beliakov accepted this apparent concern for their safety with proper appreciation, but they knew a forced landing in the rugged mountains of western Canada would be something easier said than done.

The moment they learned of Stalin's decision, Chkalov and Baidukov called Sasha Beliakov away from the Air Academy and together they went directly to Sholkovo Aerodrome to take a look at their plane. The hangar door was rolled back, revealing a low-slung monoplane with a huge 122-foot red wing and a gray fuselage that extended 44 feet from nose to tail. Entirely of metal construction except for the fabric on the wing, the *ANT-25* had been designed by Professor A. N. Tupoleff,

chief engineer of Moscow's Central Aero-Hydrodynamic In-
stitute, and the plane derived its name from his three initials.
Especially engineered for long-distance flying over the Arctic,
the Soviet-made 12-cylinder, 950-hp engine was one of the
largest in use at the time. Streamlined with retractable landing
wheels and fuel tanks built into the wings, the plane weighed
about 12½ tons when fully loaded with crew, equipment, and
nearly 2000 gallons of gasoline. Under normal conditions, the
cruising speed ranged between 85 and 100 miles an hour. Immediately behind the engine was the pilot's cabin, complete
with all modern instruments including those for blind flying.
Next came a sleeping compartment, and then the navigator's
cabin. Toward the rear was still another compartment equipped
with a set of emergency controls which could be used while
changing pilots in flight.

For the next three weeks, preparations were made at almost
a frantic pace. Emergency supplies were loaded on board, including a tent, electric stove, food, rifles and cartridges, sleeping bags, and other survival items should they be forced down
in the Canadian wilds. Sasha Beliakov gathered together all the
available charts and navigational material and, while stuffing his
duffel bag, he noticed a copy of Vilhjalmur Stefansson's book,
The Friendly Arctic, lying on a table. It was a big, heavy volume, and should he take it along? He picked the book up and
placed it in the bag with the other material.

Six hours before the scheduled takeoff time, Sasha hurried
to a barber shop for a shave and a haircut, with Baidukov
accusing him of plotting to charm a female walrus in case they
should have to land on the ice. Later, just after Sasha returned to
quarters, Valery Chkalov arrived and gave both his flying mates
a bawling out in some choice purple Russian for their failure
to get a few hours of precious sleep. The tension mounted as a
big touring car drove up to carry them to the airport and, when
they arrived on the runway, a great crowd was on hand. Then
the *ANT-25* was rolled to the end of the runway and the fliers,
clad in caps and turtle-neck sweaters, leaned from the cabin

doors to bid the crowd farewell. Russia's number one aeronautical engineer, Professor Tupoleff, his hands trembling, embraced
each of the aviators in turn. There were more handclasps, more
embraces, and then Chkalov climbed into the pilot's cabin and
took the controls.

A white flag flashed across the runway, and the roar of the
engine split the silence as the plane began to roll down the
concrete strip. In moments, the *ANT* was in the air, soaring past
the nearby factory smokestacks, and then up into the clear
blue above Moscow. The date was Thursday, June 17, and the
clock read 5:05 P.M., Pacific Coast Time, as the Russian flight
to America began.

Chkalov took the plane to 1300 feet, far above the mist-
covered river valleys that wound their way through the green
woods and fields of the collective farms. The moment the plane
was airborne, Sasha tumbled into a sleeping bag and Baidukov
took over the navigator's cabin—the first shift in their planned
schedule of duty rotation. The cities of Kaliasin and Kashin
passed beneath, then the lake country, stretching away toward
the Barents Sea and the North Pole more than 2000 miles distant. Chkalov puffing on his pipeful of strong Russian tobacco,
climbed to 6500 feet only to see the weather go sour as a
heavy bank of clouds appeared on the northern horizon.

Beliakov, unable to sleep his full eight hours, awoke ahead
of time and Baidukov relinquished the navigator's cabin to get
a few hours' rest himself. Barely ten minutes after closing his
eyes, he felt someone pulling his leg and dragging him from
the bunk. It was Sasha, shouting, as he pointed to the floor.

"The oil is leaking somewhere!"

All around the navigator's hatch and radio apparatus the floor
was flooded with oil. Baidukov leaped to his feet and rushed
forward to inform Chkalov. Then, returning to the cabin,
Baidukov grabbed a rubberized bag and began mopping up the
oil, a process that clearly revealed the source of the "leak."
A thin stream of fluid was coming from a radiator but it was
merely the drainage, caused by pumping the oil line too far

above the halfway mark in the tank—not nearly so serious a condition as he had feared. Within minutes, the trickle died away and Baidukov returned to his sleeping bag, for soon now he was due to relieve Chkalov in the pilot's cabin.

The plane was cruising steadily at 6500 feet as it approached a massive cloud bank over the Kola Peninsula, the last neck of Russian mainland before the open Barents Sea. A stiff cross wind was blowing in from the west, harbinger of a cyclone the Moscow weathermen had warned would sweep the peninsula during the late evening hours. The heavily loaded plane was still flying too low to clear the clouds and when Baidukov awoke and took the controls, a white mist closed in around them.

Still smoking his pipe, Chkalov made his way back to the sleeping quarters and stretched out, but he couldn't close his eyes. Baidukov, as he settled into the pilot's chair, noted that the outside temperature was minus-3 degrees Centigrade. Flying blind now, he also saw a thick white frost gathering on the wings and creeping across the windows. Turning, he yelled to Chkalov who came forward, his eyes red from lack of sleep.

"Work the de-icer. Quick!" shouted Baidukov.

"Right away!" Chkalov yelled in reply as he headed for the pump.

The alcohol spurted from the nozzles, clearing the frozen glaze from the windows and the propeller blades, but ice was forming on the tail assembly—a condition that could send the *ANT* out of control. Baidukov, fighting to escape the clutches of the white devil, opened the throttle wide to begin a slow climb and when the plane reached 8200 feet, the rays of the sun broke through the clouds to the west. In minutes they emerged into the bright sunlight where the solar heat rapidly melted the ice from the tail.

Far below now, through the rifts in the clouds, Baidukov caught fleeting glimpses of the ice and snow on the Barents Sea. The Russian mainland was behind them and, from his post in the navigator's cabin, Sasha saw elbow-macaroni-shaped Novaya Zemlya gliding by to his right. These islands were a checkpoint in the sea, telling them they were on their course straight for the North Pole.

As they passed their thirteenth hour in the air, Chkalov returned to the pilot's cabin while Baidukov went aft to take over the navigation table. There he found Sasha with his head bowed wearily over the charts, his eyes bleary from exhaustion. Worse still, the sextant had been damaged.

The sun was still above them, but soon the skies to the west began to darken with another formidable array of clouds. Baidukov reached for the damaged sextant and found that, fortunately, it still contained a small bubble, just enough to permit a quick sighting on the sun. It showed they were drifting slightly off course to the east on a track that would take them over the western edge of Franz Josef Land, another group of Russian islands in the Arctic. Chkalov took the plane to 13,000 feet, swinging the course even more to the east to avoid the gathering storm. Still, the clouds rolled relentlessly around them and even though five hours remained on his shift, Chkalov decided to turn the pilot's chair over to his blind-flying expert, Baidukov.

"You take this stretch," Valery told him, "and anyway, my leg aches terribly."

Baidukov inwardly cursed this arrangement but he noticed that Chkalov's cheeks were hollow and drawn. Fatigue was clearly getting the better of him, and he crawled into a bunk to instantly fall asleep. With the visibility gone, Baidukov ascended to 13,600 feet and once again they were above the clouds. He had to fight off the temptation to put on the oxygen mask, knowing their supply had to be saved for possible emergencies ahead.

Chkalov awoke after only a few hours and Baidukov, his turn to be weary now, made his way back to the sleeping compartment. He slept only briefly before he was aroused by shouts from the pilot's cabin.

"Land! Land!"

It was Chkalov, pointing to the islands of the Franz Josef

Archipelago. He nosed the plane upward to 14,000 feet and more islands came into view, while Baidukov went back to the navigator's cabin where he found Sasha using the oxygen mask.

"How long before we reach the Pole?" Baidukov asked.

"Strong head winds," Sasha answered, removing the mask and handing it to Baidukov. "Probably not for another four or five hours."

Chkalov's game leg was still bothering him so he soon recalled Baidukov to the controls, and by now the plane was rapidly approaching the Pole. Here they were facing an interesting navigational challenge—the problem of precisely zeroing in on 90 Degrees North—the charted location of the North Pole. They were flying through a region where the meridians of longitude intersect at a tiny dot on the surface of the globe, and where the magnetic lines converge and cross in a welter of confusion. To navigate successfully, they must remain on their true course, fly across the Pole, and then pick up the 123rd meridian southward over Canada to California. Even the slightest deviation might send the plane far off its path, and their fuel supply couldn't last forever.

In the navigation cabin, the instruments were twirling and dipping crazily. Sasha wrote a note and took it forward, asking Baidukov to use the sun compass attached to the engine cowling directly in front of the pilot's chair—the same type instrument Byrd had used eleven years before on the *Josephine Ford*'s flight to the North Pole. A quick sighting on the high-riding sun confirmed the course and at exactly 8:10 P.M., Pacific Coast Time, the *ANT* was 13,600 feet above the Pole—27 hours after the takeoff from Moscow.

The clouds rolled beneath the wings again, blocking the ice-crusted sea from view. It would be impossible now to see Comrade Papanin and the others on the ice below. They couldn't be far away, but even the opportunity to talk with them was lost for as they had drawn near the Pole, the plane's radio went dead.

As the plane flew on southward toward the Arctic islands north of Canada, a tail wind developed and increased the speed to 125 miles an hour. Still, the rising layers of cumulus forced Baidukov to climb to 16,400 feet to maintain visibility. Chkalov came up to take over the cockpit, but his leg was still bothering him and Baidukov remained at the controls. Baidukov now was beginning to feel the grind himself and he resorted to the oxygen mask as he climbed even higher to stay above the ascending clouds. The *ANT* reached its ceiling at 18,700 feet and Baidukov still had to reckon with a massive white barrier of vapor that blocked his way. For nearly an hour he weaved the plane to and fro, trying to find a way through the wall, but it was futile and he had no recourse except to descend to lower altitudes.

In the downward glide a sudden spray of steam from the radiator doused the windscreen and froze into a solid layer of ice, shutting out the forward view. Reaching through a side window into the 100-mile-an-hour wind, Baidukov used a pocketknife to chop the ice away, only to be confronted with a new and more alarming hazard. The water-level gauge on the radiator had fallen to zero, raising the specter of a burned-out engine. Aroused by Baidukov's shouts, Chkalov quickly came to the rescue and poured new water into the tank until a normal condition was restored. Then, Fortune smiled not only once, but twice. Just as the pump began to draw again, the clouds cleared away, revealing a host of islands on the southern horizon and the Canadian mainland only a few miles away.

It was now 8 o'clock, Saturday morning, and for the first time since leaving Moscow it occurred to Chkalov and Baidukov that they were hungry. They pulled a few apples and oranges from a knapsack—but the fruit was frozen solid.

Even though the signals were faint, the radio had come to life and Sasha sent a message to the nearest Canadian station, reporting they were on course for the California coast with Oakland Airport near San Francisco as their goal. Crossing Banks Island and the Amundsen Gulf, they reached the Canadian

mainland at Cape Parry. Then, they flew on over the northern
Barren Lands to Great Bear Lake and soon picked up the trail
of MacKenzie River.

As they soared up the MacKenzie Valley, flecks of white
clouds drifted through the skies around them, and soon a great
storm was moving across their path from the east. The tanks
still contained enough fuel for at least twenty hours of flying,
but their oxygen supply was running low, and without it they
surely would find it impossible to take the higher altitudes over
the Canadian Rockies just ahead. If a lack of oxygen should
force them lower, the visibility hazards of a storm would be
fraught with danger.

As the clouds rolled in front of them, Baidukov climbed to
18,000—still, no sun. Faced with a desperate situation, he decided to change course and fly directly west to cross the Rockies
immediately. If all went well they would be above the Pacific
coastline by nightfall, and the problems of oxygen and altitude
would be behind them. As they passed the oxygen mask around,
the gauge showed barely an hour's supply left—mainly because
Chkalov had found it necessary to use it so often.

When the plane reached 20,000 feet Chkalov came forward
with his nose bleeding profusely, and nearly collapsed as he
relieved Baidukov at the controls. The moment he left the cockpit, Baidukov grabbed the oxygen mask again himself. The
time now was 3 P.M. They had been in flight 46 hours, and
began to wonder where it would all end—or if it ever would.

The exhausted Chkalov remained in the pilot's cabin exactly
one hour, then called for relief again. "Get up!" he urged
Baidukov, pulling him from the bunk. "Look how the clouds
are gathering." Then he crawled away as Baidukov wearily
took over again.

Now the plane was flying through clouds that hid the mountains, and Baidukov had to use the instrument panel to find his
way. Maintaining an altitude of about 20,000 feet, he was trying
to keep the plane on course in the turbulent gales when Sasha
passed him a note. It said all the oxygen was gone. No longer

could they remain at such heights, so Baidukov nosed the plane down with a fervent hope that the Rockies were behind them. The descent continued for a full hour until the altimeter read 13,000 feet. Then the clouds were no longer beneath them, and—there was the Pacific Ocean.

The coastline was to the east, hidden behind the clouds, but Chkalov was able to take a sextant reading in the setting sun. It placed their position above the Queen Charlotte Islands, 700 miles northwest of Seattle. As darkness fell over the sea, they were flying at night for the first time since takeoff. Even so, they had the reassuring knowledge it was only the ocean beneath them. No more mountains. But the clouds gathered around them again, battering the *ANT* with hail, sleet and rain. Confident over the open sea, Baidukov climbed the plane to 14,700 feet where the moon and stars were shining above.

Shortly before dawn the clouds cleared away, but the dwindling gasoline supply forced a revision of their plans. They still had enough gas for about five more hours, but they were bucking a head wind and no longer could they hope to reach Oakland. By stretching the fuel to the limit, there was a good chance of making it to Portland, Oregon. In the navigator's cabin, Sasha asked the Seattle radio operator for the frequency of the beacon at Bellingham, Washington. Then he passed a note to Baidukov: *Watch your radio-compass, and head for Bellingham.*

Flying southward over Washington with the plane at 10,000 feet, they approached Seattle. New clouds arose in the distance and Baidukov once again turned to the instrument panel, knowing that lofty Mount Rainer was somewhere near. Soon they were homing on the Portland radio-beacon, but they encountered heavy rain and had no way to check their course. Still, the radio signal was growing in intensity and soon it became so strong they were sure they must be right over Portland.

Baidukov glanced at the gasoline gauge and it showed the tanks were virtually empty. No choice now. They must descend

The Russian fliers, (from left to right) Alexander Beliakov, navigator; Valery Chkalov, pilot; and Georgi Baidukov, co-pilot, after landing at Vancouver, Washington, June 20, 1937. A fuel shortage had forced them to land en route to Oakland, California, from Moscow. (*Wide World Photos*)

The Russian fliers' single-engine *ANT-25* monoplane after being forced down at Vancouver, Washington, en route to Oakland, California, from Moscow. Premier Joseph Stalin had approved the flight to the U.S. after a successful non-stop 6000-mile trip across Siberia. (*Wide World Photos*)

through the clouds and hope to find an airport. Gradually, Baidukov eased the *ANT* downward until he spotted the Columbia River and, nearby, the city and suburbs of Portland. The airport appeared much too small for their plane, but on checking his map he saw there was another landing field just across the river at Vancouver, Washington. Baidukov promptly swung the plane in that direction and, with Chkalov standing nervously behind him, they began the slow descent to the runway.

"Give her some gas!" Chkalov shouted, apparently forgetting that the gauge already showed zero.

A light rain was falling as the wheels touched the soggy American earth and rolled across a roadway that intersected the landing strip. And so the first non-stop flight between Moscow and the United States had ended—600 miles short of its goal, still the Russians had flown 5288 miles. They had been in the air 63 hours and 17 minutes, finally coming down virtually out of gas, water, and oxygen.

The three sleepy-eyed Russian fliers stood beside their plane on the runway at Pearson Field, the U. S. Army's airfield at Vancouver Barracks across the river from Portland. American soldiers came running through the rain toward them, and there was a barrage of questions but no answers—the Russians could speak no English. As the fliers stood glumly in the crowd, trying to make themselves understood by sign language, George Kozmetsky, an American-born son of Russian parents, broke the ice by saying "hello" in their native tongue.

The time was 8:30 Sunday morning, and the commanding officer at Vancouver Barracks turned out to be none other than Brigadier General George C. Marshall who came forward to greet his unexpected guests from beyond the North Pole. With Kozmetsky joining the group as an interpreter, Marshall invited them to his home where they used the general's razor to remove their heavy beards and enjoy the luxury of a bath. In the kitchen, Mrs. Marshall was preparing a breakfast of bacon and eggs, and she increased the portions to include a trio of

Having their first breakfast since leaving Moscow are Russian fliers (left) Beliakov and (first from right and right) Chkalov and Baidukov. First from left is Soviet Ambassador Alexander A. Troyanovsky and in the center is United States General George C. Marshall, whose wife prepared the breakfast. Fruit the fliers had carried with them to eat had frozen over the North Pole. (*Wide World Photos*)

hungry fliers who had eaten little in more than 60 hours. At the same time, the general sent orderlies scurrying around the base for cognac—the drink the Russians said they wanted most.

Soon the highway bridge between Portland and Vancouver was jammed with traffic as thousands converged on the Army base to see the plane and the fliers. Within an hour after breakfast, the Russians were sound asleep in the Marshall home, and the general would permit no one to disturb them—not even a swarm of newsmen who arrived on the scene. A message of congratulations arrived from Joseph Stalin, President Franklin D. Roosevelt sent his best wishes, and the following day Chkalov, Baidukov, and Beliakov were guests of honor at a

Chamber of Commerce luncheon in Portland where they rode in a motorcade through streets lined with thousands of cheering Americans.

Even though the flight had failed to break the world's non-stop distance record, it was the second longest in history. The record was held by two French fliers, Maurice Rossi and Paul Dodos, who had flown more than 5600 miles non-stop from New York to Syria in 1933. Less than a month after the Russian fliers reached Vancouver Barracks, another Soviet plane took off from Moscow and flew non-stop to Los Angeles, a distance of 6262 miles—breaking the record of the two Frenchmen. This Russian plane also carried three fliers—pilot Mikhail Gromov, co-pilot Andree Yumashev and navigator Serge Danilin. Then, on August 12, 1937, Sigismund Levanevsky and five companions took off from Moscow in a four-motored plane on still a third flight to America. Soon after they crossed the North Pole, their radio went silent and the six men disappeared, never to be heard from again, although Sir Hubert Wilkins and a number of other famed Arctic pilots flew thousands of miles looking for them.

And what of Ivor Papanin and his three companions who were left adrift on that polar ice floe? For 274 days they floated across the Arctic Ocean, taking depth soundings and gathering other valuable scientific information, until finally on January 19, 1938, all four were taken safely on board a Russian vessel off Greenland—bringing another epic saga of the Arctic to an end.

Valery Chkalov plunged to his death on December 15, 1938, while testing a pursuit plane in Russia. He was given a state funeral in Moscow, with Premier Stalin leading the dignitaries in attendance. Georgi Baidukov continued his career with the Red Air Force, advancing to the rank of lieutenant general, and during World War II, he was in command of an aerial combat unit. Alexander (Sasha) Beliakov went on to achieve much success as an aeronavigation specialist and he, too, eventually attained the rank of lieutenant general.

Wilkins and Eielson had crossed the Arctic from America to Europe in the 1920s. The Russians had spanned the Arctic from Moscow to the U.S.A. But strange as it may seem, and strange indeed it was, more than four decades were to roll by before airmen would fly across the Antarctic. Finally two huge turbo-prop planes made it all the way from Africa to Australasia by way of "the Bottom of the World."

CHAPTER XV

First Across the Antarctic from Africa to Australasia*

What would Amundsen and Scott have said had they been there? The scene was the South Pole where an unusual change-of-command ceremony was taking place under cloudless skies in temperatures of 34-below. A crowd of eighty-five scientists, United States sailors and newsmen stood on the lofty ice capped plateau, watching as Admiral James R. Reedy assumed command of Operation Deep Freeze—the U. S. Naval Support Force in the Antarctic. Among those shivering through the ceremony were Theodore Hesburgh, president of Notre Dame University, and Dr. Lawrence Gould who had been Byrd's second in command at Little America.

I had flown down a few days before with Admiral Reedy, who was due to take command from retiring Admiral David Tyree in a simple ceremony at the bottom of the world, right at the Pole. As the two parka-clad admirals read the orders, saluted each other and shook hands, an American flag fluttered from a staff marking the geographic location of the Ultimate South—there on that flat plain of snow and ice stretching to the horizon in every direction—all being True North, of course, from that spot. The ceremony took place at the Amundsen-Scott South Pole Station on November 26, 1962. It was one of seven bases the United States had established in the Antarctic some six years before to help set the stage for the International

* First person reference in this chapter is Lowell Thomas, Senior.

Geophysical Year (IGY)—a worldwide program of scientific study in which the scientists of sixty-six nations participated.

The first commander of Operation Deep Freeze had been Admiral Byrd who, as a special honor, held the post briefly. Only three months after arriving in the Antarctic to assume command, ill health forced Byrd's return to the United States where he died in 1957 at the age of sixty-eight. For three decades, Admiral Byrd had dominated the great age of Antarctic exploration and his achievement of lifting the veil of secrecy from some 2,000,000 square miles of the earth's surface ranks along with the voyages of Columbus, Vasco da Gama, and Captain James Cook.

Even though the IGY came to an official conclusion in 1958, that did not mean the end of international cooperation in scientific study of the Antarctic. Instead, it provided the momentum for an even broader program of international teamwork which continues to this day. National jealousies and the whole concept of boundary lines have been put aside, at least temporarily, as scientists from all over the world work together in an effort to tap the Antarctic's resources "for the good of mankind." From the abundant marine life of the waters surrounding the south polar continent, could come the food to help meet the needs of the world's expanding population. The mineral resources of that ice-covered land are yet to be fully evaluated, and they could be enormous. The United States and eleven other nations signed a treaty in 1959, guaranteeing that for a period of thirty years, there will be no militarization of the Antarctic and freedom of scientific inquiry will prevail without territorial claims by any country. Also, Operation Deep Freeze would continue as the United States government's support for American studies on the southern continent.

In taking his first Antarctic duty assignment at the age of fifty-two, Admiral Jim Reedy had already logged an impressive amount of naval experience in both war and peace. Born in 1910 at Cleveland, Ohio, he entered Annapolis in 1929 and was captain of the football team. Like many other Navy fliers before him, Reedy received flight training at the Pensacola Naval Air Station and won his wings in 1935. During the early months of World War II, he served as an instructor in dive-bombing at the Corpus Christi Naval Air Station in Texas before going overseas to England for combat duty. There, he was placed in command of a bombing squadron, charged with search-and-destroy missions against German submarines in the Atlantic, and his outstanding record in this assignment won for him the Air Medal, Distinguished Flying Cross, and the Bronze Star Medal. He was advanced to the rank of rear admiral in 1961, and now as leader of Operation Deep Freeze he had become an important figure in the world's largest scientific community—Antarctica. It also spurred him to consider the possibility of new flights of exploration across the white continent, many parts of which still remained unseen by human eyes.

Ever since 1928 when Sir Hubert Wilkins and Ben Eielson became the first men ever to fly an airplane over the south polar regions, the aerial conquest of the Antarctic had been moving steadily forward, gradually pulling back the mantle of mystery from the last great unknown territory on earth. The Wilkins flight was a daring one, covering a round-trip distance of about 1300 miles along the eastern coast of the Antarctic Peninsula, and back again to the takeoff point on Deception Island in the South Shetlands. Only a few weeks later Byrd began his extensive exploration of the Antarctic with three airplanes, a campaign climaxed by the historic flight to the South Pole.

After Wilkins and Byrd, the airplane became, by far, the most important vehicle for mapping and exploring the Antarctic —which had to be explored and mapped if only because it was there. During the 1930s, Lars Christensen of Norway made several flights over the uncharted territories of Wilkes Land and Queen Maud Land. In 1935, Lincoln Ellsworth, Amundsen's former comrade-in-adventure, teamed up with a Canadian pilot, Hollick-Kenyon, to fly a single-engine plane from an island off the tip of the Antarctic Peninsula all the way to Little

America on the Bay of Whales. With three landings en route, they covered a distance of more than 2000 miles in twenty-two days, although they had to complete their journey on foot after abandoning their plane 20 miles from Little America. The aircraft was eventually retrieved, and taken on board a ship.

Eleven years later, in 1946, Rear Admiral Richard H. Cruzen led a U. S. Navy task force of 13 ships, 21 airplanes, and 4000 men to the Bay of Whales to train naval personnel in cold weather operations. Captain Finn Ronne of the U. S. Naval Reserve launched an aerial research expedition that same year and logged nearly 350 hours of Antarctic flying time over a three-year period. Late in 1955, four U. S. Navy planes flew from New Zealand to McMurdo Sound and for the next several weeks, exploratory flights were made over unknown parts of the continent. Another long-range flight came in 1962 when an American Navy plane covered the distance from McMurdo Sound to Punta Arenas, Chile, by way of the South Pole.

Still, none of these aerial journeys were flown all the way across the bottom of the world between the mainland of South America and Africa or Australasia. In fact, no plane had ever made the great long-distance flight that would connect two or even three continents across the vast expanse of Antarctica. But in 1963, the year after General Jimmy Doolittle and a few of us had made our first trip to the South Pole, Admiral Reedy decided the time had come to try that long flight from Africa. There was now equipment available that could do the job.

His plan called for the flight of two huge Navy C-130 turbo-prop ski-planes from Cape Town near the tip of South Africa across 4700 miles of the Antarctic Ocean's widest part, then on across the continent by way of the South Pole to the U.S. base at McMurdo Sound where they would land. From there, the planes would continue another 2400 miles to Christchurch, New Zealand—completing the first flight in history from continent to continent over the width of the south polar plateau, partly over areas never seen before.

The primary purposes of such a flight were these: It would

be another important long-range first, and seek to prove the feasibility of a new air route between South Africa and Australasia. Commercial planes flying between those two parts of the planet were doing it by way of a long and circuitous route. Swinging northward up the east coast of Africa the planes flew across the Middle East to India and thence southeast to Singapore, on over Indonesia and the Timor Sea to Darwin, south across Australasia, finally to reach New Zealand—a total of 13,705 miles in about 35 hours. But the distance from South Africa to New Zealand directly across the Antarctic was only 7100 miles and could certainly be flown in much less time, almost cutting it in half. In addition to forging a new air route, the trans-polar flight would have two other objectives. The exploration of uncharted territory, and the investigation of a mysterious auroral belt which often caused atmospheric interference in radio communications between South Africa and that part of the Antarctic coast bordering the Ross Sea.

One afternoon at a meeting of Operation Deep Freeze's staff officers, Admiral Reedy launched his idea as a conversational trial balloon. He outlined his arguments in favor of such a flight and asked for opinions.

"You're talking about unknown quantities," one officer told Reedy. "No one has ever flown directly to the South Pole from the mainland of either South America or Africa."

Another officer spoke up and he, too, had some misgivings. "Plenty of flights have crossed distances just as great," he said, "but not over 4700 miles of empty ocean and a continent covered with ice. You'll be flying above the most inaccessible and inhospitable area on earth."

Still sold on his idea and hopeful of finding positive support from some of his officers, Reedy turned to his Air Squadron leader, Commander George R. Kelly, and asked him:

"But can we do it?"

Kelly's answer came quickly, with just a hint that his Irish dander was up over the suggestion that naval airmen couldn't do the job.

"Yes, sir, I think we can."

With that, the "ayes" carried the day and within a few weeks preparations for the flight were in full swing. Two big turbo-prop transport planes were placed on special detail from the Navy's Air Development Squadron 6. They were designated *Navy-318* and *Navy-320,* and both were equipped with special landing gear—skis and wheels which could be lowered and used interchangeably according to the terrain.

I knew nothing of all this until one day in September I happened to be talking to Admiral Reedy on the phone. I've entirely forgotten whether I called him or he called me. All that was overshadowed by the postscript to our conversation when I said: "Admiral, anything new and exciting in your world?"

Then he told me about the great flight he was planning. When he finished, I said the obvious: "Don't you think I ought to go along?" In reply, he said the two planes would be "flying gas tanks," with virtually no extra space on board. The next day, to my astonishment, he phoned me to say: "Lowell, we've decided to drop one of our pilots and take you instead." And that's how I happened to make two flights to the South Pole within twelve months. Also how, as an unimportant bit of aviation history, I became the first human being ever to fly from Africa across the Antarctic, to Australia.

On September 19, two big Lockheeds were flown from Andrews Air Force Base near Washington across the Atlantic to Cape Town, the jumping-off point for the south polar flight. They were based at Malan Field on Cape Town's outskirts and for a week Navy crews bustled about the engines, tuning them up, checking the radio communication systems and preparing for a September 30 takeoff date. When fully loaded, each plane would weigh 145,000 pounds. Although this would be 10,000 pounds more than the flying weight recommended for the C-130, no real trouble was anticipated in taking off. Nearly 9600 gallons of JP-4, a gasoline-based jet fuel, would provide enough for 17 hours of flying time. Part of the JP-4 was stored in huge special tanks that nearly filled the cavernous C-130's cabins.

Rear Admiral James R. Reedy with Lowell Thomas who accompanied Reedy on the first historic flight from Africa across Antarctica to Australasia. Their flight time varied only one minute from Reedy's original schedule.

The South African Navy, cooperating fully with the project, sent one of its frigates far out into the Antarctic Ocean some 1200 miles south of Cape Town, to stand by as a navigation marker and, if the need arose, to serve as an emergency rescue ship. Masses of weather data were run through a computer for analysis and favorable tail winds were forecast throughout most of the flight. And the new computerized age was given a vote of confidence on Monday, September 30, 1963, when dawn came up with the skies clear and brisk.

I was privileged to be among those who made this historic flight with Admiral Reedy and rode with him on the lead plane, *No. 318.* Among those with us were Professor L. C. King, a geologist from the University of Natal who represented the South African government, and Otis Imboden, staff photographer for National Geographic. Our plane was piloted by Lieutenant Commander Richard G. Dickerson of Pocatello,

Idaho, with Commander Kelly, who hails from El Dorado, Illinois, as the co-pilot. The second plane, *No. 320*, was piloted by Lieutenant Commander William B. Kurlak of New York City, and among those on board with him was Allyn Baum, photographer-reporter for the New York *Times*. Altogether, including the crews, there were twenty-nine of us on both planes.

A crowd of several hundred South Africans were on hand to cheer us on our way, including a dozen or more of my own age who had flown the primitive open cockpit planes of the World War I era when you got a thrill every time you went up. The night before, they had given a party in my honor, because I had made my first flight with one of their pals, Major Emmett—a South African who was one of Allenby's pilots in the war against the Turks. The South Africans marveled at these big Lockheeds in which we were about to make the first trans-Antarctic flight.

A South African Air Force plane, sent out at the last minute to check meteorological conditions, radioed that the flying weather was perfect—and it was shortly before 2 P.M., Greenwich Mean Time, when we went on board. As the two Lockheeds taxied out to the runways, their aluminum and red colors glinting in the sun, we could actually see the wings drooping from the heavy load of fuel that made up nearly half the total weight. We could literally *feel* the huge planes hugging the ground. The big question was: Can we get off the runway with 10,000 pounds of excess weight?

We would soon know.

With the takeoff time barely a minute away, Dick Dickerson checked his controls, then the brakes were released as he gave the engines full throttle and the wheels began to roll.

"Sixty knots . . . Ninety knots . . . One eighteen!"

Commander Kelly was calling the airspeed, and now the plane was pounding down the runway, straining to get up and away. Dickerson eased back on the controls and the nose angled up ever so slightly as the wheels got the message and gradually began leaving the ground.

The crews of both C-130s shortly before departure on historic non-stop flight from Cape Town across the Antarctic. In front row (left to right) Lieutenant Commander R. G. Dickerson (plane commander of lead plane); Rear Admiral James R. Reedy, Commander G. R. Kelly, Lieutenant Commander W. B. Kurlak (plane commander of second plane). (*Official U. S. Navy Photo*)

"Man, she looks like she'll do it," was Dickerson's only comment, but to our ears his words were set to music.

"Wheels up!"

Slowly, the landing gear began withdrawing into its housing as the planes continued to gain altitude by the second. Then suddenly—there was trouble.

"No lock light on nose gear."

The nosewheel and its ski had retracted into their housing, but apparently had failed to fasten securely in place. If this meant something was wrong with the plane's hydraulic gear, we'd have to call off the flight and head back to Cape Town.

As the plane climbed higher and higher, Dickerson set his course toward the South Pole, while the landing gear was lowered again for another try at pulling it back into place. This time the safety lights flashed the welcome signal, "wheels locked." So we were on our way.

Soon, we heard from the pilot of the other plane, Bill Kurlak, who reported that his *No. 320* was off the ground and on course, holding visual contact with us. Table Mountain, second only to Gibraltar as a landmark, was the last familiar sight to fade in the distance as we headed south from Africa. Then, as we passed the Cape of Good Hope, we continued a steady climb to 22,000 feet, wondering if we would see the South African frigate, *Transvaal,* somewhere between us and the continent of ice.

We were two and a half hours out of Cape Town when the sun began to drop behind the horizon. Outside the temperature was 24-below, and a tail wind of 50 knots were boosting us along. Beneath was the cold and stormy Antarctic Ocean, formed by the confluence of those three great oceans—the Indian, the Atlantic, and the Pacific. At 5 P.M. a bright blip appeared on our radar screen, indicating we were nearing the *Transvaal* on the lonely sea below us, and a few minutes later we were directly overhead. Its skipper, Commander William Hogg, radioed Admiral Reedy a message of "Godspeed" as our plane roared on southward, and the admiral replied with an expression of thanks to the *Transvaal* and its crew for the long 2000-mile voyage they were making to help us—just in case.

By 7 P.M. the temperatures had tumbled considerably and we began to feel the first blasts of that cold air from the southern polar ice cap. So we began putting on some of our special Antarctic clothing as the planes neared the PSR—Point of Safe Return—about 2300 miles south of the tip of South Africa. As we approached the shores of Antarctica, our navigators, Marine Staff Sergeant Arthur Kring and Lieutenant (jg) Don Miller, were busy with the sextant, having the planet Saturn and the stars of Canopus, Altair and Antares as their only guides.

We were at 30,000 feet and a thick frost was forming on the windshield when we passed the PSR at 8:45 P.M. Now, there could be no turning back. About half an hour later, a mountain range showed up on the radarscope and the Antarctic coast was beneath our wings. The Sor Rondane Mountains were on our left, and the Wohlthat Range stretched away to our right. Almost immediately, the radio began crackling with messages from our South Pole Station and other points around the Antarctic Continent. McMurdo came in on voice radio, relaying a message from Russia's Mirnyy Station whose commanding officer offered his congratulations and said our plane was welcome to use his landing facilities. Admiral Reedy sent his thanks and best wishes, but explained that the plan was to continue on across the South Pole to McMurdo—and in an aside to me he added that our planes were too big to land at the small Mirnyy runway anyhow.

By 10:30 P.M. we had passed the area of known mountain ranges and were flying over uncharted territory, but an undercast had developed beneath us, shutting out nearly everything. Even so, strong radar echoes appeared, indicating the possibility that undiscovered mountain peaks were below, and Admiral Reedy made a note that he wanted to return someday for another look at that terrain in clearer skies.

Before long we began receiving reports of bad weather ahead. Captain Roy Shults radioed from McMurdo that the weather there was showing signs of closing in. The South Pole Station reported wind-blown snow was decreasing the visibility there to less than a quarter of a mile. The temperature was around 28-below—warm for the South Pole where it often goes below minus-100.

"Typical day at the Pole," Dick Dickerson remarked. "Hot and dusty."

It was 12:30 A.M. and the midnight sun was beginning to rise as we neared Amundsen-Scott Station which was located under the ice. The *No. 320* now came winging up on our port side and, despite the blowing snow, we soon could see the outlines of the Pole Station's landing strip. Twenty-two men were wintering-over down there in those tunnels, and Admiral Reedy radioed our greetings, assuring them that planes would be coming in to take them out as soon as possible.

With the Pole behind us now and the plateau beneath obscured by whirling and drifting snow, our goal, McMurdo, was still more than two hours away. The sun was well up in the sky, forcing all of us to wear dark glasses. Soon it was obvious that Admiral Reedy and his navigators faced an important decision. With the weather at McMurdo growing worse, it was doubtful whether we should risk a landing there if the visibility continued to deteriorate. There were several alternatives. We could return to the South Pole, or swing far to the east toward Byrd Station 800 miles away, or possibly fly on past McMurdo to Hallett Station if the visibility failed to cooperate. Even so, the fuel supply would be marginal for any of these and there would be the danger of landing on the rugged ice without the aid of ground controllers.

The decision was made to press on toward McMurdo, and by 4 A.M. we were on its very high frequency homer beacon, but the undercast was growing thicker with each passing mile. About fifteen minutes later, McMurdo reported that both our planes were on their radar and we were given new bearings for an approach.

By this time the snow was blowing fiercely, making it impossible to see where to land even though we knew McMurdo was right below us. The ground controllers began talking us down to within a hundred feet of the runway, and within a few minutes our own radar revealed that, luckily, we were zeroed in between the rows of gasoline drums that lined McMurdo's landing strip.

"We've got the barrels!" Commander Kelly sang out when he spotted the twin rows of drums, and then he added: "We've got the threshold!" This meant he could see the end of the runway. Swiftly now the plane's skis swooped down to meet the hard-packed snow, and a few seconds later we slid to a stop.

"All right, boys," Admiral Reedy called out. "You're all a bunch of ruddy heroes."

Bill Kurlak brought *No. 320* down only moments behind us, and more than a hundred of the McMurdo winter populaton greeted us as we emerged from the two C-130s—in summery temperatures of 35-below. Among them was Colonel Ronald A. Tinker, leader of New Zealand's nearby Scott Station.

Crew of the mission that in the fall of 1963 completed the first non-stop flight in history from continent to continent over the entire Antarctic. Pictured at McMurdo Sound Air Force Base after arriving from Cape Town, South Africa, are (from left to right) Lieutenant Commander W. B. Kurlak, Lieutenant Commander R. G. Dickerson, Rear Admiral James R. Reedy and Commander George R. Kelly. (*U. S. Navy*)

"Ron," the admiral told him, "I'm happier than usual to see you today."

The flying time from Cape Town to McMurdo had been 14 hours and 31 minutes, exactly one minute off the flight plan Admiral Reedy and his aides had drawn up in Washington several weeks before.

We had carried a large consignment of fresh steaks on our record-breaking over-the-pole flight, and a few hours later we all sat down to a banquet in one of the big Quonset huts. Before the coffee was served, Admiral Reedy gave us this word: "Relax, all of you. There'll be no speeches tonight!"

Just the same, New Zealand's Antarctic commander, Colonel Ron Tinker, was in a speech-making mood. After all, he was one of the hosts, wasn't he? I don't recall when he started his speech, but it seemed that hours after he had gotten underway I headed for my bunk. Even at 4 o'clock in the morning, as the storm continued to howl outside, I could hear the eloquent Kiwi commandant—and he was still going strong.

After a brief stopover at McMurdo, we took off for the uneventful remainder of the flight—the 2400 miles to Christchurch, New Zealand. But what did this first continent-to-continent Antarctic flight accomplish? Said Admiral Reedy: "We proved our communcations could satisfy requirements for regular flying into, or over, the Antarctic from Africa. And I have no doubt that the day will come when planes will fly this route across the South Pole, just as transports routinely fly great circle routes across the top of the world."

There is one other unimportant postscript to add. From Christchurch I flew on, alone, to Australia, and when I arrived in Sydney, genial six-foot-four Hercules McIntyre met me. "By the way, Lowell, you are the first ever to cross the Antarctic, by way of the South Pole, from Africa to *Australia.*"

So said my friend Hercules.

Finally, at long last comes the aerial adventure that inspired this book, the flight that brings to a close one of the major eras in the life of Man, the flight airmen had talked of, and dreamed of for more than half a century, the circumnavigation of the planet, within the earth's atmosphere, by way of both the North and the South Pole.

CHAPTER XVI

Around the World
by Way of Both Poles

The ancient Greeks considered the Earth to be a heavenly body and therefore spherical. This was because they regarded heavenly bodies as perfect, and the most perfect shape is a sphere. The farther south you went from the Greek world, your approach would bring you closer and closer to the burning heat of the tropics. And, similarly, by going too far north you would arrive in the frozen zone where the cold was no longer endurable. Under this general view, the people of the North Temperate Zone were like rats in a revolving cage, free to move east or west, but imprisoned by a wall of flame to the south and a barrier of ice to the north. This being the case, it was always theoretically possible to go around the Earth, east or west, and many Greek philosophers took it for granted that someday, someone would do it. But that anyone would ever go around the Earth from north to south, was absurd beyond discussion.

Vilhjalmur Stefansson

And yet, on the afternoon of Sunday, November 14, 1965, millions of Americans who tuned in on the CBS Radio Network heard these words, so full of meaning for the history of aviation:

"Hello everyone. This is Lowell Thomas, Jr., reporting from the *Polecat,* a jet plane which is at this moment 31,000 feet above the blue Pacific, heading westward to begin the first flight that has ever been made around the world from north to south, over both the North and South Poles. A few hours ago we left Palm Springs, California, and now we're bound for Honolulu, the official takeoff point for the last great flight yet to be made on this planet, a Double Pole flight never before attempted. We'll be on the ground at Honolulu International Airport no more than two or three hours, just long enough to refuel the plane. Then we'll be off again, and heading due north on the longest leg of the whole trip around the world— the 7400 miles from Honolulu up over Alaska, across the Arctic Ocean to the North Pole, then down to London. The present plan is to fly from London to Buenos Aires, then on across the South Pole to Christchurch, New Zealand, and from there back to Honolulu, completing a globe-circling journey of more than 26,000 miles.

"While our mission is to make this the last great aviation 'first,' the flight does have a number of important scientific goals and Dr. Serge Korff, a world-renowned physicist and leading authority on cosmic research, will have something to say about that as we proceed. Also, the *Polecat* and its crew are out to set at least five world speed records for jet transports, including the fastest times from point to point, from pole to pole, and around the world. And this is a plane that can get places in a hurry. It's a brand new but even larger version of the Boeing 707 on lease from the Flying Tiger Line, and when the flight is over it will go back to its regular job of hauling cargo to various corners of the globe.

"The *Polecat* has a range of about 8000 miles, at a cruising speed of 600 miles an hour. Powered by four Pratt & Whitney jet engines, it has a wing span of nearly 146 feet, and from nose to tail it's half as long as a football field. Up front is the cockpit with places for the pilot, co-pilot, navigator and flight engineer. Next comes the large forward cabin area with sleeping bunks, broadcasting facilites, and a motor generator that supplies power for the special scientific equipment on board. Farther back is the center cabin area where the Air Logistics Corporation has installed two huge, rubberized tanks, holding an additional 4000 gallons of fuel and bringing the total capacity to 27,908 gallons. Every ounce will be needed to wing the

Polecat across these vast stretches of the planet. In the rear cabin area we have our flying weather bureau, and more scientific equipment, including some highly precise instruments for measuring cosmic rays. For the moment, that should be enough to let you know what this flight is all about, but I'll be reporting again in a few hours, so—so long for now from the *Polecat*, high over the Pacific on its way to Honolulu."

I'd like to explain why an around-the-world flight by way of the two poles was never made until 1965. The primary reason was, up until recently, airplanes simply didn't have enough range to make it a safe proposition. In the old days it would have been virtually impossible, if not downright fool-hardy, to attempt such a flight because of the problems of landing and refueling in the vast snows and ice of the Arctic and Antarctic. It also called for extremely skillful navigation to keep a plane from going astray over the North and South Poles, and polar navigation is a critical factor in global flying even in this modern age.

As far as my being on the flight goes, well—it was really just a stroke of luck. I happened to be in the Los Angeles area on a speaking tour when word came that I could go along as official historian. So, naturally I climbed on board in a hurry. But the man who really should have been on the *Polecat* instead of me is my father, because he was the official historian of the first flight around the world and has always followed the history of aviation very closely. The first global flight, you'll remember, was made by a team of U. S. Army fliers back in 1924, flying in the conventional west-to-east directon. Four single-engined airplanes took off from Lake Washington near Seattle and proceeded westward around the globe, but only two of them actually completed the flight of more than 26,000 miles. And that, interestingly enough, was about the same distance the *Polecat* flew in circumnavigating the globe over the two poles. But the big difference was that the Army fliers made it in about six months, while we did it in less than three days.

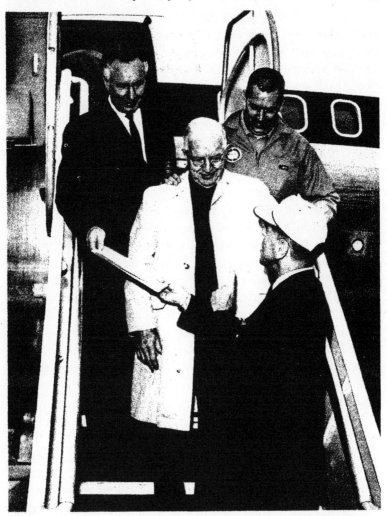

Pilots Finch and Austin receiving honors from General Joseph D. Caldara, USAF (Ret.), of the Flight Safety Foundation. In the center is Colonel Willard F. Rockwell whose firm, Rockwell-Standard, was the principal sponsor of the first air circumnavigation of the globe via both poles.

There were forty people on board the *Polecat,* including five pilots, three flight engineers, three navigators, and a communications man who had a standby associate. Dr. Korff led a team of nine scientists who studied the problems of high altitude flying in an effort to make aviation safer for us all. Then there were . thirteen observers, headed by Colonel Willard F. Rockwell of Pittsburgh, whose firm, the Rockwell-Standard Corporation, enabled the flight to get off the ground with a financial grant of $200,000. For this reason our aerial expedition was officially called "The Rockwell Polar Flight," in honor of its principal benefactor. Also on board was that great explorer-aviator and the first man to pilot a plane over both poles, Bernt Balchen. This global flight would take Bernt over the North Pole for the twenty-sixth time, and over the South Pole for the second. Appropriately enough, he was given the assignment of selecting the survival gear for our Double Pole flight. The Army and Air Force sent its Arctic survival kits, and from these Bernt chose such items as emergency rations, boots and parkas, snow-saws and so on. With us also were five editors, writers, cameramen and newsmen, including Wayne Parrish, the founder and editor of *American Aviation Magazine,* who has flown more than 1,700,000 passenger miles during his long career.

The way the Double Pole flight got started in the first place is a story in itself. The two men who dreamed up the flight, and worked with untiring zeal to get it into the air, were the *Polecat*'s two flight commanders, Captains Fred L. Austin and Harrison Finch, both of whom are Trans World Airlines pilots. For nearly two years they spent hundreds of hours of their own time, and much of their own money, trying to make their dream a reality. They had to find a plane big enough and with sufficient range to do the job, but that was only part of the problem. Scientific equipment was needed to make the project meaningful for the future of aviation. Great care had to be taken in choosing the members of the expedition, with special attention to the professional capabilities of the flight crew and scientific team. And, like Lindbergh, Kingsford-Smith, Wilkins, and others who wanted to achieve a flying "first" on this globe, Austin and Finch had to work long and hard to get financial support for their plans. There were moments of discouragement, then moments of triumph, and time and again, just when it seemed they were ready to go, something would happen to throw them off the track. But they had what it took to get the job done.

This was no attempt at heroics. Never for once did Austin and Finch indulge in any make-believe about the "dangers" involved in a flight around the world over the poles, for they knew it would be a "cinch." Given the capabilities of a high-speed jet plane, an accurate rendering of weight and load, fuel capacity and length of runways, they knew the flight could be accomplished with virtually no risk in this advanced age of aeronautical technology. The main point was—there had never been a flight around the world over the poles. Austin and Finch wanted to be the first to do it, and they were.

Fred Austin, a fifty-one-year-old resident of Los Angeles, had studied commercial law at Glendale Junior College before turning to an aviation career and receiving his pilot's license in 1934. Five years later he joined Trans World Airlines as a first officer and has held many TWA flight administration positions along with his duties as a pilot. Throughout his career he has logged more than 17,000 hours of flying time, most of it over the TWA's far-flung domestic and international routes.

Harrison Finch, Austin's long-time friend and partner in organizing the flight, is a fifty-year-old native of Du Bois, Pennsylvania. After attending Pennsylvania State University where he majored in mechanical engineering, he began flying in 1936 and has spent more than 18,000 hours at the pilot's controls. Like Austin, Finch joined TWA in Kansas City, and soon was promoted to flight captain. During World War II, he trained pilots for the Army's Air Transport Command, and since 1946 his base has been New York where he flies TWA airliners between the United States and Europe.

The story began about midnight one evening in the spring of 1964 when the telephone rang in Harrison Finch's modern home in the woods overlooking Lloyd's Harbor near Huntington, Long Island. His wife and young daughters were asleep, and it was perhaps a late hour for the telephone to ring in New York, but the caller was Fred Austin in Los Angeles where it was only 9 P.M.

"Hello, Harrison," Austin began, "this is Fred. Forgive me for disturbing you at this late hour. But thought I'd better call to let you know that I'll definitely be in New York to attend the Explorers Club dinner with you."

"Fine," Finch replied, "and I know John DuBois will be glad to hear that. It's the Club's 60th annual dinner, you know, and it should be a gala affair. Even though you and I are not members, it's sure thoughtful of John to invite us to attend these dinners as he's done through the past several years."

"That's right," Austin agreed, "and we're grateful to him for it. So I'll see you in a couple of days. And by the way, Harrison, before we hang up, there's something I want to talk to you about. I'll go into more detail when I get to New York, but right now let me say it's an idea for a flight that has always intrigued me, one that's never been done before. There've been a lot of around-the-world flights, but none by way of the North and South Poles."

"That does sound intriguing," Finch told hm. "Go on, tell me more."

"It'll take quite a bit of time, effort, and money to accomplish it," Austin continued, "but such a flight could contribute a lot to aviation safety if we have the proper scientific equipment on board to study such problems as high altitude turbulence, cosmic radiation, and other hazards both you and I are aware of. We would have to line up an excellent team of scientists and the best flight personnel we can find, and another thought occurs to me—taking John DuBois along on such a flight would be one way of repaying him for all the courtesies he has shown us."

They brought the conversation to a close and, after he hung up the phone, Finch found it impossible to sleep. The idea began to grow on him as he got up and began pacing the floor. The possibilities were almost endless. In the old flying days, an airplane's biggest enemies were temperatures and air conditions, but these no longer provided a really hostile environment. Instead, modern jet planes were flying at extremely high altitudes, in the upper areas of the earth's atmosphere where the scientists were still stumped by a lot of problems. What are the sources of these problems? A study of severe wind patterns and turbulence could be correlated with what we already know about radiation, wind direction, and velocity in an effort to find a way of measuring causes. A barometer, for instance, used to be the major instrument in determining flying conditions. Now, we want to know what makes the barometer act the way it does.

For the next several months, the Explorers Club in New York became a kind of organizational base and sounding board for the proposed flight. The club's president at the time was Dr. Korff, and he gave his full support by carefully planning the flight's scientific goals. My father, Lowell Thomas, Sr., went from member to member, using his influence to generate interest in the project. Talbert Abrams of Lansing, Michigan, and Dr. Richard Dominick of New York were among the members who lent their full support and wanted very much to be on the plane, but when the time came they could not be taken along because of weight limitations. The flight captured the imagination of John DuBois who gave Austin and Finch many helpful suggestions as they literally "explored" every possible avenue in the search for a plane, and, even more important, the money to fly it with.

However, it was slow going, and for months the two pilots used every contact at their command in an effort to charter a suitable plane, but to no avail. Nevertheless, Austin and Finch felt the prospects were so encouraging that they formed their own corporate organization to handle the details. Chartered in

Los Angeles, it was called "Geo-Atmos Explorations," with Finch as president and Austin as vice-president. And it marked the birth of a new scientific exploration company that's still in business today.

It was John DuBois who first suggested that Colonel Rockwell might be interested in becoming the financial "good angel" for the flight. There was certainly an area of common interest. Rockwell was board chairman of the Rockwell-Standard Corporation, a firm which manufactures a complete line of private and business aircraft. For years also the company had been one of the nation's leading suppliers of parts and equipment to the automotive industry. Born in Boston in 1888, Colonel Rockwell received his education at MIT and, as a highly successful businessman, he had become a director of several banks, insurance companies, railroads, and a television station. And his interests extended far beyond his Pittsburgh home. He was a sponsor and past president of the World Trade Council, a former member of the Army and Navy Munitions Board, and a colonel in the Army Ordnance Reserve Corps.

On November 4, 1965, Harrison Finch was in Pittsburgh, trying to reach a financial agreement with Rockwell-Standard, when Fred Austin telephoned from Los Angeles with the news that the Flying Tiger Line would definitely make one of its Boeing 707 jets available for the flight. With unexpected suddenness, the airplane problem was solved and it marked a turning point. Only two days later on November 6, Rockwell-Standard decided to finance the whole venture with $200,000. The contracts were signed with the Flying Tiger Line agreeing to supply the plane and all the fuel for $150,000. And in a statement to the nation's press, radio, and television, Colonel Rockwell announced that his firm was financing the flight "in the interest of broader research in the field of intercontinental aviation."

Austin and Finch had already set their sights on the men they wanted as pilots and, being pros themselves, they knew how to choose the pros. The ultimate in flying skill was needed.

If it became necessary, every pilot on board would have to know how to land with zero ceiling and zero visibility. In addition to themselves, they chose three others who would take their turns at the controls.

As chief pilot they selected Captain J. L. (Jack) Martin, a forty-five-year-old aviator who had just become System Chief Pilot for the Flying Tigers. Martin had learned to fly early, while he was still in high school at Oklahoma City. He served in the Army Air Corps and later spent three years on the faculty of the University of Southern California's College of Aeronautics before joining the Flying Tiger Line. And he was pilot operations manager when the airline took an important role in building the famed Dewline Early Warning System in the Arctic.

Chosen also was Captain Robert N. Buck, another TWA pilot and one of the outstanding aviators of our time. During World War II, he was cited by the Air Force for his pioneerng work in global thunderstorm research, bringing him recognition as one of the world's foremost weather pilots. A fifty-one-year-old native of Elizabeth, New Jersey, Buck had taken his first solo flight on his sixteenth birthday, and in 1930 he set a junior transcontinental speed record. He had also conducted much research in blind and instrument landing systems, and served as adviser to the President's Supersonic Study Committee.

To complete the pilots' roster, Austin and Finch selected Captain James R. Gannett, the Boeing Company's senior engineering test pilot, whose talents included an ability to wring every bit of performance out of the takeoff of a plane. Born at Lyons, New York, in 1923, Gannett began his flying career at the University of Michigan, and during World War II he served as a pilot instructor with the Air Force. The war over, he returned to the university and received a Master's degree in aeronautics. Then he went on active duty with the Air Force again to fly fifty-five missions as a combat pilot in the Korean fighting.

The official takeoff from Honolulu was scheduled for Novem-

ber 14, only eight days after the Rockwell-Standard contract
was signed. But the plane designated for the flight was still
overseas on a regular military transport mission for the Flying
Tiger Line. And it was November 10 when the big Boeing 707,
henceforth to be known as the *Polecat*, was made available to
the flight crew and mechanics at Burbank, California. This left
the space of only four days in which to install two extra fuel
tanks and some 5000 pounds of scientific equipment before the
takeoff. Under normal conditions, this would require weeks
or even months, but the *Polecat* had to be ready to go within
a deadline time of one hundred hours. It seemed an almost
impossible task, and there were sleepless nights for the entire
ground crew, but somehow they got the job done.

"Hello everyone. This is Lowell Thomas, Jr., reporting from
the *Polecat* high over the Pacific between the California coast
and Honolulu. We're making a ground speed, or I should say
'a sea speed,' of only 420 miles an hour because of a strong
head wind. Also, we're up in the jet stream and that's not
helping, but we should land at Honolulu within the next 30
minutes or so. It might be of interest to know how these
reports are reaching the radio listening audience. We have some
very sophisticated radio equipment on board and it's located
right here in the forward cabin area along with other navigational
and scientific instruments. This remarkable radio was produced
by the Collins Radio Company of Cedar Rapids, Iowa, and is
being used on several MARS frequencies (Military Affiliated
Radio System).

"I know very little about it, but John Demuth, the radio
wizard on board, explains it this way. He says that because of
a 'single sideband' feature, we're putting four times the normal
power into the voice transmission. These broadcasts are being
received at Collins Radio headquarters in Cedar Rapids, and then
relayed to points where they are taped and placed on the air.
John has been with Collins Radio for nearly twenty-five years
and he's highly qualified for his job as flight radio operator.

In the past, while on special assignment as a field research engineer for the Armed Forces, he traveled to many parts of Europe, Africa, and the Far East. And we should have no trouble keeping the *Polecat* in touch with the world as we fly around it. The word from up front is that soon we'll be getting ready to touch down at Honolulu, but I'll be reporting again within a few hours. So—so long from the *Polecat*."

It was raining, but the cloud ceiling was high and the visibility good when we came down to land at Honolulu International Airport after the flight from Palm Springs. As we climbed down from the plane and walked toward the terminal building, the official greeters, a couple of eye-catching Hawaiian girls, came forward with the usual assortment of leis and kisses. It was quite a change from the old days. Back in 1924, the Army fliers had trouble finding an Eskimo to rub noses with when they made their first landing.

We were soon ready to go, but a hitch had developed. Originally, the plan had been to land at London's big Heathrow Aerodrome. However, just before leaving Palm Springs, we were notified that the long runway at Heathrow was closed for construction work. So a decision was reached to head for London's Stanstead Airport which had a runway only 10,500 feet long—barely enough room for the *Polecat* to take off with a full load of fuel.

The tried and tested methods of human navigation by conventional sextants, celestial observation, radio direction finding and loran were, of course, used throughout the flight. But one of the sponsoring firms, Litton Systems of Woodland Hills, California, also went to much time and expense to place its highly scientific Inertial Navigation System on board the *Polecat*. While in flight, the INS relates all the forces which act upon a plane and tend to make it change its course or speed. These forces may include cross winds, turbulence, power, or a number of other factors. Working like an automated watchdog, the INS senses these changes and gives the navigator the course he's *actually* flying, instead of the one he may *think* he's flying. Never before had the INS been used in a flight over both poles, and Litton Systems assigned three of its top men, Dr. David Bjorndahl, Peter Mesquita, and James Furuya, to the job of testing and evaluating its global capabilities.

The plane's navigation was under the direction of John Larsen of Garden City, New York, a former chief navigator for TWA and one of the most highly experienced navigators in the world. He's associated with the Weems System of Navigation. Assisting him were E. A. Hickman, the Flying Tiger Line's chief navigator, and Lauren DeGroot of Grand Rapids, Michigan. DeGroot, head of navigation for Lear Siegler, Inc., was on the *Polecat* to develop a method that would give astronauts an on-board capability of determining both altitude and position by celestial observation. To accomplish this, he and Larsen brought along a Plath Marine Sextant, one of the most accurate instruments of its type available, and it was used together with the plane's conventional sextant in making observations throughout the flight.

There was a very real need for an emergency navigational system during space flights. Only a few months before, two astronauts had lost the services of their on-board navigational computers because of a power failure. In the emergency, ground control radioed them their exact height and position for rocket retrofire as they prepared to splashdown in the sea. If there had been a breakdown in radio communications at that critical moment, the astronauts could not have received this vital information and, not knowing when or where to fire the retros, they might have landed far from the designated recovery area.

We were on the ground at Honolulu nearly three hours before the refueling chore was completed and the tanks were brimming full with 27,908 gallons of aviation-grade kerosene. It was raining hard as we boarded the plane, and the streets of Honolulu were flooded by one of the worst storms in recent months. Big puddles were on the runway, creating something of a tactical problem for the *Polecat*'s takeoff because pools of standing water can be a drag on a heavily loaded plane. But pilots Jack Martin and Jim Gannett had no trouble and we were off for the North Pole, still wearing our leis and nourishing a large bunch of fresh tropical flowers which had been placed on board. When we left, it was Sunday, November 14, by the Honolulu calendar, but it was already Monday, November 15, and 5:54 A.M., Greenwich Mean Time, which was to be our official time reference for the world flight.

"Hello everyone. This is Lowell Thomas, Jr., reporting once more from the *Polecat* on this record flight over the North and South Poles. We're presently cruising at 32,000 feet over the Pacific somewhere north of Hawaii. We left Honolulu about an hour and a half ago, and should land at London in

Full crew of the *Polecat* in front of their plane. The Boeing 707, powered by four Pratt & Whitney engines, had a cruising speed of 600 miles per hour and a fuel-carrying capacity of 27,908 gallons—specifications that would have stunned earlier flight pioneers!

about another twelve hours. But first we'll fly up to the North Pole, where we'll make a slight right hand turn that'll place us on a course due south to England. It's still dark outside, and it'll stay pretty much that way until we're well beyond London and out over the Atlantic on the flight to South America.

"Let me tell you now about some of the people on board the *Polecat*. We have three flight engineers—Dino Valazza and James M. Jones, both of TWA, and Eugene Olson of the Flying Tigers. With us also is the founder and president of the Flying Tiger Line, Robert W. Prescott, who was a member of the famed 'AVG'—The Flying Tigers, back in 1941. As a pilot with General Claire Chennault's volunteers, he carried supplies over the Hump to aid the Chinese in their struggle against the Japanese invaders. He took part in five major campaigns, and shot down six Japanese planes.

"In addition to Colonel Rockwell, two of Rockwell-Standard's top officials are also on board. One is Edward J. Williams of Pittsburgh, vice-president of Manufacturing and Facilities, and a year ago he held the same position with General Dynamics, a firm which has contributed much to the development of America's nuclear submarine and missile program. The other Rockwell-Standard official is Earl D. Johnson of Greenwich, Connecticut, a member of the firm's Advisory Board. A native of Hamilton, Ohio, Mr. Johnson served as assistant chief of a geographical expedition to the Arctic back in 1929. Later, he received flight training at Randolph and Kelly Fields, and during World War II advanced to the rank of colonel in the Army Air Force. In the early 1950s, he was Assistant Secretary of the Army.

"With us also is William Schulte of El Reno, Oklahoma, general chairman of the International AeroClassic, a worldwide aviation exposition now being held at Palm Springs. And incidentally, our unofficial takeoff from Palm Springs was arranged to make the Double Pole flight a part of the AeroClassic program. Bill Schulte is also a former Assistant Administrator of the Federal Aviation Agency. On board, too, is the National

Aeronautics Association Timer, Bert Locanthi, who has his eye on the clock as the *Polecat* goes after a flock of speed records. Among the writers, broadcasters and cameramen we have Clete Roberts of Los Angeles, one of the West Coast's most widely known television newsmen. Clete once obtained Generalissimo Chiang Kai-shek's first TV interview by the simple process of knocking on the door and asking for it. The team also includes a veteran news cameraman, Joseph Longo of Canoga Park, California, and two staffers of *Life* magazine, Donald Moser and J. R. Eyerman.

"Our altitude is now 35,000 feet and we're flying at a speed of 575 miles an hour. At this moment we're passing to the west of Anchorage, Alaska, my home town, and I'm hoping this message will be relayed to Radio Station KFQD—that I'm sorry I can't stop in to say 'hello' to Tay and the children. Although I've been away for over a month, I'll have to continue on around the world before returning home. It's like being on a satellite in orbit around the poles. But tell my wife that I'll try to talk to her on the radio some time later as we fly southward over the Atlantic. Did you get that, KFQD?

"Before signing off for now, there's another member of our party I want to tell you about. He's Dr. Randolph Lovelace of Albuquerque, New Mexico, the National Space Agency's director of space medicine. In other words, he's the family doctor for our American astronauts. A one-time Mayo Clinic surgeon, he developed the first satisfactory oxygen mask for high altitude flying, and was chosen to screen the original Project Mercury astronauts. Dr. Lovelace's achievements have long been in the forefront of aerospace research and development, and his pioneering work is making flying safer for us all. It's a privilege to have him aboard.

"Our route is going to take us just west of Point Barrow, the northernmost point of Alaska, and we should be over the North Pole by about 2:30 P.M., GMT. I'll be reporting again soon and until then, so long from the *Polecat*."

We were passing over the northern coast of Alaska in the vicinity of Wainwright, and flying at about 37,000 feet when an "incident" occurred to break the routine. It was still dark outside, but the weather was essentially clear with temperatures of about 60-below. At 12:15 P.M., Captain Finch was talking with Colonel Rockwell in the forward cabin area when a faint tinge of light blue smoke was seen coming from a fresh-air vent over a window. The fumes were almost inconspicuous, but Finch detected the smell of hot insulation, that familiar electrical odor that comes from burning wire and rubber. There was no need to push the panic button, but a great deal of extra wiring had been strung through the cabin to supply power for the scientific equipment, and Finch knew that some of these lines went right past the fuel tanks. Excusing himself, he hurried forward to the cockpit where Jim Gannett was at the controls with navigator John Larsen and flight engineer Dino Valazza.

"We seem to have an electrical problem," Finch told Valazza, "and maybe we'd better knock off the unessential power until we straighten it out."

Valazza immediately pulled the circuit-breakers, disconnecting all electricity except the power for flight instruments, and the radio and lighting equipment. Larsen asked about the circuit-breakers for the Inertial Navigation System and Finch ordered the same procedure, pending clarification of the trouble. By now, the entire forward cabin area was filled with a blue haze of smoke, and Finch also told Valazza to decrease the cabin pressurization and step up the air flow as much as possible to evacuate the fumes.

Within only a few minutes, Valazza pinpointed the trouble. A ventilating fan motor had burned itself up, probably because of a faulty bearing, and the smoldering insulation had caused the bluish fumes. With the trouble isolated, all electrical power was turned on again, and the cabin pressure was returned to normal levels as soon as the smoke was cleared. Even so, it became necessary to watch the operation of the scientific equip-

ment very closely because some of it had been cooled by the
fan motor that went on the blink. It also meant that the
Inertial Navigation System could no longer give position information because of a break in electrical continuity. But this
loss was only temporary. The INS would be realigned and
restored to normal working order as soon as we reached London. For the time being, however, the *Polecat*'s human navigation was left without a confirming system.

"Hello everyone. This is Lowell Thomas, Jr., reporting from
the *Polecat* as it draws near the North Pole. We should be
there very soon now, in only a few minutes. Our altitude is
35,000 feet with a solid undercast down there below, so there
isn't anything to see except the moon, and it's only half a moon
at that. Captain Bob Buck is in the pilot's seat. He took over
just after we left the vicinity of Point Barrow and with him
is Jack Martin as co-pilot.

"Flash! It's about 2:30 P.M., and the word is that we're over
the North Pole right now. We still can't see any of the ice
pack because of the undercast. Almost everybody is up in
the forward cabin. That's where a large navigation chart is
spread out on the wall. Up front, too, is Bernt Balchen who
calls the Arctic Ocean the 'Mediterranean of the Future' because it's right in the middle of most of the world's developed
nations.

"There's a little ceremony in progress as we fly over the
Ultimate North. Harrison Finch and Fred Austin are being
inducted into the Explorers Club by its president, Edward C.
Sweeney, and past president, Dr. Serge Korff. Ed Sweeney is
also president of the National Aeronautics Association, and
through the years he has made several trips into the Arctic
and Antarctic. He holds a Defense Department Antarctic Service
Medal for his contributions to these expeditions. Also taking
part in the ceremony is John DuBois, a retired industrialist of
Du Bois, Pennsylvania, who during the 1940s spent several
years with an Air Force geodetic squadron making aerial maps

of nearly all the South American countries. So when we arrive over South America, he'll certainly be above familiar terrain.

"Well, that's all to report at the moment, except that we've gotten over the first pole and there's still one more to go with a lot of mileage in between. So long from the *Polecat*, over the Arctic and heading southward to London."

Soon after passing the North Pole, we had the unusual experience of seeing both a sunrise and a sunset within only about an hour of each other. From our position, the sun actually began rising in the *west*, then went back down again and that was all the daylight we saw on Monday. It was just a red glow that stayed below the horizon, a tricky phenomenon resulting from our flight path's relation to the earth's rotation. In one of his plays, Shakespeare describes the dawn by saying: "Jocund Day stands tiptoe on the mountaintop." In this case, Jocund Day not only failed to stand on the mountaintop—he didn't even get a foot in the door.

As the *Polecat* approached the northern part of Scotland, the weather information from London forced another change in the flight plan. An ice-fog had developed over Stanstead Airport where we had intended to land, lowering the ceiling there to about a hundred feet. There was some talk on the flight deck about going on to Paris, but a stop at London was necessary in order to qualify for the designated speed records. So Austin and Finch decided to land at London's Heathrow Airport, even though the only available runway there was just 9300 feet long, or less than the minimum required for taking off with a full load of fuel. Because of this, a refueling stop would have to be made at Lisbon, Portugal, instead of flying directly from London to Buenos Aires as originally planned. So we headed for Heathrow Airport and it was still Monday, dark, and very cold when Bob Buck brought the *Polecat* down to the runway at 7:48 P.M., GMT. We had made the 7413-mile flight from Honolulu over the Pole to London in 13 hours and 54 minutes, a transport speed record for the course.

As soon as the plane rolled to a halt, we learned the sad news that Robert Prescott's eleven-year-old son, Peter, had been killed in an airplane crash on Sunday, the very day our flight began. The bodies of young Peter Prescott II and seven other persons were found in the wreckage of a twin-jet plane, about six miles north of Indio, California. Grief-stricken by his tragic loss, Bob Prescott parted company with the flight in London, and immediately took a plane back to New York. It was a sad moment for us all, and our hearts were with him as he started the long journey home.

Heathrow, located about 14 miles west of London, is one of the world's busiest airports. It was built for the Royal Air Force during World War II with its eventual development as London's main airport in mind. More than 10,000,000 passengers, including ourselves, passed through Heathrow in 1965, and the number is expected to reach 15,000,000 by 1970. There were signs of constant expansion all around us while we remained there a little more than three hours, just long enough to realign the Inertial Navigation System and take on 10,000 gallons of fuel for the short flight to Lisbon.

"Hello everyone. This is Lowell Thomas, Jr., reporting from the *Polecat* over the English Channel, bound for the Portuguese capital of Lisbon. Up until a few hours ago, our stop at Lisbon was unscheduled, but now it's necessary because a short runway at London prevented a takeoff with enough fuel for the long haul to Buenos Aires. We're still flying in darkness, and soon it'll be Tuesday morning in this part of the world. The flight to Lisbon should take only about two hours, and right now I want the head of our scientific team, Dr. Korff, to tell you about some of the things his group is trying to accomplish as we fly around the world.

"Dr. Korff has been on the faculty at New York University since 1941. A native of Finland, he received his Bachelor's and Doctor's degrees from Princeton. In the 1930s, he was leader of a cosmic ray expedition to Mexico and Peru, and for three years served as adviser to the U. S. Antarctic Service Expedition. He's also a former consultant to the United Nations Atomic Energy Commission. Dr. Korff is a leading authority on cosmic rays, and has some very elaborate research equipment in the rear cabin area.

"Dr. Korff, why is it important to study cosmic rays on this Double Pole flight?"

"Well, Lowell, first of all, it's never been done, simply because this type of flight has never been made before. About twelve years ago a study of cosmic rays was made around the world east-to-west by way of the Equator, but it's never been done over the polar route. On this flight, we're flying at heights ranging from 31,000 to 41,000 feet, and it's important to measure the variations in cosmic ray bombardment at the various altitudes. Also, these measurements should be made within a rather short space of time, and our speedy jet plane makes this possible."

"But, Doctor, can't all this be done a lot better by our high flying satellites?"

"Certainly, the satellites make these studies, too, but they can't measure the effect within the atmosphere. The cosmic radiation that comes from outer space generates a great deal of very complicated secondary radiation when it hits the earth's atmosphere. And this is very important, because during the coming age of supersonic transport, perhaps within the next twelve years or so, man will be flying at altitudes of from 60,000 to 70,000 feet. At those heights the pilots and passengers will be exposed to more and more cosmic radiation, and this will be especially true of flight crews in those altitudes on almost a daily basis. We want to know what kind of radiation this is, and how much of it man will encounter. This, of course, is just a start. Sooner or later these same studies will be made at higher altitudes, but for the moment we have to hold it to 30,000 or 40,000 feet."

"Dr. Korff, what kind of equipment are we using in this research?"

"Our cosmic ray equipment from New York University is on board the plane. A fast neutron counter and a slow neutron detector are making a continuous record of cosmic radiation levels at the various cruise altitudes. One of my colleagues, William Sandie of N.Y.U., is also on board, aiding us in these studies. But that's only part of our total research effort. William King of the National Aeronautics and Space Administration is conducting what's known as a 'radiation absorption' experiment. For this purpose, he has a NASA 'plastic phantom,' a sealed chamber which contains synthetic body tissue simulating that of a 180-pound man. Two ionization meters are being used, one to record radiation levels inside the plane, the other to measure radiation inside the 'plastic phantom,' and the results will be compared. It's experiments such as these that help determine the biological effects of radiation upon the human body."

"*Does the Space Administration have any other equipment on board?*"

"Yes, Lowell. NASA is also using a radiometer to measure the amount of radiation which is scattered back from the earth's atmosphere. The radiation we receive from the sun is mostly in the form of light and heat. Some of it is retained and it warms up the earth, making it hotter in some places and colder in others, depending upon how much solar radiation is received. And this is the story of the world's weather. But some of this light and heat is reflected back into space, and our radiometer is pointed downward to measure the extent of this reflected radiation at various points around the globe. Father Anderson Bakewell is operating this particular instrument."

"Thank you, Dr. Korff. And we'll be talking with you again later on about our scientific goals. But soon now we'll be landing at Lisbon, and before signing off I want to tell you about Father Anderson Bakewell whom Dr. Korff just mentioned. Father Bakewell is our 'flying chaplain,' you might say. And he's assistant pastor of Holy Trinity Church in Washington. Even before he was ordained in 1951, he was a mountain climber and explorer, and he has continued to pursue a life of adventure ever since. Years ago he made the first ascent of Pico Cristóbal Colón, the highest peak of the Sierra Nevada in Colombia, a mountain known to the Indians as the 'Throne of the Dead.' Once, also, he was on an expedition to Mexico to locate specimens of the only python believed to be in the Western Hemisphere, and he personally collected a number of live reptiles on the slopes of Colima Volcano and presented them to a zoological society. As you can see, Father Bakewell is a combination of priest, scientist and explorer. Time to sign off now as we approach the airport at Lisbon, so it's so long for now from the *Polecat*, and I'll be reporting again soon."

We landed at Lisbon's Portela Airport at 1:31 A.M., GMT, on Tuesday, November 16, the second day of our journey. We had covered the distance from London in two hours and 19 minutes, and this, too, was another transport speed record, one of eight the *Polecat* would eventually establish. Next would come the long 6000-mile flight across the South Atlantic to Buenos Aires over much of the ocean trail blazed by Major Ramón Franco some forty years before. A capacity fuel load was required, and our flight engineers immediately went to work directing the refueling operation and checking the equipment.

And while we were on the ground at Lisbon, a funny thing happened to several *Polecat* crewmen on their way to the airport operations office. Captain Buck, Jim Gannett and about five others walked into the terminal building to file a flight plan, and they crowded into a small elevator that was supposed to carry them to the upper floor. But when they pressed the button, it blew a fuse, and instead of going up, the elevator went down to the basement which happened to be a bonded customs area with a big padlock on the elevator gate. It was one of those open-cage elevators and our flying companions were in plain view, trapped behind the metal bars while outside a frantic search went on for the padlock key. But the hour was well past midnight, and a mild-mannered airport official didn't help matters when he said: "I'm very sorry, but the man with the key won't be here until later in the day."

They were stuck in the cage for about an hour and Clete Roberts, ever on the prowl for a good news story, asked a cameraman to take a picture. That did it, for, just as the photographer aimed his camera, Captain Buck grabbed the cage with his hands and yelled out:

"Knock off that silly picture-taking business and get us out of here!"

A big barrel-chested Portuguese Army officer finally showed up with a hack-saw and cut through the padlock. By that time, though, all the victims had lost their senses of humor, and no one dared mention the incident for hours afterwards.

"Hello everyone. This is Lowell Thomas, Jr., reporting from the globe-prowling *Polecat*. We left Lisbon a short while ago and now we're off the west coast of Africa, heading south toward the bottom of the planet with Buenos Aires our immediate destination. And for the first time on this flight, we expect to be in broad daylight as soon as we pass the Cape Verde Islands. Harrison Finch and Fred Austin have been pretty busy with their jobs as flight commanders, but they're taking the pilot's seat now and then, just to keep in touch with the controls.

"All of us are getting in a little sleep when we get the chance, either in the bunks or on the collapsible rubber fuel tanks which, by the way, are great to curl up on for a short nap. Jim Jones, one of our flight engineers, keeps his bedding in the forward baggage compartment and, just a while ago, he came out after sleeping about six hours. Captain Austin met him in the companionway and asked him:

" 'How do you feel now, Jim, after that long nap?'

" 'Terrible,' Jim yawned in reply. 'I had a good sleep but I dreamt I was awake.'

"And that's the way it goes on this polar flight. When you're asleep, you sometimes think you're awake. Incidentally, we have a practicing psychiatrist on board—Dr. Walter Gartner of Los Angeles, and his job is to take a look at the problems of people working intensely in cramped quarters where the levels of fatigue can be high. He represents a firm called Serendipity Associates, a group engaging in research and development activities for government and industry. We'll be thrown together in tight quarters on this polar orbiting plane for nearly three days, but everybody seems to be holding up very well. No short tempers, no 'nervous nellies,' or anything like that. So that's about it for now, but I'll be reporting again soon from the *Polecat*, somewhere over the South Atlantic on our way to Buenos Aires."

We were well out over the South Atlantic with the sun above us for the first time when I had a two-way radio conversation with my wife, Tay, in Anchorage, Alaska. We talked directly through the Collins Radio control station in Cedar Rapids where they made a "phone patch"—plugging the receiver into a telephone line to Alaska. Our conversation across thousands of miles of land, water, ice, and snow went something like this:

"Hello, Tay. Can you hear me? Over."

"Yes, I can just perfectly. Over."

"We're above the South Atlantic, almost halfway between Lisbon and Buenos Aires. Have you heard any of my reports? Over."

"Oh yes. We've been glued to the radio all day. It sounds terribly exciting, and we think of you all the time, wondering what you're doing while you're flying so much. Over."

"Well, we're busy, taking notes and pictures and trying to get a little sleep every once in a while. And we're being served hot meals, pancakes, steak, peas, carrots—none of those squeeze tubes the astronauts use for food because there's plenty of gravity on this plane. Goodwin Lyon is filling in as the official chef but he's getting a helping hand from Melvin McKinney who's a bank vice-president from Sherman Oaks, California. Hank-from-the-Bank, we call him. And we're making good time across the ocean, although we were delayed a bit in Lisbon when some of our party got stuck in an elevator. Over."

"It just goes to show that you're much safer up in the air. Over."

"You can say that again. Over. Are you still there?"

"Yes, I'm still here. Can you say 'hello' to your daughter who's awake and right here? Over."

"Right, put her on. Hello, Anne. How are you? Over."

"I'm fine."

"Well, I'll see you, I hope on Thursday, but I can't get home until this plane has gone all the way around the world. So lots of love to you all, and now we'd better sign off. Tay? Is there anything else? Over."

"Nothing else. But we're thinking of you, and send all of our love."

And that's how it was out over the South Atlantic. Home, sweet, home was only a turn of the radio dial away. Just about the same time, I had another two-way radio talk, this one with General Hunter Harris, commander of the American Air Force in the Pacific, who was on a jet plane approaching Manila. Now the Philippines are exactly halfway around the world from the South Atlantic, about 12,000 miles distant, and I thought that Collins Radio had performed a modern miracle with a conversation between two planes in flight, with half the globe between them.

"Hello everyone. This is Lowell Thomas, Jr., reporting from the *Polecat* somewhere over the Atlantic Ocean south of the Equator. We're still quite a distance from Buenos Aires, our present destination, but the weather is beautiful and I'm sure we'll get there on schedule. Right now I want Dr. Korff to tell you more about the scientific work on board the plane, for there's plenty of it in progress.

"*Dr. Korff, one of the big problems of high altitude flying, of course, is the sudden turbulence that often occurs in what appears to be perfectly clear atmosphere. Are we investigating this during our flight?*"

"Yes, Lowell, we certainly are, although this clear-air tur-

bulence is a dangerous phenomenon for which no warning
systems have yet been devised. We simply know very little about
it. A jet plane traveling at, say, 600 miles an hour, can be badly
shaken and even forced off its course. And this can happen in
a cloudless sky. We're using what's known as a single axis ac-
celerometer to measure turbulence effects for comparison with
pilots' reports of turbulence at various degrees of intensity."

*"Well, Doctor, we've been flying through the jet streams. Do
they have anything to do with turbulence?"*

"Yes, turbulence often occurs at the edge of a jet stream.
There are two jet streams, one in the Northern Hemisphere
and the other in the Southern, but very little is known about the
one in the South where there are relatively few meteorological
stations. A jet stream sometimes has speed in excess of 150 miles
an hour, and a pilot would like to know how to get into it if he
wants a tail wind, or how to get out of it to avoid a head wind.
Our Double Pole flight will intersect the jet streams four different times as we go around, and by periodic recordation of air
pressures, temperatures, and wind velocity we hope to expand
our knowledge in this field."

*"While we're on the subject of weather, Dr. Korff, what
role is the U. S. Weather Bureau playing in our flight?"*

"A very important one. The Bureau has provided on-board
equipment to measure the amounts of carbon dioxide and ozone
in the atmosphere at various flight levels. There's only a relatively small amount of carbon dioxide in the atmosphere but
its presence has great significance, mainly because it gives the
earth's atmosphere some of the qualities of a greenhouse. As we
all know, the sunlight can get into a greenhouse, but the heat
can't get back out. And so it is with carbon dioxide in the
atmosphere. It lets the heat from the sun in, but the earth gets
hotter when the heat can't get back out, and this could possibly
throw the globe's natural forces out of balance. Interestingly
enough, most of the carbon dioxide in our atmosphere comes
from man-made industries. Enormous quantities of it are belched
from blast furnaces, smokestacks, and other industrial structures.

And, since most of the world's industrial complexes are located in the Northern Hemisphere's middle latitudes, the Southern Hemisphere derives comparatively little carbon dioxide from this source. Even so, we know very little about the extent of carbon dioxide in the Southern Hemisphere's high altitudes. For instance, is there enough mixing? Is it uniformly distributed north and south? Is there enough wind drift to bring this about? The Weather Bureau's Director of Aviation Affairs, N. E. Lieurance, is conducting this phase of our work. He has an air sampling device on board to measure the content of carbon dioxide and ozone in the atmosphere."

"Dr. Korff, that carbon dioxide 'greenhouse' sounds like it could become a very hot place at times, but not too hot, I hope. Before signing off, a word about Mr. Lieurance who heads this study. Serving as a weatherman on scientific and exploration flights is nothing new to him. During World War II, he was meteorologist on flights that helped develop weather services for the Naval Air Transport Command in the Pacific and the Far East. Back in 1952, he made a global survey of aviation weather on an around-the-world flight that originated in Washington. And he's been with the Weather Bureau for nearly twenty years. We're rapidly approaching the Ezeiza Airport at Buenos Aires now, and soon we'll be taking off for the South Pole. I'll be reporting again, but until then, this is Lowell Thomas, Jr., saying so long for now from the *Polecat*."

The Argentine skies were clear and the temperature was 89 degrees as Jack Martin brought the plane in to land at Buenos Aires where government officials were waiting to greet us. We had flown the 5957 miles from Lisbon in 11 hours and 56 minutes, another speed record. And, counting the ground time at Lisbon, the flight from London had taken 16 hours and 41 minutes, still another record. So far, the *Polecat* had established four speed marks. We spent three hours on the ground at Buenos Aires, and for a good part of that time Bernt Balchen sat on the steps outside the plane, soaking up the sun and getting one of the brownest suntans of his life.

We were about to begin a journey full of memories for Bernt who, as you know, was Byrd's pilot on the first plane—a Ford tri-motor—ever to fly across the South Pole back in 1929. Since that time, Bernt has become a kind of elder statesman of aeronautical exploration. He had flown Byrd across the Atlantic in 1927, and during the 1930s he was chief pilot of Lincoln Ellsworth's Antarctic Expedition. In the early years of World War II, Bernt served with the RAF Ferry Command before transferring to the U. S. Air Force and advancing to the rank of colonel. At the height of the war he directed aerial combat operations against the German occupation forces in his homeland of Norway and received many decorations including the Congressional and Distinguished Service Medals. Now retired from military service, he's aviation consultant to General Dynamics in New York City.

The *Polecat*'s crew now faced one of the most critical takeoffs of the entire flight. The distance from Buenos Aires across the South Pole to Christchurch, New Zealand, was about 7000 miles, but most of the flight would be across the desolate ice and snow of the Antarctic Continent. It would, of course, require a capacity fuel load, and the runway at Buenos Aires was 11,500 feet long—barely within the *Polecat*'s takeoff capabilities at maximum weight. However, the temperatures were around 90 degrees, and hot weather increases the takeoff problems of a heavily loaded plane. There were misgivings, and some fingers were crossed as Captain Bob Buck took the controls with Jack Martin by his side, but the *Polecat* rolled swiftly and smoothly along the runway, then rose toward the Antarctic skies.

"Hello again, everyone. This is Lowell Thomas, Jr., reporting from the *Polecat*, bound for the South Pole. We left Buenos Aires just a few moments ago and the Pole is about 4000 miles away. The weather is perfect, and we're flying well above 30,000 feet as we head down the Argentine coast toward the open Atlantic. We're not sure what kind of weather we'll run into over the Antarctic, for the reports are rather sketchy. But conditions so far are favorable, and all weather stations are alerted along the way.

"A few moments ago I was talking to our flight commanders, Harrison Finch and Fred Austin, both of whom are greatly relieved over the *Polecat*'s performance in getting off that hot runway at Buenos Aires with a full load of fuel. This will be the first time a plane has ever flown from Buenos Aires across the South Pole to New Zealand, and our flight's sponsor, Colonel Rockwell, has his eye on a record of his own. At the age of seventy-seven, he believes he'll become the oldest man ever to fly over both the North and South Poles. Colonel Rockwell also says it's a pleasure to be on a flight with men who are experts in their fields, and to see so many chiefs working like Indians. That's all for now, but soon I'll be reporting again as we fly over the South Pole. So it's so long for now from the *Polecat*."

About an hour after we left Buenos Aires, I had another two-way radio conversation. This time, with my father, who was at his desk in New York.

"Hello. This is L.T., Sr. How are you? Over."

"Well, hello there. Greetings, what a surprise. I had no idea you were on the line. Everything is going along just fine. Over."

"Where are you at this moment, and how long will it be before you reach the Pole? Over."

"Well, just a second. I've written it down somewhere. Here it is. Let's see. We should be there in about six hours. Over."

"Fine. When you fly over the Antarctic Peninsula, I don't want anybody to go out of their way. But if you could get a look at those L.T. Mountains named for me by Finn Ronne, it would be kind of fun because I've never seen them. So it's up to you. Over."

"Yes, we're going to try to sneak over and take a look, although we don't know what the weather is like ahead. But if it's clear at all I'm pretty sure we'll be able to see them. From the technical point of view, this is the most critical part of the

flight. Once we leave South America behind, there's no place
to go in an emergency. As you know, it's a very long haul and,
so far, we have no reliable information on the weather over the
Antarctic, especially the winds. Over."

"In an emergency couldn't you land, make a belly landing, at
the South Pole itself? Flying the Antarctic can be plenty risky
as you know. And isn't it possible for you to land at McMurdo
where there's a landing strip on the ice? Over."

"Er—well, I imagine McMurdo Sound would be an emergency
possibility, but the flight crew doesn't like the idea because it
would pose some terrific problems, like servicing the plane
and getting started again. The ultimate emergency of course
would be a belly landing somewhere on the ice cap. But no one
is even thinking about that. The plane is operating beautifully,
no problems whatsoever. Over."

"O.K. That's all very interesting. I'll sign off now, and try
to contact you again later on. So long and good luck."

Not long after I talked with L.T., Sr., we passed over the
first icebergs and reached the outer limits of the Antarctic
Continent. But a cloud cover developed beneath us and we
could see none of the icy terrain and, because of this factor
along with time, distance, and fuel, we had to abandon our
plans to get a look at those mountains we talked about. As
we sped over the ice fields we sent a message to President Johnson in Washington, telling him about our flight objectives and
expressing hope that it would further man's scientific knowledge
in the realm of aviation.

When we were well over the polar plateau, Bernt Balchen
went forward to the cockpit and sat beside Captain Buck who
was piloting the plane. We were flying well over 30,000 feet,
and the *Polecat* had none of the problems Balchen had in climbing above the 12,000-foot Antarctic horst when he flew that
Byrd plane back in 1929. You'll recall they had to kick a lot
of emergency food supplies out the door in order to get their
plane over the mountains. As a matter of fact, as the *Polecat*
neared those same mountains, I thought I saw Bernt taking a

careful look at some of our food supplies in the galley, but perhaps this was only my imagination. Shortly after passing the Antarctic Peninsula and reaching the main coastline itself, the clouds rolled back and the visibility was unlimited. Bob Buck told me that Bernt, sitting up front in the co-pilot's seat, was the world's most qualified tour guide for a flight across the Antarctic. As we reached a point within 40 miles of the Pole, virtually every man on the plane was up in the forward cabin, watching the blue lights of the Inertial Navigation System as the big moment drew near at a speed of 550 miles an hour.

"Hello everyone. This is Lowell Thomas, Jr., reporting from the *Polecat*—over the South Pole at this very moment! We've just completed the first historic flight from the North to the South Pole. Our altitude is 37,000 feet and we're in bright sunshine over the U. S. Amundsen-Scott Station where some 40 men are based and living beneath the snow and ice. Despite all our advanced navigational technique, our pilot, Bob Buck, still needed an assist from the ground in order to hit the Pole right on the nose. Over the radio he asked someone at the station:

" 'Can you see us? Over.'

" 'No,' came the answer, 'but I'm under the ice. Wait, I'll come out.'

"There was a brief pause, and then came the same voice, again:

" 'Now I can see you. You're west of the Pole. Turn a little to the left and you'll make it fine.'

"The observer down below had spotted our contrails in the sky, and from the plane we could then see the antennas at the station very clearly. A plane had actually landed at the South Pole for the first time only three years before in 1962. It was an American Navy ski-plane, commanded by Rear Admiral George J. Dufek, who landed there to start the ball rolling for Operation Deep Freeze. And to him went the honor of planting the Stars and Stripes where only two other flags, the Norwegian and the British, had been planted before. Perhaps you can hear a little of the cheering in the background. Everybody on the *Polecat* is most appreciative of this opportunity to fly over the South Pole, and it's a moment to be remembered. Our five pilots are taking turns at the controls, sharing the privilege of flying over this southernmost point on the globe. And there's a birthday ceremony in progress, too. Someone brought a cake along to give our flight engineer, Jim Jones, for this is his forty-seventh birthday. As we circle over the Pole, Father Bakewell is reading a prayer over our radio to the men down below, blessing the South Pole Station and all its members. So that's it for now. I'll be reporting again soon as we climb back up the other side of the globe."

Leaving the South Pole behind, we flew on across the vast polar plateau, the scene of some of exploration's most stirring episodes. And there's still a lot to be learned about that mammoth continent of ice. Even today, for instance, there remains a controversy over the proper pronunciation of the word "Antarctic." Some people pronounce it "Ant-ark-tik," while others say "Ant-art-ik." But you can take your choice, because Webster quotes it both ways in that order. Fully 90 percent of the world's accumulation of snow and ice was on the land and seas beneath us. Should Dr. Korff's carbon dioxide "greenhouse" ever get hot enough, all that snow and ice might even melt. And if that happened, all the oceans would rise about 200 feet. There would be no port city left in the world and the Atlantic coastline of the United States would be somewhere in central Pennsylvania, with everybody running for the hills. Not even science fiction can match that for a scary story.

The distance from the Pole to Christchurch was about 3000 miles and Jim Gannett took the controls as we headed toward McMurdo Sound where the United States maintains a base on the Antarctic coast. About half an hour after leaving the Pole I had another two-way talk with my father in New York.

"Hi there. This is L.T., Sr. How's it going? Over."

"Hello, hello there. It's going exceedingly well. We just passed over the South Pole Station a short while ago and could actually see it down below on the ice. And we've established another speed record, flying from pole to pole in 34 hours and 46 minutes. Over."

"Well, that's fine. By the way, I talked to Dr. James Mooney, deputy commander of Deep Freeze, in Washington tonight and he said that, in an emergency, he was sure your plane could land at McMurdo and take off. Over."

"Roger. Roger. The crew has that information, but we're in good shape now. Unfortunately, Dad, there was an undercast and we didn't see your mountains after all. But right now, looking down to the starboard, I can see an immense range of mountains covered with snow and ice. We're only about one hundred miles from the Pole itself and on the 170th meridian to Christchurch. Over."

"Fine. It's great to know things are going okay. So long."

As we passed over McMurdo Sound, unable to see it, our pilot talked to the base commanding officer by radio and there was the usual exchange of greetings. Then we headed on north over the Pacific toward Christchurch, our next-to-last port of call.

"Hello everyone. This is Lowell Thomas, Jr., on the round-the-world *Polecat* somewhere over the South Pacific. We're on our way to Christchurch, New Zealand, and should be there in about an hour and a half. Looking out the window at the moment there's lots of water, but no ice. The Roaring Forties are behind us now. It won't be too long before we'll be bringing this flight to an end, but we hope its scientific achievements will linger on for the future safety of aviation. The chief of our scientific team, Dr. Korff, has been very busy, but I believe he has one more phase of his activity to tell you about.

"*Dr. Korff, I understand we're taking pictures of cloud formations as we go along.*"

"That's right, Lowell. The purpose is to correlate these photographs with the ones being relayed to earth from those Tiros
satellites now in orbit. The difference is that the Tiros pictures
are being taken looking straight down on top of the clouds,
while ours are being made sideways from the horizontal position. By correlating the Tiros vertical pictures with our horizontal ones, we'll get a fuller perspective of these cloud formations. This time-lapse photography is being directed by Dr.
Donald Goedeke of the Douglas Aircraft Corporation."

"Thank you, Dr. Korff. Dr. Goedeke, by the way, has a long
record of scientific research in the Antarctic where, only a few
years ago, he established a geophysical laboratory at McMurdo
Sound. We should be arriving at Christchurch soon now, but,
for the moment, it's so long from the *Polecat* over the South
Pacific."

It was dark again when we came down to land at Christchurch International Airport at 9 A.M., GMT, on Wednesday.
And we had established another speed record by making the
flight from Buenos Aires across the South Pole in 14 hours 17
minutes. We remained on the ground only about two hours,
and then took off across the Pacific on the last lap, the 4861-mile
flight to Honolulu. Shortly after leaving Christchurch, I had
one more two-way radio conversation with my father in New
York.

"Hello, this is L.T., Sr. How's it going now? Over."

"Hi there. It's still going fine. We just took off from Christchurch, and we're on our way to Honolulu. Our flight is almost
over, and so far we've survived the dangers and hazards that
our early aviators faced on their great flights from point-to-
point. But just the same, the penalties for failure would have
been just as extreme as they ever were, with all that snow
and ice in the Arctic and Antarctic, not to mention all the
oceans we've been flying over. If we had been forced down, or
had we crashed, survival for 39 people, some of them along in
years, might have been a pretty grim proposition under those
conditions. Over."

"That's true. On many of these first time flights we had tragedies, and whenever you set out to accomplish something like this, you must calculate the risk along with everything else. There're still unsolved mysteries as to what happened to some of those who took part in these flights. They simply vanished. On the Double Pole flight, at least you had excellent preparations, plus the fact that you have on board the world's Number One expert in Arctic rescue, Bernt Balchen. He has rescued more aviators in regions of snow and ice than any other person.

"Furthermore, you and some of your friends up there in Alaska now have your own unofficial rescue organization. And if anything had happened to the *Polecat* in the Arctic, some of your friends like Don Sheldon and others, who have their own planes, would have been on their way to drop supplies or pick all of you up from the ice floes, if possible. As for the Antarctic, rescue work there has come a long way since the development of those big ski-planes, the C-130 turbo-prop transports. Admiral Bakutis commands our Navy and Air Force planes in the Antarctic and they'd have been on their way to undertake a rescue in a hurry. Even if they had been unable to land, they could have dropped emergency supplies, like tents, foods, and sledges, and maybe even a doctor or two would have parachuted down. So the chances for polar rescue are much better now than they ever were, especially since the past four or five years. Over."

"It's encouraging to know that, but I'm sure glad nobody had to blow the rescue whistle for the *Polecat*. As it is, the plane is doing fine, and home is just a few more hours away. Over."

"It's been a great flight, and I'm looking forward to seeing you soon. So long."

"Hello everyone. This is Lowell Thomas, Jr., reporting from the *Polecat* some 33,000 feet above the South Pacific. The weather on this global flight has been excellent, but we did run into some terrific thunderstorms over Samoa about an hour or so ago. The towering thunderheads of the inter-tropical front reached up to 45,000 feet, well above our operating ceiling, but we steered our way through them and now we're rapidly approaching Honolulu. All I can say at the moment by way of summation, is that this has been the thrill of a lifetime for all of us on board. The Boeing 707 and its Pratt & Whitney engines, Collins Radio communications, and the Inertial Navigation System, all performed marvelously throughout the flight. We're greatly indebted to all of those who made this global journey possible, particularly Captains Fred Austin and Harrison Finch who had the inspiration and energy to pull this whole thing together. Colonel Rockwell said at the beginning that his firm was financing the flight in the interests of broader research in intercontinental aviation. And his dedication to this goal has been an inspiration to us all. This is Lowell Thomas, Jr., saying goodbye from the *Polecat*."

The same Hawaiian girls who had given us the sendoff welcomed us again when we landed at 12:41 P.M., Pacific Standard Time, on Wednesday. We had left Honolulu on Sunday evening, but the tropical flowers we had taken on board were still fresh when we returned. Among those who greeted us was General Erik Nelson, one of the heroes of that first round-the-world flight in 1924. The Honolulu customs officials greeted us, too, and gave us something of a hard time. They couldn't understand that we'd circled the world without leaving the premises of the airports on the way around, and staying with the plane all that distance just didn't make sense to them.

And a final word about speed records. When the *Polecat* began its flight, we were after five jet transport records, but we actually wound up with eight. The distance from Christchurch to Honolulu was covered in 9 hours and 1 minute, a record. And for the big one, we traveled 26,230 miles around the world over both poles in a record 62 hours, 27 minutes and 35 seconds. The actual time in flight was 51 hours, 27 minutes. And would you believe it? Our flight commanders, Fred Austin and Harrison Finch, had predicted that 52 hours of flying time would be required for the journey.

Crew of the 1965 Double Pole flight stands in front of their jet, the *Polecat*. Harrison Finch, (second from left) and Fred L. Austin (second from right), both TWA commercial pilots, commanded the flight. The great aviator-explorer Bernt Balchen (center), holds one end of the plane's flag. Lowell Thomas, Jr., historian of the flight, is on the far right. (*J. R. Eyerman*)

If you happen to be an authority, or even a near authority on aviation, at this moment you may be saying, "but what about the flight of so and so, and the one by so and so?" If so you are right, for we could go on and on. In fact there are two or three we were so reluctant to leave out we are including them in an epilogue—just to ease our conscience, and also as a salute to the scores of others whose stories would fill many books. You may find them the most exciting of all.

Epilogue:
A Salute to Those Who Failed

(With a Bow to a Few Others Who Succeeded)

We have told the stories of some of the airmen who made the first important point-to-point flights on this planet—flights that were milestones in the history of aviation. However, as we pointed out in our "Before the Takeoff" prologue, the stories of the "also-rans" often surpassed the others for sheer excitement and adventure. The fliers who came in second, third, or last received little recognition. This thought was expressed rather well by Charles L. Lawrence, the man who perfected the Wright Whirlwind engine that carried Lindbergh, Kingsford-Smith, and so many others triumphantly to their goals. When someone reminded Lawrence of the little credit he had received for the brilliant performance of his engines, he replied:

"Who ever heard the name of Paul Revere's horse?"

So as a salute to the hundreds of airmen of all nations who received little recognition for their part in these great long-distance races, we have decided to mention a few who tried to get there first but didn't. In fact, we will give you some of the story of perhaps the most madcap adventure of all, the flight of two young airmen who crossed the finish line months after one of the greatest of these air races was over.

Before embarking on these narrations, we also would like to make a bow in the direction of those who did achieve "firsts," but are not included here because of space limitations, or because we simply haven't their stories. For example, we know almost nothing about long-distance flights made by the Russians prior to June 1937, when Chkalov, Baidukov, and Beliakov startled the world with their flight over the North Pole to the U.S.A. Also, throughout World War II, there were many spectacular flights over vast distances but we heard little about them, mainly because of military security.

The story of one of these wartime flights became fully known only in recent years. It was one that established a new aerial link between Australia and Ceylon at a time when Japanese combat planes were roaming the skies above the Indian Ocean. By early 1942, the Japanese military juggernaut had overrun Southeast Asia, cutting asunder the British Empire's aerial routes between Australia and England. This was a devastating blow to Allied communications through the air, and high-ranking officials in both London and Australia met far into the night to chart a course of action in the emergency. The answer became obvious. An air link must be established across the 3500-mile stretch of Indian Ocean between Perth, on Australia's west coast, and the island of Ceylon. This long, lonely, barren expanse of water became known—only to a few—as the Kangaroo Route. Even as late as 1942, no plane had ever flown it non-stop.

In April of that year, only four months after the Japanese attack on Pearl Harbor, the plans to bridge the Indian Ocean were set in motion. The managing director of Qantas Empire Airways, Hudson Fysh, asked the Australian government for permission to establish the link with Catalina flying boats, if such aircraft were available. But A. B. Corbett, Director-General of Australia's Civil Aviation, didn't think much of the idea.

"I'm afraid you will obtain no support for your proposal to start an Empire service to Ceylon at present," Corbett wrote in a letter to Fysh. "The area is not regarded as safe for flying boats. The prospect of obtaining Catalinas is remote. And my reaction is that the proposal would be little short of murder."

Still, Hudson Fysh was not easily swerved from his views. First, he borrowed a Catalina from the British government. Then, Qantas completed a survey flight from Perth to Ceylon, with the plane landing on Koggala Lake south of Colombo. In 1943, Captain R. B. Tapp commanded the first Catalina to make a regular civil flight over the Kangaroo Route. For the next two years these flying boats made a total of 270 crossings. Even so, the first one hundred flights were completed before the public learned that an Empire air link had been secretly re-established by way of Ceylon.

Flight certificates were issued to those who flew the Kangaroo Route, admitting them to the "Rare and Secret Order of the Double Sunrise"—a reference to the length of the clandestine flights since they averaged more than 24 hours in the air. Because of the danger of Japanese planes, each flight was made with the radio silent, even though the crewmen could still receive—but not send—messages en route. Sometimes the Catalinas would land on Cocos, a small island in the Indian Ocean midway between Perth and Ceylon. Japanese bombers often flew over Cocos, but for the most part they failed to interrupt the new air link.

The Catalinas made their last flights over the secret Kangaroo Route in July 1945, after achieving the vital task of carrying top-ranking officers, couriers, diplomats and mail—much of this American—between Australia and Ceylon at the height of the Pacific War. This was truly another major "first" in aviation annals.

As we have seen, Major Ramón Franco became the first to fly across the South Atlantic from Spain to Brazil in 1927. Before that, however, two Portuguese naval officers completed a South Atlantic crossing in 1922, wrecking two planes on the way and being forced to travel part of the distance by steamer. Rear Admiral Gago Coutinho and Captain Saccadura Cabral took off from Lisbon, Portugal, on March 30, arriving at Pernambuco, Brazil, more than two months later. In order to complete their 4000-mile journey they eventually had to use three seaplanes, all of the same type—Fairey models, with a 360-hp Rolls-Royce engine. Captain Cabral was pilot while Admiral Coutinho attended to the navigational duties, a field in which he had distinguished himself for nearly 30 years. Although Coutinho was fifty-three years of age, he tackled problems of aerial navigation with all the enthusiasm of youth and the South Atlantic flight served as a test for his new techniques.

Flying their first plane, the *Lusitania*, they reached the Cape Verde Islands. Two weeks later rough seas made it impossible to take off with a full load of fuel for the long South Atlantic flight to Fernando de Noronha Island. Deciding to risk it anyway, they left on the morning of April 18 but only a few hours later noted with alarm that the gasoline supply was rapidly dwindling.

For nearly an hour, Coutinho and Cabral argued over what to do—land in the sea while it was still daylight and hope that some passing ship would pick them up, or continue on to the St. Paul Rocks, a point on the route to Fernando de Noronha. They decided to head for the Rocks. They arrived in darkness with their gas tanks empty, and when they came down to land in the sea, huge waves wrecked the plane. Luckily, the two fliers were picked up by a Portuguese cruiser standing by for just such an emergency.

Nearly a month passed before a new plane arrived so they could resume their flight. After only a few hours in the air, engine trouble developed to force them down at sea again. Fortunately, the British steamer *Paris City* was in the vicinity and rescued them, though their second plane also became victim of the heavy seas and went down to Davy Jones. When the steamer landed them at Fernando de Noronha they awaited the arrival of their third plane. Then on June 5, they finally took off on the 279-mile flight to Brazil, completing a transatlantic journey that had been as agonizing as it was heroic.

Shortly after Lindbergh flew from New York to Paris in 1927 —followed days later by Clarence Chamberlain who made it all the way to Berlin—Byrd, Balchen, Acosta, and Noville made their dramatic flight in the *America*, landing in the surf off the French coast near the village of Ver-Sur-Mer. Part of the story of what happened aboard their plane on the way over has never been chronicled. In fact, some of the drama and near tragedy on almost every expedition remains untold out of consideration for the feelings and sensitivities of others. Many of the airmen and explorers who undertook these hazardous feats were prima donnas—men of unusual talent in one direction, but not necessarily gifted in other fields. As a result, there are personality clashes on many expeditions, the stories of which seldom reach the public.

One of the wisest of them all, Sir Hubert Wilkins, avoided this problem by keeping the personnel of his expeditions to an absolute minimum. Still, other famous explorers, including Admiral Byrd, took many men into the field and then had endless personnel problems to solve. The strain and tension of months of isolation often is too much. I recall one expedition on which a friend of mine went on the air from down near the South Pole. One day, when in direct voice radio contact with New York, he told his employer who was on the other end: "Boss, if you don't get me away from here, I'm going to shoot this S.O.B.!"

There was, as we know, a personality clash between Roald Amundsen and Umberto Nobile during the flight of their dirigible, *Norge*, across the polar regions from Spitsbergen to Alaska. This resulted in much bitterness. Even so Amundsen subsequently went to his death in the Arctic, trying to aid Nobile and his companions aboard the dirigible *Italia*.

Then, there is the untold human interest story of the famous Arctic explorer who once remained an extra winter in the North because he was infatuated with a woman whose life story could well be the basis of a lurid novel. While he has been dead for some years now, at last reports she was still alive. Also, if you visit those parts of the Arctic inhabited by the Eskimos, don't be surprised if you find among them some whose features are hardly Mongoloid. These are the sons and daughters of celebrated Arctic travelers—another tale that will never be told.

Now, for the story of one of the strangest flights of all time
—we come to the aerial odyssey of Parer and McIntosh, which
had its beginning in a London pub. The year was 1919, with
Hounslow Aerodrome the bustling base for the Great London-
to-Australia Air Derby. Many Australian aviators wanted to enter
the competition and win the large cash prize offered by the
Australian government. As usual, some fliers were having trouble
securing a plane, to say nothing of financial backing. Having,
perhaps, the most difficulty of all was Lieutenant Raymond
Parer, an Australian airman who was more or less stranded in
London at the end of the First World War.

Ray Parer, twenty-five years of age, a quiet little man from
Melbourne, was known as "The Pocket Hercules" among his
friends in England. He literally had grown up with airplanes.
Even before joining the wartime Australian Flying Corps while
still in his teens, he was designing engines, aircraft and successful gliders. Parer, who was something of a genius with
engines, went directly into the AFC as a mechanic where his
superiors soon discovered he was also a skillful pilot. To his
sorrow he failed to be assigned to a combat squadron because
an AFC doctor said his heart was not strong. So he should never
be allowed to fly higher than 10,000 feet! Nevertheless his skill
as a pilot was not to be set aside lightly, and he was given the
assignment of testing the newer combat planes—a job with a
mortality rate of more than 50 percent.

For weeks during that summer of 1919, Parer had been hoping to get a plane and find a financial "angel" for the London-
to-Australia Derby, all with no success. Then one evening he was
in a London pub, trying to plot his next move over a drink.
Beside him at the bar was a tall Scot in flying uniform. As two
men are wont to do under such circumstances, they conversed.
The convivial Scot was Lieutenant John Crowe McIntosh, an
RFC veteran who had been wounded in the Gallipoli campaign.
As a youth, McIntosh had journeyed to western Australia where
he worked as a timber-cutter. Then, at the outbreak of war he

enlisted with the Australians, and eventually was transferred to the Royal Flying Corps. Later, he even invented an aerial bomb that was accepted by the War Office. With the war now over he was attached to a training squadron near London.

Ordering a new round of drinks, Parer told McIntosh about his futile efforts to enter the big race. The Air Ministry had surplus planes up for sale though, try as he might, he could find no one ready to put up the money. Being an extrovert and in high spirits at the moment, McIntosh listened to Parer's tale of woe with lively enthusiasm.

"Just a minute," the Scotsman interrupted, "if I can raise that money, will you take me on as a partner for this halfway-round-the-world race?"

"Certainly," Parer replied. There would be nothing to lose, although he wondered how McIntosh could get his hands on the necessary cash.

From then on they were a team. As the days passed, Parer realized that McIntosh had many of the qualities he himself lacked, including boundless optimism, intuitive judgment, and the knack of saying the right thing at the right time. Still, finding a financial backer seemed to be no easier and all prospective "angels" continued saying "no"—until one day a friend suggested Peter Dawson, the millionaire Scottish distiller.

Since Scotland was McIntosh's home ground, he set out for Glasgow where he encountered no trouble at all in closing an agreement with his sports-minded, generous, fellow Scot. Peter Dawson not only put up enough money to buy a plane, he also promised more financial help if and when it was needed.

Said Dawson, "After all, if you and Parer can risk your lives, surely I can risk a few thousand pounds."

Whereupon, they purchased a DeHavilland-9 biplane with a 6-cylinder, 240-hp Puma engine, and named it the "P.D." in honor of their benefactor. Meanwhile time was running out with other planes already racing toward Australia, 11,000 miles away. In fact, by the time Parer and McIntosh were ready, Ross Smith and his crew had landed their Vickers-Vimy at Port

Darwin. This meant the race actually was over. Even though Parer and McIntosh no longer could win the prize, they still might set some records and Peter Dawson was in complete agreement.

Their first task was to fly their plane from the Aircraft Disposals Depot near London to Hounslow where a longer runway would permit a heavier load of fuel on takeoff. Getting to Hounslow in itself became the first of an endless series of adventures. They left the Depot at dusk, and even before arriving over Hounslow they lost their way in the semidarkness. Spotting a clearing surrounded by trees they came down to land, missing a fence by inches. That night as they tried to sleep in a haystack, a heavy rain drenched them, while at Hounslow the wiseacres were saying:

"How can they expect to reach Australia if they can't even find Hounslow?"

After reaching the official starting point on a typical dark

Lieutenants John McIntosh and Ray Parer in front of their war-surplus single-engine biplane before takeoff from England to Australia in January 1920. Though they finished last in the race by taking six months to complete the flight, their adventures brought them fame.

day in January 1920, they finally loaded the "P.D." with gas and supplies. One important item aboard was a bottle of Peter Dawson's well-known whiskey which their sponsor told them to hand to "Billy" Hughes, the Prime Minister of Australia.

Heading first for Paris, they climbed above the clouds to 5000 feet and crossed the Channel without seeing it. Some minutes later while over France, bad weather forced them down near Beauvais where they nearly crashed into trees, bouncing hard enough to lose a wheel. While McIntosh stayed with the plane, Parer started for Paris in a peasant's cart, hoping to find a replacement. Two days later at Le Bourget he talked some French airmen into loaning him a wheel, the only one they could find. Then, on returning to the plane he found it wasn't the right size! Wearily, Parer made the trip to Paris again and this time he found one that would do, and that got them on to Le Bourget.

Leaving Paris on January 17, they flew on down the Rhone Valley and the Italian coast to arrive at Sarazana, near the seaport of Spezia. On this flight they discovered they were using far too much oil, a forerunner of more trouble ahead. That night at a small inn, they were regaled with a typical Italian meal, and when he awoke the next morning McIntosh complained of having a nightmare in which he was "nearly strangled in spaghetti."

Heading on down the Italian coast the plane was airborne only ten minutes when a loud report came from the engine, followed by a stream of petrol gushing from the carburetor. Flames came out and crackled along the fuselage, nearly reaching Parer at the controls. "Now," McIntosh thought, "we'll learn what it's like to go down in flames."

But Parer knew a trick or two for such a desperate situation. As he put the plane into a side-slip the flow of the air stream extinguished the fire, just as he began feeling the heat on his legs. The maneuver had worked, and a few minutes later he brought the "P.D." down at Forte di Marmi, an abandoned aerodrome where they made repairs. By the time they got to Rome nearly a month had elapsed since their takeoff at Hounslow. All this meant spending more money than they had expected and they were obliged to send the first of many SOSs to Peter Dawson.

A week went by before a reply came, giving them a chance to see the sights of Rome and have a gay time. Finally, they took off on February 2, heading for Naples. As they came in over Mount Vesuvius, McIntosh urged Parer to fly near the smoking crater for a picture. Parer was willing, but instead of merely flying "near," he maneuvered to a point directly above the seething crater of molten lava and poisonous gases. Suddenly, the plane dropped as though an unseen giant hand were pulling it into the crater. For a moment the engine went dead and Parer thought they were heading into Dante's Inferno. Then it picked up again and they pulled out just in time.

Leaving Naples the following day, they flew on across the Apennines toward the Bay of Taranto, sometimes climbing as high as 14,000 feet to get above the clouds. Shortly after passing the island of Stromboli with its smoking volcano, they ran out of gas and were forced down in a hay field. This time they had to walk 14 miles to Nicastra, the nearest town, where Parer took a train back to Naples. There the British Consul came to his aid, and several days later a 200-liter drum of gasoline, despatched by train, was dropped off five miles from the plane. Parer and McIntosh then had the opportunity to engage in a new sport—rolling a drum full of gasoline for miles along a dusty Italian road. Although the experience at Nicastra was a rugged one, it did have its enjoyable moments. During their stay they were befriended by a young Italian baron who even put on a fiesta in their honor—with McIntosh entertaining the crowd with an exhibition of jujitsu, using the friendly baron as his willing victim.

Their plan had been to fly from the Bay of Taranto directly across the Ionian Sea to Athens, but it wasn't going to be that easy. Soon after takeoff, one of the fuel pumps froze. Then, a sudden gust of wind sent all of their maps sailing out of the cockpit. After an emergency landing at the Adriatic seaport of Brindisi to repair the pump, they flew on to Athens, coming in to land on a field near the Acropolis. Next came the long overwater leg to Africa, and when they reached the African coast they had set at least one record—it was the first time a single-engine plane had ever flown across the Mediterranean. They had made one stop on the island of Crete, and while flying the remaining 220 miles of open sea they expected every moment to be their final one, for the engine kept backfiring, forcing them to fly dangerously close to the water.

Their "P.D." was badly in need of an overhaul when they reached Heliopolis, the main aerodrome at Cairo. Also, they faced a new problem. The British officers and mechanics at Heliopolis were busy and gave them the brush-off, suggesting that they fly on to Helioun several miles away. There, they had better luck. Lord Milner, one of the top British pro-consuls of that period who had just landed at Helioun, took an interest in their predicament and urged the RAF to do everything possible for them. When mechanics examined the plane, they told Parer and McIntosh that if they had flown thirty minutes longer the tail assembly would have broken loose and they both probably would have been killed. Also, to cheer them up even more, the British officers at Helioun urged them to abandon their plans. They were told it would be impossible to cross the desert from Palestine to Baghdad. Parer and McIntosh laughed this off and when the British realized they were determined to continue, they gave the fliers hand grenades to carry along with their revolvers should they be forced down in the desert. Once again out of funds they managed to borrow enough money to get out of town, and on February 26, took off across the Suez Canal and the Sinai Desert for Palestine.

Ramleh, in the Plain of Esdraelon, had been an important air base full of memories for those of us who had been there during the First World War. It had been one of Allenby's airfields, and I landed there when I flew up from Egypt to join Allenby's army. During those days Ross Smith also used Ramleh as his base for combat flights against the Turks. Here again, Parer and McIntosh were advised to call off their 640-mile flight on to Baghdad. Although the cruising range of their plane was only 500 miles, they had no intention of letting that stop them. Parer was sure that somehow they could complete the journey— with a favorable tail wind. So after refueling and taking on some tins of bully-beef, biscuits, and two flasks of brandy, they flew on east toward Baghdad.

When they reached a point far out over the desert, the engine once again began backfiring with flames shooting from the carburetor. Narrowly missing some boulders while landing, they fixed the motor and were off again. By this time, night was approaching and Parer decided to descend once more to wait until morning. They collected some desert shrubs and bedded down on the sand behind the tail assembly, and when they awoke at dawn a rough-looking Arab was standing near the plane. Within minutes more Arabs came out of nowhere, and they didn't look any friendlier. Faced with what could become a fight for their lives, the two fliers drew their revolvers and McIntosh, just to give the Arabs a fright, pulled the pin from a grenade. The explosion sent the Arabs reeling back, giving Parer and McIntosh time to jump into the cockpit. As the "P.D." took off, the Bedouins shouted at them in language which the fliers suspected would not be found in the Koran.

Despite all the dire predictions about their trans-Arabia flight, they arrived safely at Baghdad. Then on March 2 they headed on east, flying far out over the Persian Gulf part of the time to avoid a sandstorm. From the date port of Bandar Abbas they continued on across desolate Baluchistan to Karachi, in those days a small city on the Arabian Sea. Just before taking off across the Sind Desert for Delhi, they were told to avoid flying over the harem of the Maharaja of Jaipur. From Delhi, their route followed the course of the River Jumna to Allahabad on the Ganges, thence on to Calcutta where they landed, tired, and once again—broke.

In order to complete their flight to Australia, two things were needed—petrol and money. So they decided to remain in Calcutta long enough to bolster their finances by taking on some kind of work. A former major of the Indian Army offered to act as their agent and approached a number of business firms with plans for an aerial advertising campaign. So for the next two weeks Parer and McIntosh were busy dropping leaflets over the city—as well as into the Hooghli River. They also gave flying exhibitions until finally they had enough cash to continue on across the Bay of Bengal to Rangoon. Just before leaving they were astonished to learn that all their work had been unnecessary, for their benefactor in Scotland had not forgotten them. Peter Dawson already had cabled them a credit balance of a thousand pounds, payable by his agents in Calcutta!

After stopping at Akyab on the Burma coast, they took off for Rangoon and once more engine trouble plagued them, forcing them down on a sandbar in the Irrawaddy. Luckily, some hundreds of natives helped them push the plane across the shallow water to the river bank. The next day, their friends turned up with sheets of bamboo matting which were spread along the muddy ground for a runway—the same arrangement that had worked so well for Ross Smith on his journey through the Netherlands Indies a few months before.

While spending ten days at Rangoon for an engine overhaul, they were approached by a Chinese multi-millionaire who offered them a dowry of $30,000 each if they would marry his two daughters. Said Parer: "The girls were beautiful, but we figured we were having too many aeronautical problems to take on matrimonial ones." Leaving Rangoon, and the Chinese lovelies, they took off across the Gulf of Martaban on the short flight to Moulmein where their epic journey almost came to an abrupt end.

Approaching Moulmein, the engine let them down again and this time the trouble was really serious. Even worse, a great crowd had gathered in the field outside the city, forcing Parer to bring the plane in on terrain so rough it broke the propeller, wrenching off the undercarriage and crumpling the fuel tanks into a pile of junk. Neither he nor McIntosh was injured. However, they surveyed their damaged plane with sinking hearts, knowing it would take weeks to make repairs and maybe even then the "P.D." would be unable to fly again.

A crew of mechanics came down from Rangoon to help, and anything resembling an airplane part was used to put the "P.D." together again, including two automobile radiators. Even Burmese elephants were pressed into service to help move things about. Their intelligence fascinated Parer and McIntosh. As they watched, an elephant would pick up a log with his trunk, put it down again, and then turn around to see if it was just right. If not, he would give it a kick to set it straight, and then plod away.

It took all of six weeks to complete the overhaul and before they departed the Burmese gave them a farewell party that lasted far into the night. By now it was late in May as they took off and headed southward toward Penang, in Malaya. When they arrived, the motor was groaning again and Parer hurriedly came down in the middle of a polo game! It was a good question when the Polo Club's president rode up on his pony to ask: "What right have you to land here?"

Flying on down the Malay Peninsula by way of Singapore, their sometimes faithful "P.D." carried them across the islands of the East Indies, even though the temperamental engine continued to give them frequent trouble. After several more forced landings, including one in Java with another smashed propeller, they reached the island of Timor—jumping-off place for the final 400-mile overwater flight across the lonely Arafura Sea to Australia. More than six months had elapsed when they arrived at Port Darwin where the entire population turned out to give them a roaring welcome.

Ross Smith and his crew had made the flight from London in only twenty-eight days. Even so, Parer and McIntosh received a far more overwhelming and tumultuous reception on their way across Australia. In a way, this was not surprising for their countrymen had followed their fortunes and endless misfortunes ever since the takeoff from London many weeks and months before. They had been in trouble so many times and so much had appeared in the papers of Sydney, Melbourne, and other cities that no one really thought they'd ever make it in their flimsy, beaten-up single-engine plane. Everybody "Down Under" from Brisbane to Adelaide and on across to Kalgoorlie, Coolgardie and Perth marveled at their dogged courage and the way they continued their flight against all odds.

Even though they did come in last in the race halfway round-the-world, they did establish several aviation "firsts." For example, in addition to being the first to fly the Mediterranean in a single-engine plane, and also the Sea of Arfura, they won a similar distinction for their feat in flying from England to Australia. After all, Sir Ross Smith, his brother Sir Keith, and their two mechanics had two engines on their big Vickers-Vimy.

After the landing at Darwin came one of the most grueling parts of the flight—the garden parties, banquets and official receptions which followed in endless procession as they flew south across their home continent, with McIntosh regaling audiences with the incredible and humorous story of the flight. In Melbourne, then the capital, they were welcomed by Prime Minister "Billy" Hughes and a half-million people. They, at long last, personally presented the bottle of Peter Dawson Scotch that somehow had survived all their crashes and other adventures. Telegrams and cables of congratulations arrived from all parts of the world, including one from Geoffrey de Havilland, designer of their plane, who praised them with these words:

"Yours is certainly one of the finest endurance flights ever made. I hope you will write a book because it must have been crowded with interesting facts which would be of great use as data for the design of truly commercial machines. I have no doubt that you had every trouble possible to an airplane and engine, many times over!"

It so happened that I was in Australia at this time and I finally convinced Ray Parer that he himself should do a book. It was a modest volume called *Flight and Adventures*, and came

McIntosh and Parer on their arrival at Melbourne, Australia, where they were welcomed by the Prime Minister and cabinet and a vast throng of Parer's fellow countrymen.

about as close to being a modern *Odyssey* as anything since Homer's classic tale of the wanderings of Ulysses.

Alas, there is a tragic postscript to add about John McIntosh, the man who rounded up the money, who did so much to keep up his partner's spirits, and who also proved to be a born after-dinner speaker. "Mac" went into the airplane business and on Easter Monday, 1921, he crashed to his death at Pithara near Kalgoorlie in the southwestern Australian desert.

As for Ray Parer, he has gone on and on as an adventurer. He and his brother, Kevin, were aviation pioneers and explorers in New Guinea—one of the wildest regions on this planet. Early in World War II when Japanese planes began dropping bombs on New Guinea, Kevin Parer helped to evacuate women and children from the north coast, Lae, Madang, and Wewak. He was shot down—becoming Australia's first casualty of the war. Ray Parer, the London-to-Australia flier and perennial adventurer, now lives on a ranch at Mount Nebo near Queensland in the Land Down Under.

This completes our accounts of those fabulous flights through "Cayley's Ocean," otherwise known as the air—that navigable sea that reaches every man's door, so named for Sir George Cayley, a nineteenth-century British aeronautical theorist. He was alleged to have been the first to figure out the scientific principles of heavier-than-air flight, the principles that enabled all these bold young men to write their names in history—and change the world.

So long.

Bibliography

BOOKS

Aero Club, 1901–1951. Iliffe & Sons, Ltd., London, 1951.

Aircraft Year Book, 1919–1962. Issued by Manufacturers Aircraft Association. Doubleday, Page & Co., New York.

Allen, Richard S. *Revolution in the Sky.* Stephen Greene Press, Brattleboro, Vt., 1964.

American Heritage History of Flight. American Heritage Publishing Co., New York, 1962.

Amundsen, Roald. *My Life as Explorer.* Doubleday, Page & Co., New York, 1927.

Baidukov, Georgi. *Over the North Pole.* Harcourt & Brace, New York, 1938.

Balchen, Bernt. *Come North With Me.* E. P. Dutton & Co., New York, 1958.

Bennett, Cora Lillian. *Floyd Bennett.* W. F. Payson, New York, 1932.

Bibliography of Aeronautics, 1909–1937. National Advisory Committee for Aeronautics.

Bluebook of Aviation. Edited by R. W. Hoagland. Hoagland Co., Publishers, Los Angeles, 1932.

Bruno, Harry. *Wings Over America.* Robert McBride Co., New York, 1942.

Bryden, Helena Grace. *Wings: An Anthology of Flight.* Faber & Faber, London, 1942.

Byrd, Richard E. *Little America.* G. P. Putnam's Sons, New York, 1930.

———. *Skyward.* G. P. Putnam's Sons, New York-London, 1928.

Caras, Roger A. *Antarctica—Land of Frozen Time.* Chilton Books, Publishers, Philadelphia & New York, 1962.

Churchill, Allen. *The Year the World Went Mad.* Thomas Y. Crowell, New York, 1960.

Clark, Harold T. *Episodes of the Amundsen-Ellsworth Arctic Flights.* Cleveland Museum of Natural History, 1928.

Cobham, Alan J. *My Flight to the Cape and Back.* A. & C. Black, Ltd., London, 1926.

———. *Skyways.* Nisbet & Co., London, 1926.

Coughlan, Robert, and the Editors of *Life. Tropical Africa.* Time, Inc., New York, 1962.

Croft, Andrew. *Polar Exploration.* Adam & Charles Black, London, 1947.

Davis, Kenneth S. *The Hero: Charles A. Lindbergh and the American Dream.* Doubleday, New York, 1960.

Davy, M. J. B. *An Interpretive History of Flight.* His Majesty's Stationery Office, London, 1937.

DeLeeuw, Hendrick. *Conquest of the Air.* Vantage Press, New York, 1960.

Dorman, Geoffrey. *Fifty Years Fly Past from Wright Brothers to Comet.* Forbes Robertson, 1951.

Dufek, Rear Admiral George J. *Operation Deep Freeze.* Harcourt, Brace & Co., New York, 1957.

Ellison, Norman. *Flying Matilda.* Angus & Robertson, Sydney, 1957.

Encyclopedia Americana. 1958 Edition. Americana Corporation, New York-Chicago-Washington.

Encyclopaedia Britannica. 1953 Edition. Encyclopaedia Britannica Corp., Chicago-London-Toronto.

Euller, John. *Antarctic World.* Abelard-Schuman, London & New York, 1960.

Fife, George B. *Lindbergh, the Lone Eagle.* World Syndicate Publishing Co., New York & Cleveland, 1933.

Franco, Ramón and J. Ruiz de Alda. *De Palos al Plata.* Madrid: Espasa-Calpe, 1926.

Fraser, Chelsea Curtis. *Famous American Fliers.* Thomas Y. Crowell, New York, 1941.

———. *Heroes of the Air.* Thomas Y. Crowell, New York, 1946.

Gibbs-Smith, Charles H. *A History of Flying.* Frederick A. Praeger, New York, 1954.

———. *The Aeroplane—A Historical Survey.* Her Majesty's Stationery Office, London, 1960.

Goldberg, Alfred. *A History of the United States Army Air Force, 1907-1957.* Van Nostrand Co., Inc., Princeton, N.J., 1957.

Grierson, John. *Challenge to the Poles.* Archon Books, Hamden, Conn., 1964.

Harper, Harry. *Riders of the Sky*. Hodder & Stoughton, Ltd., London, 1936.

———. *Twenty-Five Years of Flying*. Hutchinson & Co., London, 1929.

Hayes, James G. *Conquest of the North Pole*. The Macmillan Co., New York, 1934.

Heinmuller, John P. *Man's Fight to Fly*. Funk & Wagnalls, New York, 1944.

Hodgins, Eric and F. *Alexander Magoun*. Sky High. Little, Brown & Co., Boston, 1929.

Hodgson, J. E. *The History of Aeronautics in Great Britain*. Oxford University Press, London, 1924.

Holland, Rupert S. *Historic Airships*. Macrae, Smith & Co., Philadelphia, 1928.

Horvat, William J. *Above the Pacific*. Aero Publishers, Inc., Fallbrook, Calif., 1966.

Hurren, B. J. *Fellowship of the Air—Jubilee Book of the Royal Aero Club, 1901–1951*. Iliffe & Sons, Ltd., London, 1951.

Kingsford-Smith, Charles. *My Flying Life*. A. Melrose, Ltd., London, 1937.

Kingsford-Smith, Charles and C. T. P. Ulm. *The Flight of the Southern Cross*. R. M. McBride & Co., New York, 1929.

Lindbergh, Charles. *The Spirit of St. Louis*. Scribner's, New York, 1953.

———. *We—Pilot and Plane*. G. P. Putnam's Sons, New York-London, 1928.

Magoun, F. Alexander and Eric Hodgins. *A History of Aircraft*. Whittlesey House, McGraw-Hill Book Co., New York & London, 1931.

Mann, Carl. *Lightning in the Sky*. R. M. McBride Co., New York, 1943.

Mitchell, General William. *Skyways*. J. P. Lippincott Co., London & Philadelphia, 1930.

Mollison, James. *The Book of Famous Flyers*. Collins Clear-Type Press, London & Glasgow, 1934.

Morris, Lloyd and Kendall Smith. *Ceiling Unlimited*. Macmillan & Co., New York, 1953.

Murphy, Charles J. V. *Struggle: The Life & Exploits of Commander R. E. Byrd*. Frederick A. Stokes Co., New York, 1928.

Nobile, Umberto. *My Polar Flights*. G. P. Putnam's Sons, New York, 1961.

Ocean Flight, May 20–25, 1919. Newspaper clippings on Alcock-Brown Flight. Mounted and bound by the New York Public Library.

Official Pictorial History of the Army Air Force. Historical Office of the Army Air Force, Duell, Sloan & Pearce, New York, 1947.

Parer, Lt. Raymond J. P. *Flight and Adventures.* J. Roy Stevens, Printer & Publisher, Melbourne, Australia, 1921.

Partridge, B. *Amundsen.* Frederick A. Stokes Co., New York, 1929.

Post, Augustus. *Skycraft.* Oxford University Press, New York & London, 1930.

Reynolds, Quentin. *The Amazing Mr. Doolittle.* Appleton-Century-Crofts, New York, 1953.

Richards, Barbara V. *The Long and Lonely Kangaroo Route.* Bee-Hive, Quarterly Publication of United Aircraft. East Hartford, Conn., Fall 1966.

Sheil, Beau. *Caesar of the Skies.* Cassell & Co., London, 1937.

Smith, Henry Ladd. *Airways.* Alfred A. Knopf, New York, 1942.

Smith, Sir Ross. *14,000 Miles Through the Air.* Macmillan, London, 1922.

Stefansson, Vilhjalmur. *Arctic Manual.* The Macmillan Co., New York, 1957.

Still, Henry. *To Ride the Wind.* Julian Messner, Inc., New York, 1964.

Sykes, Sir F. H. *Aviation in Peace and War.* E. Arnold & Co., London, 1922.

Taylor, Sir Gordon. *The Sky Beyond.* Houghton Mifflin Co., Boston, 1963.

Taylor, John W. R. *A Picture History of Flight.* Pittman Publishing Corp., New York-Toronto-London, 1956.

Thomas, Hugh. *The Spanish Civil War.* Harper & Row, New York, 1961.

Thomas, Lowell. *Sir Hubert Wilkins—His Life of Adventure.* McGraw-Hill, New York & London, 1961.

———. *The First World Flight.* Houghton Mifflin Co., Boston & New York, 1925.

Turner, C. C. *Marvels of Aviation.* Lippincott, Philadelphia, 1917.

———. *The Old Flying Days.* S. Low Marston & Co., London, 1927.

Vaeth, J. Gordon. *To the Ends of the Earth.* Harper & Row, New York, 1962.

Victor, Paul-Emile. *Man and the Conquest of the Poles.* Simon & Schuster, New York, 1963.

Vivian, E. C. and W. L. Marsh. *History of Aeronautics.* W. Collins & Sons, London, 1921.

Whitten-Brown, Arthur. *Flying the Atlantic in Sixteen Hours.* Frederick A. Stokes, New York, 1920.

Wilkins, Sir Hubert. *Flying the Arctic.* Putnam, New York, 1928.

Winslow, Kathryn. *Alaska Bound*. Dodd Mead Co., New York, 1960.
Yearbook & Almanac of Newfoundland, 1919.
Zahm, A. F. *Aerial Navigation*. D. Appleton & Co., New York & London, 1911.

MAGAZINES

Aerial Age

Aero

Aero Digest

Aeronautics

Aircraft

Airway Age

American Aeronautics

Automobile

Aviation

Aviation Week

Collier's Weekly

Commonweal

Current Opinion

Flight

Fly

Flying

Harper's Weekly

Independent

Literary Digest

Mechanical Engineering

Motor Life

National Geographic Magazine

Natural History

Newsweek

New Yorker

Popular Aviation

Popular Mechanics

Popular Science

Reader's Digest

Review of Reviews

Saturday Review

Scientific American

The Aeroplane

Time

U. S. Air Service Bulletin

Woman's Home Companion

NEWSPAPERS

London Times

New York Daily News

New York Herald Tribune

New York Times

INDEX